# COGNITIVE FOUNDATIONS
# OF CLINICAL PSYCHOLOGY

## Chris R. Brewin

*MRC Social Psychiatry Unit,*
*Institute of Psychiatry, London*

LEA LAWRENCE ERLBAUM ASSOCIATES, PUBLISHERS LEA
Hove and London          dale (USA)

Reprinted 1990, 1993

Lawrence Erlbaum Associates Ltd., Publishers
27 Palmeira Mansions
Church Road
Hove
East Sussex, BN3 2FA
UK


British Library Cataloguing in Publication Data

Brewin, Chris
    Cognitive foundations of clinical psychology.
    1. Medicine, Cognitive behaviour theory
    I. Title
    616.89'142

    ISBN 0-86377-098-3 (Hbk)
    ISBN 0-86377-099-1 (Pbk)


Typeset by Ponting-Green Publishing Services
Printed and bound by BPCC Wheatons Ltd., Exeter

*All unhappiness depends upon some kind of disintegration or lack of integration; there is disintegration within the self through lack of co-ordination between the conscious and the unconscious mind; there is lack of integration between the self and society, where the two are not knit together by the force of objective interests and affections.*
                                    Bertrand Russell

# Contents

# Preface

The enormous growth in the popularity of cognitive–behavioural therapies for psychological problems such as anxiety, depression, and the addictions has generally been unaccompanied by an appreciation of their theoretical basis. Whereas the foundation of traditional behaviour therapy was seen to lie in the laws of learning and in psychophysiology, the new therapies draw primarily on social and cognitive psychology. But the core articles on such topics as expectations, attributions, automatic thoughts, and emotional schemata are scattered widely and there has been little attempt to provide an integrated view of the theories behind the practice. This has led to many misconceptions about cognitive and cognitive–behavioural therapy, including a great deal of confusion over what the term "cognitive" actually means.

This book has been written for undergraduates doing an advanced clinical option, postgraduate clinical psychologists, and practising clinicians who want to understand more about what cognitive–behavioural therapies are and what they try to do. It begins by addressing basic questions about the nature of conscious and unconscious processes and the relation between them. For example, what sort of answer do therapists get when they ask patients how they are feeling? Do people have access to their mental states and can they report on the causes of their behaviour? The book also discusses cognitive influences on classical and operant conditioning and tries to describe both behavioural and cognitive therapies using a common framework.

In addition to a' major focus on theories of emotion, the book deals in detail with self-perception and self-esteem. Unlike traditional behaviour therapists, cognitive therapists pay considerable attention to people's beliefs about themselves, and altering a negative self-image is often a central part of therapy. But what is self-esteem, how does it develop, and how can it be measured? Another topic covered at some length is motivation for therapy. It's no good knowing what patients need to do to make themselves better if they are unwilling or feel unable to comply.

In the past there has been much debate about the effectiveness of different schools of therapy. In my view many of the arguments have been specious, because the therapies address different kinds of problem and have different aims. One would not expect a therapy that is effective with phobias necessarily to be good with marital problems; or a therapy that works for the believer to work for the sceptic. Clinical psychology has now progressed to the point where it attempts to modify many different problems, and the insights and observations of many different kinds of therapy are likely to be valuable. This is not to say that all therapies are right, but that they are all based on systematic observations of behaviour. It is important to keep hold of the observations (the data) while simultaneously challenging and re-evaluating the theory used to explain them. Agreement on theory is impossible unless there is prior agreement about the observations.

Many individuals have helped with advice and discussion about the ideas in this book, and I am extremely grateful for their efforts to straighten out my own errors in thinking. Although it would be impossible to mention all of them, I would like to single out for special thanks Bernice Andrews, Charles Antaki, Paul Bebbington, Brendan Bradley, Clare Bradley, Graham Davey, Jenny Firth-Cozens, David Fowler, Adrian Furnham, Paul Gilbert, Sue Henley, Brigid MacCarthy, Karen Mogg, Glenys Parry, Mick Power, Padmal de Silva, Fraser Watts, and Mark Williams.

*Chris R. Brewin*

# 1 Introduction: Cognition and Clinical Psychology

Since the early 1950s psychology has seen many significant developments. On the theoretical side, one of the most dramatic has been the decline of behaviourism and the rise of cognitive psychology, whereas on the practical side there has been an enormous expansion in the clinical applications of psychological knowledge. Much of the subject matter of clinical psychology, such as distressing thoughts and memories, delusions, and fixed ideas, is of course cognitive in nature, and in the last century psychoanalytic theories of psychopathology attempted to explain such phenomena. Breuer and Freud (1893), for example, attributed many hysterical symptoms to the presence of disturbing ideas or memories that had been repressed and made inaccessible to conscious awareness. Cognitive theories are not new, therefore, but it is only comparatively recently that they have come to play an important role in clinical psychology, backed up by the findings of systematic empirical research. In this chapter I want to outline briefly some of the ways in which cognitive theories, drawn from social psychology as well as from the experimental study of mental processes, can help to explain clinical phenomena and guide clinical practice.

The approach taken in this book is that psychological problems usually have multiple causes—personal, environmental, and sometimes constitutional. Often problems arise in the context of very real social difficulties, threats to well-being, and agonizing personal choices, either past or present. Sometimes situations that appear relatively non-threatening to the average person cause great distress or provoke an extreme reaction in a particular individual. Even in the case of severe environmental stressors, however, people seem to differ greatly in the nature and intensity of their reaction and in their ability to cope. This means that it is necessary to assess, not just what has happened in the eyes of a neutral observer, but how the person experiencing the event has understood it, what has been learned from it, and what the consequences are thought to be for the future. These subjective assessments are based on the integration of situational information with the person's prior knowledge about the world. The judgements made in turn become incorporated into that knowledge, thereby affecting future judgements. The task of the various branches of cognitive psychology is to explain how knowledge is acquired, how it is internally represented and integrated with existing information, and what kinds of knowledge affect people's feelings and behaviour. The task of the clinical psychologist is to apply this understanding to the enhancement of human potential and to the alleviation of suffering.

The theme of knowledge and its acquisition will be central to this book. In practice, the knowledge people require to evaluate stressful situations properly and decide on the appropriate course of action is often missing, or forgotten. Simply telling people relevant facts about the frequency of the problem or its most likely outcome may be extremely helpful to them. Even if relevant knowledge is available, the inferences that people are called upon to make about themselves and their circumstances are often complex and difficult, and human judgement is known in many cases to be all too fallible. For example, parents trying to explain why their child is truanting may have to integrate a huge amount of information about school circumstances, the behaviour of peers, current sources of stress, their own attitudes towards school and disciplinary styles, and so on. There is now a great deal of evidence that even in simple situations people's ability to recognize the interdependence of events, identify causes, estimate the degree of control they have, and draw valid conclusions from a set of data, are quite limited and prone to be influenced by a variety of factors (e.g., Nisbett & Ross, 1980). It is known that people are strongly affected by prior expectations, that they are subject to various errors and biases, and that they tend to rely on simple rules or heuristics when faced with large quantities of information. Under these circumstances erroneous and premature judgements, made either by the patient or by the clinician, are likely to flourish, sometimes with the most unfortunate consequences.

It is equally evident that people are not always consciously aware of the knowledge they possess, and that their behaviour may be influenced by events that occur out of awareness (see Chapter 2). We shall therefore be examining the issue of unconscious knowledge as well as considering the sort of conscious judgements people make, how accurate they are, their consequences, and how they can be altered. But before going any further it is necessary to give some idea of the range of problems and situations to which today's clinical psychologist is expected to contribute.

## CONTEMPORARY CLINICAL PSYCHOLOGY

In the early days of behaviour therapy the main clinical focus was on anxiety neuroses, and in particular phobic and obsessional disorders. In terms of the then current (behaviourist) learning theory, disorders such as insect or height phobias were conceptualized as conditioned fear responses that had been acquired accidentally and that were elicited by contact with the conditioned stimulus (see Chapter 3 for a fuller account of conditioning theories). A variety of techniques, such as extinction and counter-conditioning, were available for overcoming such examples of learned avoidance, and aversion therapy was also used to combat learned approach behaviours such as alcohol addiction and transvestism (Wolpe, 1973). This conditioning model, which was to lead to many innovative treatment strategies and to prove very influential in clinical psychology, was characterized by a concern with maladaptive habits and behaviours rather than with thoughts and feelings. It was based on principles derived from the study of animal learning and took little account of the person's wider social and interpersonal context. It was also mechanistic in the sense that people's behaviour was considered to be primarily shaped by environmental events, and that therapeutic improvement was expected to follow exposure to a different sequence of events.

Behaviour therapy began, then, with a fairly simple conception of a limited set of disorders. These represent only a small proportion of the workload of clinical psychologists, who are now involved in such diverse activities as marital and family therapy, the management of chronic pain, preparation for surgery, skills training for the mentally handicapped, the treatment of depression in the elderly, the assessment and rehabilitation of brain-injured patients, the management of alcoholism and drug addiction, and the counselling of the terminally ill and bereaved. The original focus on disturbed behaviour has given way to a concern with many aspects of human functioning, such as people's emotional state, their thoughts, their memory and concentration, their ability to cope with difficult situations, their interpersonal problems, their sense of wellbeing or self-esteem, and their physiological health status. It is now recognized that assessment must include many or all of these areas of functioning, and that problems in different areas may require different kinds of intervention. Nor do psychologists confine their efforts to altering conditioned responses, but attempt to help people deal with the direct, unconditioned responses to major life stresses, such as going into hospital for a major operation or coming to terms with the loss of a loved one.

Cognitive theories are relevant to many of these aspects of the contemporary psychologist's role. In this book it will not be possible to cover all aspects, and I therefore intend to concentrate on a limited set of phenomena that are widely encountered. A major focus will be on the nature, origin, and modification of emotional states, particularly anxiety and depression. These are important, not just in a psychiatric context, but anywhere that people are coping with major stresses. Another topic will be self-esteem and how it is maintained. Although particularly associated with depressive disorders, low self-esteem is common and there is evidence that people's statements and actions are greatly influenced by attempts to protect and enhance their self-esteem. Motivational processes also receive a great deal of attention, as the issue of how much effort people are prepared to expend in therapy or in dealing with their problems is of concern in any area of clinical psychology. The fourth topic includes various social processes, in particular interpersonal emotions, cooperation and helping, that are relevant to understanding family and client–professional relationships. However far clinical psychological services develop, these four topics are certain to remain of central importance, whether the client groups are old or young and whatever the nature of their difficulties.

## COGNITIVE APPROACHES IN PSYCHOLOGY

The main distinguishing feature of a cognitive approach to psychological investigation lies in the emphasis given to mental processes that intervene between an environmental event and the reaction of a person or animal. Once simple reflex arcs are excluded, all events are thought to be mentally evaluated in various ways and compared to prior experiences stored in memory before being acted on. Thus, as noted by Eysenck (1984, p. 1), "virtually all those interested in perception, learning, memory, language, concept formation, problem solving, or thinking call themselves cognitive psychologists, despite the great diversity of experimental and theoretical approaches to be found in these various areas." Experimental cognitive psychology is largely concerned with explaining how people perceive, attend to, classify, store, and remember information, and how they then use this information to make decisions. Typically the aim has been to develop general models of these processes, and little account has been taken of individual differences or motivational variables. Because the processes of interest are usually unavailable to introspection, inferences about their nature are often derived from computer simulations or from measures of human performance on experimental tasks. "Social cognition" refers to the relatively recent extension of this approach to the study of how social stimuli, such as information about oneself and other people, are registered and processed.

The idea that there are mental processes that intervene between stimulus and response is historically associated with the Gestalt school of psychology. Their theories were not only influential in explaining how objects in the physical world are perceived, but were soon extended to the perception of social objects and hence influenced the course of social psychology as well as the study of perception and thinking. Throughout the period when behaviourism was in the ascendant, social psychologists such as Lewin, Heider, and Festinger continued to emphasize the importance of conscious perceptions and evaluations in determining human behaviour. These theories invoked such mentalist concepts as expectancy, level of aspiration, balance, consistency, causal attribution, and cognitive dissonance, which did not correspond to directly observable behaviour but rather to hypothetical processes designed to account for behaviour. Unlike the theories stemming from experimental cognitive psychology, they were very much concerned with motivational processes, individual differences, and with the specific content of the information available to the person. Many current theories in clinical psychology, such as social learning theory (Bandura, 1977a) and learned helplessness theory (Abramson, Seligman, & Teasdale, 1978; Seligman, 1975), have their roots in this work.

Clinical psychology can therefore draw on both experimental cognitive psychology, with its focus on such processes as memory and attention, and cognitive social psychology, whose emphasis is more on conscious attitudes, expectancies, and beliefs. In addition clinicians themselves have come up with influential cognitive theories to account for the wide individual differences they meet in their work. For example, Kelly (1955) proposed that people have unique systems of personal constructs with which they categorize the objects in their world, interpret the events that happen to them, and predict the future. One of the main purposes of therapy, he suggested, is to help people free themselves from the restrictions imposed by their own construct systems. Ellis (1962) and Beck (1967) have also argued that dysfunctional emotions such as anxiety and depression follow from people's perceptions and evaluations of the events in their lives rather than from the events themselves. Ellis' Rational–Emotive Therapy and Beck's Cognitive Therapy are both designed to alter these perceptions by a number of techniques, including challenging faulty underlying assumptions such as "I cannot live without this person" or "Nobody will ever speak to me again if I make a fool of myself".

This brief overview is intended simply to give the reader some idea of the diversity of cognitive approaches relevant to clinical psychology. In the following chapters the various theories will receive much more detailed treatment and the evidence for and against them will be discussed. The important point to bear in mind is that, although all cognitive theories emphasize the importance of intervening mental processes, there is no one "cognitive approach". Theories may deal with *processes* such as selective attention, or with *structures* such as "schemata" or "associative networks" that describe the organization of material in memory. They may be concerned with specific kinds of *content*, such as ideas, images, expectations, and attitudes, and this content may be accessible or inaccessible to consciousness. They may assert different kinds of causal relation between mental processes, emotions, and behaviour. This diversity means that the potential contribution of cognitive theories is considerable. In the rest of the chapter I illustrate this by discussing some major aspects of the onset a course of illness.

## COGNITIONS AS PRECIPITATING FACTORS

The major factor associated with the onset of a wide range of physical and psychiatric disorders is life stress (e.g., Brown & Harris, 1978; Dohrenwend & Dohrenwend, 1974; Totman, 1979). Stress is thought, for example, to cause or exacerbate acne, anxiety, asthma, amenorrhea, arthritis, cancer, the common cold, coronary heart disease, diabetes, depression, duodenal ulcer, epilepsy, glaucoma, hypertension, insomnia, low back pain, leukaemia, migraine, neurodermatitis, premenstrual tension, post-operative infection, schizophrenia, stroke, tension headache, and ulcerative colitis. In spite of these numerous findings, simply counting the number of events, commonly regarded as stressful, that a person has experienced does not allow one to predict whether he or she will become ill with any great accuracy. Even responses to very serious stressors such as earthquakes or being interned in a concentration camp show enormous individual variation. Many authors have concluded that this is because the stressfulness of events depends, at least in part, on how they are evaluated or appraised by the individual (e.g., Lazarus, 1966).

Considerable research effort has therefore gone into describing the characteristics of stressful situations, and animal studies have consistently identified a number of factors leading to behavioural disturbances and abnormal physiological activity. Among the most common are threat of pain or other punishment, the frustration of goal-directed behaviour, conflict between equally attractive or equally unattractive goals, approach–avoidance conflict, helplessness, and loss of or separation from other animals. Although these characteristics can be defined as properties of a situation, they can also be treated as psychological states that are aroused in individuals to varying degrees. Research presented in Chapters 3 and 4 indicates that the response of animals and human beings to these situations often depends on the integration of a wide range of relevant information. For example, physiological responses to stimuli signalling shock vary according to whether an escape or avoidance response has previously been learned or is believed (erroneously) to be available (Miller, 1979). Such findings imply a need for some account of how different kinds of information are registered, stored, and integrated.

Outside the laboratory, too, most examples of human stress can be categorized as involving threat, conflict, loss, and so on. However, some of the events one person would find threatening, such as being offered promotion at work, others would find challenging. People also differ greatly in their response to loss and conflict. The enormous variety of goals that people can aspire to means that apparent frustration or conflict in one area may be relatively unimportant because of the presence of substitute goals, a topic that is covered more fully in Chapters 5 and 8. So, although certain situations may have profound physiological and behavioural consequences for both people and animals, those situations cannot be defined without considering the state of the organism as well as the state of the environment. According to the cognitive theorist, this internal state represents the outcome of various forms of appraisal and evaluation.

These points are illustrated in detailed research by Brown, Bifulco, and Harris (1987) on the kind of life events that tend to precede depression in female community residents. They point out that whereas on average four-fifths of depressed women have experienced a major stressor, only about one in five women experiencing such a stressor go on to become depressed. This association can be strengthened by considering only severe events that correspond either to ongoing difficulties (D-events), to particular areas of strong commitment (C-events), or to areas where role conflict exists (R-events). The significance of D-events is presumed to lie in the high levels of helplessness that accompany them, while C-events and R-events can be readily understood in terms of goal frustration and conflict. Brown et al. give, as an example of a C-event, a woman with a strong commitment to her role as a mother experiencing her son being put on probation for violent behaviour. The authors conclude (p.41): "The role of matching difficulties and commitments indicates the importance of the loss of something upon which one has heavily staked a part of oneself... The findings of course underline the importance of social environment and cognitive factors in the aetiology of depression".

## COGNITIONS AS VULNERABILITY FACTORS

The wide variability in people's response to stressful life events has also led to the suggestion that events only have severe consequences for individuals who are in some way permanently vulnerable. These diathesis–stress models, as they are sometimes known, include as potential vulnerability factors the experience of particular events in the past as well as the possession of particular genes, particular types of nervous system, particular types of personality, and particular cognitive characteristics. In practice these various models are not mutually exclusive but may be thought of as describing vulnerability at different levels within a complex system. For example, life events are more likely to lead to the onset of depression in women who have lost their mothers early in life and who have no current intimate relationship. Brown and Harris (1978) suggest that vulnerability is not directly attributable to these environmental factors themselves, but rather to the consequent reduction in levels of self-esteem, a cognitive/personality factor. Similarly, genetic vulnerability to develop specific psychiatric disorders appears to be limited to a small number of conditions such as schizophrenia and manic-depressive psychosis. But it is likely that hereditary factors also exercise some influence on more general characteristics of the nervous system, such as fearfulness (Gray, 1971), and on cognitive/personality factors such as aggression and altruism (Rushton et al., 1986) and locus of control (Miller & Rose, 1982).

The personality dimension most often considered to be a vulnerability factor for psychological disorder is almost certainly neuroticism, which reflects differences in the strength and reactivity of emotional responses. Neuroticism (N) scores have been found to be elevated in many groups of psychiatric patients (Eysenck, 1967). The notion that people have stable, highly consistent personality traits that influence their behaviour across many situations has, however, come under increasing criticism in recent years. One reason is that, in general, people do not behave with a high degree of consistency in different situations, and it appears more useful to think of behaviour as the product of complex person–environment interactions (Mischel, 1973). This is not to say that certain individuals do not demonstrate consistency in certain areas of their life, but the fact remains that the ability of trait scores to predict behaviour in the individual is rather low. To cite Mischel (1973, p. 262):

> No one suggests that the organism approaches every new situation with an empty head, nor is it questioned by anyone that different individuals differ markedly in how they deal with most stimulus conditions. What has been questioned is the utility of inferring broad dispositions from behavioral signs as *the* bases for trying to explain the phenomena of personality and for making useful statements about individual behavior. The available data do *not* imply that different people will not act differently with some consistency in different classes of situations; they *do* imply that the particular classes of conditions must be taken into account far more carefully than in the past, tend to be much narrower than traditional trait theories have assumed, and

for purposes of important individual decision making, require highly individualized assessments of stimulus meanings.

Mischel's solution was to integrate personality research with the approach of cognitive and social learning theory, shifting the unit of study from global traits inferred from behavioural signs to the individual's cognitive activities and behaviour patterns, studied in relation to particular circumstances. The variables he identified as likely to be important in predicting behaviour, including abnormal behaviour, were competencies, encoding, and categorization of events, expectancies, subjective values, and self-regulatory systems and plans. Many of these variables have now been considered as potential vulnerability factors by cognitive and social learning theorists. For example, people with an external locus of control, i.e., who believe they have relatively little control over the positive and negative events that happen to them, have been thought to be more at risk of becoming anxious or depressed (see Chapter 7 for a more detailed discussion of locus of control). Other vulnerability factors suggested for anxiety include the tendency to attend selectively to threat stimuli. Vulnerability to becoming depressed has been linked to maladaptive attitudes and beliefs, low self-esteem, blaming misfortune on characterological defects, and preferential processing of negative information about the self.

Many of these cognitive and personality variables correlate highly with one another, but there is as yet little agreement about the most fruitful way of describing vulnerability. Another problem is that self-report measures of neuroticism, maladaptive beliefs, the self-attribution of blame, and self-esteem are noticeably mood-dependent, scores becoming more pathological as the person becomes more anxious or depressed and returning to normal as mood improves. These short-term changes mean that it has been difficult to establish the presence of the consistent long-term individual differences that would characterize true vulnerability factors. The evidence that people vulnerable to psychological disorders differ on cognitive measures during normal mood as well as during abnormal mood is discussed in Chapter 5.

A final vulnerability factor shown to be relevant to a wide range of physical and psychological disorders is the absence of social support. Although this is normally considered as a social variable, absence of support may in some cases be related to cognitive characteristics of the person. For example, people who have low expectations of being able to form relationships, who do not expect others to be supportive, or who believe that others are unlikely to understand the unique nature of their problems, may actually avoid potential sources of support. The relationship between cognitions and social behaviour is the subject of Chapter 9.

## COGNITIONS AS FACTORS IN RECOVERY

Whether or not cognitive factors contribute to the onset of a problem or emotional disorder, they may be involved in determining how the person responds to it and hence how long it lasts. For example, experiencing emotions such as anxiety or depression may bring back memories of previous times when these emotions were felt, memories that may themselves upset the person still further and exacerbate feelings of sadness or helplessness. Recovery may therefore be affected by the number or the intensity of memories that are accessible in different mood states (see Chapter 5 for further discussion). Exacerbation may also occur because unwanted behaviours such as stuttering, insomnia, or impotence are attributed to personal defects and inadequacies (Storms & McCaul, 1976; see Chapter 6). Compared to external attributions, for example to a temporarily stressful situation, such self-attributions are likely to be distressing, to provoke further anxiety, and to make the problem worse. It has also been suggested that mood disturbance and other features of depression can be exacerbated when inability to deal with current stressors produces a state of heightened self-awareness. Feeling increasingly self-aware and unhappy, it is suggested, breaks through people's normal tendency to see themselves and the world in a positive light (Lewinsohn, Hoberman, Teri, & Hautzinger, 1985).

Cognitions are also an important part of the coping process. In most cases there are likely to be a range of more or less effective coping strategies that people in distress will choose between. Lazarus (1966; Lazarus, Kanner, & Folkman, 1980) distinguishes between strategies aimed at altering a problematic situation, such as getting one's doctor to support an application for transfer to better accommodation, and strategies aimed at regulating the person's own emotional response, such as confiding in a sympathetic friend. In the case of both problem-focussed and emotion-focussed coping the sort of methods people most commonly use, according to Lazarus, are information-seeking, direct action, inhibition of action, and intrapsychic methods such as denial (pretending the problem doesn't exist) and intellectualization (thinking about the problem in an emotionally detached way). The analysis of people's choice of coping strategy, and what determines the persistence with which they pursue it, comes within the scope of research on motivation. The important factors here are people's views about the cause of the problem, their knowledge and beliefs about the range of appropriate strategies, their estimate of the resources, both personal and environmental, that they think are available to carry out these strategies, and the existence of values and goals that are in opposition to particular coping strategies or coping efforts in general. Faulty analysis of the cause of a problem, ignorance of an effective strategy, and overestimation of the difficulty involved, could all lead to giving up coping attempts prematurely.

Causal beliefs, and their relationship to coping, are the subject of Chapter 6. Causal beliefs also influence the formation of expectancies, for many years a central concept in theories of human motivation. A person's motivation to perform an action has been thought of as the product of two major factors, the value of the goal that the action is designed to attain, and the expectancy that the action will achieve that goal (e.g., Feather, 1982). The more important the goal, and the higher the expectancy of success, the more vigorously should the action be performed. This "expectancy-value" framework, as mentioned previously, has given rise to a number of influential theories in clinical psychology. Learned helplessness (Seligman, 1975), in which motivational deficits are related to the expectancy that actions will have no effect on outcomes, is discussed in Chapter 6, and Bandura's (1977b) self-efficacy theory, which deals with the role of expectancies in the outcome of psychological therapy, is evaluated in detail in Chapter 7. The influence of values and goals on motivation is a major focus of Chapter 8.

Another example of an influential theory based on an expectancy-value framework is the Health Belief Model (Becker & Maiman, 1975; Rosenstock, 1966), which has been used to explain preventive health behaviour and patient adherence to medical regimens. According to the HBM, a person's readiness to perform some health related behaviour is related to three sets of factors: health motivations, such as a general concern about health, willingness to seek medical help, and intention to comply with the suggested action; aspects of perceived threat, such as vulnerability to a particular disorder, and the severity of the symptoms or side-effects; and the perceived effectiveness of the actions proposed. The last two sets of factors are clearly estimates of value and expectancy, respectively. A more general theory that has sometimes been applied in the clinical domain is the theory of reasoned action (Fishbein & Ajzen, 1975). This states that any attempt to perform some behaviour is preceded by an intention to do so. This intention is in turn a function of two factors, attitude toward the behaviour and the subjective norm. Attitude toward the behaviour is determined by the perceived value of the consequences and by the perceived effectiveness of the behaviour, whereas the subjective norm is a social factor referring to perceived social pressure to carry out the behaviour.

With the exception of learned helplessness, which developed from research with animals, these various motivational theories are characterized by the explicit or implicit role played by conscious intentions. Unlike a behaviourist account of people's actions, they assume that most behaviour is self-generated and that human beings first consciously evaluate and then deliberately attempt to regulate themselves and their environment. One important, and so far unresolved, issue concerns the extent to which expectancies and values are fully accessible to consciousness and can be assessed by simply asking the patient to report on them. We shall consider the limits of conscious awareness in Chapter 2 and return to the problem in Chapters 7 and 8.

## CONCLUSIONS

Even this brief survey has touched on a large number of areas where cognitive factors may be important and described many possible mechanisms by which they may affect emotions and behaviour. On the one hand we have distinguished between cognitive processes such as memory and attention, and cognitive structures such as schemata and associative networks. On the other we have considered human knowledge of the environment, whether accurate or inaccurate, in terms of values and goals, judgements about cause and contingency, and expectations of mastery and control. Each of these various aspects of cognition may be involved in the onset of emotional disorders, in vulnerability to various kinds of stress, and in coping and recovery processes, not to mention in family and professional–client interactions. The following chapters describe these processes in detail, evaluate the evidence for them, and consider the practical implications for clinical psychology.

# 2 ___ Conscious and Unconscious

The understanding of consciousness and of people's awareness of their mental states is at the heart of theory and practice in clinical psychology. Much of the impetus for the development of models of psychopathology at the end of the last century came from observations of hysterical patients whose symptoms could be made to disappear under hypnosis. These observations led ultimately to psychoanalytic theories of unconscious motivational processes, manifested not only in symptoms but also in dreams and by slips of the tongue in such a way that the patient remained unaware of their true significance. Any general theory of psychopathology, however, must account for the fact that patients suffering from such disorders as phobias and obsessional neurosis typically experience fearful sensations, images, and thoughts without knowing why they do so and in spite of the conscious, "objective" belief that there is no reason to be frightened. Similarly, individuals may find themselves responding angrily to employers, colleagues, marital partners, and sometimes their therapists, without being aware of any obvious provocation. How are we to explain the fact that people, and in particular psychiatric patients, have so many experiences that appear to be neither intentional nor desired?

In this chapter we will not be concerned with the disturbances of consciousness that follow alcoholism, poisoning, head injury, or organic brain disease, and that are often characterized by confusion and sometimes profound memory loss. Nor will we consider dissociative phenomena such as fugue states, multiple personality, and the effects of hypnotic induction.

For a contemporary cognitive account of the latter, the interested reader should consult Kihlstrom (1984). Instead we will focus on three specific questions that are of central importance to everyday clinical practice and that will recur throughout this book. These are: (1) Do people register and respond to events and experiences of which they are not consciously aware? (2) What are the limitations on people's ability to report on their internal states and on the reasons for their behaviour? (3) To what extent is behaviour consciously controlled and to what extent is it under the influence of factors that people remain unaware of? Finally, we will consider the implications for the Freudian view of the unconscious mind.

First, a few definitions are necessary. As we have noted in Chapter 1, the term "cognition" is commonly used to denote the representation within an organism of knowledge about itself or its environment, or alternatively the processes whereby this information is categorized, stored, and integrated with knowledge that is already present. In contrast, conscious thought describes a phenomenological experience of awareness, which is restricted by the inability of human beings to hold more than a few events or experiences in focal attention at one time. There are, of course, many stimuli of which we are not consciously aware because we are deliberately choosing not to attend to them. Other "preconscious" stimuli may also be accessible to consciousness if we are alerted to their presence. These stimuli have not been deliberately ignored, but are part of the enormous number of sensations, images etc., that are automatically filtered out of the material potentially available to our limited consciousness. For example, Beck (1967) has described a phenomenon found in the depressed that he calls "automatic thoughts", thoughts (such as "I must be stupid"), which occur so rapidly and spontaneously in certain situations that patients are often not aware of their existence until their attention is drawn to them by the therapist. "Unconscious" events, however, are not potentially accessible to conscious experience. Neisser (1967) has argued that people do not have access to the vast majority of cognitive acts and processes involved in the registration, transformation, and storage of stimuli, but may achieve conscious awareness of some of the products of these processes.

## PERCEPTION WITHOUT CONSCIOUS AWARENESS

Our first question, about whether people register events of which they are not consciously aware, is probably the easiest to answer. The main source of evidence is the study of subliminal perception, the evidence for and against which has been thoroughly reviewed by Dixon (1981). He describes a number of experimental paradigms in which people have been found to respond to stimuli too weak to be consciously represented. For instance, Rollman and Nachmias' (1972) subjects were shown chromatic discs at very weak intensity levels and asked on each trial whether or not a stimulus had been presented. Each time they incorrectly reported a stimulus as having been absent they were asked to guess what colour the disc might have been, and these guesses proved to be correct significantly more often than chance. Presumably the level of stimulus intensity necessary for conscious perception was higher than the level necessary for some information about the stimulus to be registered.

Electrophysiological studies confirm that subliminal stimuli are registered by the brain. Libet (1973) recorded evoked potentials from the somatosensory cortex of fully conscious individuals and found that tactile stimuli too weak to be consciously perceived still elicited the primary component of the compound evoked potential (CEP). Prolonged repetition of these stimuli did lead to conscious sensation and were associated with the later components of the CEP. Further evidence that information may be registered outside of awareness is provided by the phenomenon of "blindsight" (Weiskrantz, 1977). This refers to the ability of blind patients with certain kinds of neurological damage to detect the location or orientation of stimuli, and perform simple visual discrimination tasks, despite being subjectively unable to see the display. When asked to make these judgements such patients tend to describe "feelings" or "intuitions" about the correct answer that are unlike the sensation of seeing. These effects have been attributed to the existence of a second visual pathway, which links the retina to the temporal cortex via the mid-brain.

It is not only the physical characteristics but also the meaning of subliminal stimuli that may be registered by the brain. Among the many demonstrations of this we will consider two particular experiments, one involving visual and one involving auditory stimuli. Marcel (1983) gave subjects the task of deciding as quickly as possible whether or not a string of letters formed an actual word, and reported that this "lexical decision time" was significantly faster if subjects were first shown a semantically related word. This effect was obtained even when subjects were exposed to the associated word too briefly to be able to register it consciously. In Groeger's (1986) auditory task subjects had an incomplete sentence presented to one ear along with a choice of two alternative missing words. Subjects also received a subliminal prompt in the other ear that was either semantically related to one of the alternatives (e.g., frigate: corvette) or structurally related to it (e.g., courgette: corvette). This prompt was also presented at two intensities, one corresponding to the subjects' recognition threshold (i.e., they were able to report hearing a word but not able to identify it), and one corresponding to their awareness threshold (i.e., they were not able to report hearing anything at all). Groeger found, as expected, that when the prompt was presented below subjects' recognition threshold they were more likely to select the structurally related alternative, but when it was presented below the awareness threshold the semantically related alternative was favoured.

Although some authors are sceptical about whether certain experiments, or groups of experiments, have demonstrated that meaning can be extracted from subliminal stimuli (e.g., Holender, 1986), the existence of subliminal perception is now grounded in a large number of studies using different sensory modalities and a wide range of experimental paradigms. In the next section we will review other evidence showing that people respond to stimuli in ways that they cannot report, not because the stimuli are subliminal but because they are not recognized as being salient. Clinically these findings are very significant, since virtually all psychotherapies attempt to elicit from patients an account of events and experiences that have happened in the past or that are associated with fluctuations in their emotions, symptoms, or other unwanted behaviours. Clearly, if information can be registered without it needing to be consciously attended to, there may be severe limitations on people's ability to report the relevant facts to their therapists.

## LIMITATIONS ON SELF-REPORTS

There is general agreement that people cannot report very successfully how they perform skilled motor tasks such as riding a bicycle or executing a tennis smash. It is not immediately obvious that they should also have difficulty in verbalizing the knowledge needed for complex decision-making. In a series of experiments, Broadbent and his colleagues (e.g., Berry & Broadbent, 1984; Broadbent, Fitzgerald, & Broadbent, 1986) have investigated the relation between the ability to control complex systems with the aid of a computer and the ability to verbalize the knowledge involved in such control. The tasks have typically required subjects to reach and maintain specified target values of an output variable, such as sugar production, by altering one or more input variables, such as the size of the workforce. Input and output variables were related by a complex equation such that the same action could result in different outcomes, depending on the state of the system. The general conclusions were that practice did improve control of the system but did not have any effect on verbalizable knowledge, as assessed by the ability to answer questions. Verbal instruction, on the other hand, improved the ability to answer questions but did not improve actual performance unless subjects utilized it explicitly during the task.

It appears, therefore, that there are limitations on the ability to describe all that we can do, at any rate when the task or problem involved is a relatively complex one. It has also been suggested, on the basis of such evidence as the consistently poor correlation between people's reported attitudes and their subsequent behaviour, that similar limitations apply to our knowledge of our own feelings and internal states. One argument, which can be traced back at least as far as William James and which has since been revived many times, states that people have no direct knowledge of their internal states but infer them from self-observation. Thus, in the famous example, people are supposed to infer that they are afraid from the fact that they are running away. Other theorists have suggested that the labelling of internal states such as fear is based on the perception of physiological arousal coupled with an appraisal of environmental events (Schachter & Singer, 1962).

More recently other social and cognitive psychologists have adopted this view that when people describe their feelings or explain their behaviour they are simply making inferences designed to account for or justify their actions (e.g., Jaspars, Hewstone, & Fincham, 1983; Wilson, 1985). This recent scepticism derives from a large body of research showing that people often have poor access to their mental states and to the factors that are shaping their behaviour (Nisbett & Wilson, 1977; Wilson, 1985). Latané and Darley (1970) found, for example, that the probability of a person helping another in distress is related to the number of other people present. But individuals asked to explain why they had or had not offered help in these experiments denied that the presence of other people made any difference. Nisbett and Wilson (1977) reported a number of similar findings indicating that subjects in social psychology experiments are frequently unaware of the influences affecting their behaviour, and concluded that to ask people about their cognitive processes might be highly misleading.

Another approach to the question of the accuracy of verbal reports is to investigate the effect on attitude–behaviour consistency of introspecting to a greater or lesser degree on one's mental state. If introspection does involve access to one's mental states, then the consistency between one's reported feelings and actual behaviour should increase with greater introspection. Wilson et al. (1984) tested this hypothesis in a number of situations, including getting couples to rate how happy they were with their relationship and then finding out whether they were still dating several months later. The more couples were encouraged to introspect before rating their relationship, the lower was the correlation between these ratings and subsequent outcome. Similar results were obtained in the other situations, indicating that the attempt to analyze one's mental state tended to produce greater error, not greater accuracy.

Although Nisbett and Wilson's (1977) conclusions appear to have been overstated (Quattrone, 1985), their article has prompted discussion of the conditions that are likely to promote accurate self-reports. Morris (1981) has noted that their examples detailing the inaccessibility of mental states involve situations in which people have to account for their behaviour rather than report what they intend to do next, and he argues that there is a fundamental difference between these two types of situation. To ask people whether they are going to go for a walk (an intended action) involves a different kind of verbal report from asking them why they liked someone or whether they are going to like someone (non-intended actions). Morris accepts that Nisbett and Wilson have cast doubt on people's ability to explain non-intended behaviours, but maintains that there is no reason to extend the same scepticism to people's reports of their intentions.

Ericsson and Simon (1980) have proposed that the accuracy of self-reports depends on a number of factors, such as whether the information reported is present in short-term memory and whether the report is of a concurrent or past experience. The more people have to base their report on memories of past experiences, the less accurate reports will be. These limitations obviously apply to those reports that effectively consist of guesses about appropriate labels for internal states such as "feelings", or about the real environmental contingencies that are related to our behaviour. Sometimes they will be demonstrably accurate or be good predictors of subsequent events, for instance when the relevant stimuli are readily observable, when the cause–effect relations present correspond to the person's *a priori* beliefs, and, perhaps, when there is a premium on accurate assessment. Under other circumstances, for instance when there are a large number of relevant stimuli, when the actual cause–effect relations present are unexpected ones, and when there are other influences such as the desire to preserve a good image in one's own eyes or those of others, self-reports are less likely to be accurate reflections of environmental contingencies.

These considerations are particularly relevant to psychiatric patients, who are typically expected to give detailed accounts of their feelings, their attempts to manage complicated interpersonal situations, and the causes of salient life events. In many cases their circumstances will correspond to those least conducive to self-reports, with a plethora of relevant stimuli past and present, unexpected reactions in themselves of which they have little understanding, and the desire to give a reasonably favourable account of themselves. Such considerations have led to the emphasis on collecting a wide variety of data from patients, such as behavioural assessment of their performance in problematic situations and consideration of their response to their therapist ("transference").

# TWO COGNITIVE SYSTEMS

It has been known for a long time that under hypnosis people are receptive to information that, given the appropriate instructions, they cannot subsequently report in their normal waking state. This and many other kinds of evidence (see Power, 1986), along with the data on perception without awareness and on the limitations of self-reports, have led many psychologists to propose that there are two cognitive systems that process information in parallel. Dixon (1981) summarizes the conclusions of relevant research not only on subliminal perception but also on such topics as signal detection, sleep and dreams, binocular rivalry, dichotic listening, and selective attention. His conclusion is (p.19):

> Taken together, the data from these various sources attest to the reality of unconscious perception and preconscious processes. They provide strong support for the notion of two systems—one for information transmission, the other for conscious experience. They suggest that sensory inflow may be subjected to successive levels of analysis and have significant effects upon many sorts of psychological functioning without ever itself being consciously represented.

Similar conclusions have been formulated by investigators of human attention. Posner and Snyder (1975) distinguished between automatic processes, which are triggered by a stimulus and operate outside of awareness, and conscious or control processes, which are deliberately set in motion by the individual. Automatic processes are illustrated by studies of semantic priming. In this paradigm subjects are required to make some judgement about a stimulus, such as whether or not it is a meaningful word. When the stimulus (e.g., BEECH) is preceded by a semantically related prime (e.g., TREE), this judgement is automatically facilitated. Shiffrin and Schneider (1977) and Schneider and Shiffrin (1977) investigated the development of automatic processing in a visual search task. Subjects were given varying numbers of target stimuli and had to report whether or not they were present in a visual display. When the targets changed from trial to trial, subjects' ability to detect them depended on memory load, i.e., how many targets they had been given and how complex the display was. When a target remained the same over many trials, however, subjects were able to detect it regardless of memory load. Schneider and Shiffrin concluded that extensive experience with a particular stimulus resulted in the development of "automatic-attention responses," so that as soon as it was presented the person's attention was automatically drawn to it.

Converging lines of evidence point, then, to the existence of two forms of information processing, one under the control and one not under the control of the individual. Conscious or control processes have been described as highly flexible and adaptable but with a processing capacity severely limited by the attention span of the human being. This limited capacity means that judgements made under conditions of uncertainty or complexity are strongly influenced by *a priori* expectations and hypotheses, and by simple rules or "heuristics" (e.g., Nisbett & Ross, 1980; Tversky & Kahneman, 1974). Conscious processing is deliberate and effortful, and adaptable to new situations, but it can be easily disrupted when there are other stimuli competing for the individual's attention. Automatic processes are rapid, relatively inflexible, require minimal attention to occur, and may be activated without intention or awareness. In attributing causality, for instance, people are powerfully influenced by the fact that two events occur close together in time. They are also influenced by the salience of stimuli, preferring to see more salient stimuli as causally prior. These factors can affect attributions without the knowledge or awareness of the individual (Kassin & Baron, 1985). Automatic processes are also likely to be activated in situations with which the individual has had considerable experience, whereas novel situations are more likely to elicit the conscious deliberate type of processing.

The rationale given for psychological treatments such as Ellis' rational–emotive therapy and Beck's cognitive therapy for depression contain descriptions of both these forms of processing. First, they emphasize the importance of paying attention to the attitudes and beliefs that patients can consciously report, and assume that changing these beliefs can alleviate disturbed mood. However, the "cognition" in these cognitive therapies does not refer solely to thoughts that the patient can report. Both Beck and Ellis have emphasized that patients may not be aware of the rules that guide their behaviour, and that may only become explicit as a result of therapy. For instance, Beck, Rush, Shaw, and Emery (1979) hypothesize the presence of "core assumptions", unarticulated rules with the aid of which the person integrates and assigns value to the raw data of experience. The operation of these rules could be the clinical equivalent of the automatic processing effects described in the laboratory. The origin of these rules in early experience will be discussed in Chapter 9, and in Chapter 5 we will consider how depression influences the processing of self-related information.

How might these two forms of processing interact in patients with psychological disorders? Although this is a relatively unresearched area, some speculation is possible. We have seen that conscious attention can be directed to a particular part of the environment through the development of automatic-attention responses. That is, people's attention may come to focus automatically on certain features that they expect or with which they are familiar. This phenomenon has been noted by Beck et al. (1979, p.14) as one of the features of depressive thinking: "*Selective abstraction* consists of focusing on a detail taken out of context, ignoring other more salient features of the situation and conceptualizing the whole experience on the basis of this fragment". Similar automatic-attention effects in people with anxiety disorders are reviewed in Chapter 5.

It has also been proposed that conscious attention directed to a stimulus inhibits the effects of automatic processing of that stimulus (Posner & Snyder, 1975). Evidence for this "restricting effect of awareness" comes from numerous studies that find that a verbal stimulus of which the person is not aware (because it is presented subliminally, for instance) elicits or activates a far wider range of associates than does one of which the person is aware. Conscious focus on a stimulus, in other words, seems to impose restraints on the ability of ideas that are weakly associated with that stimulus to enter awareness. Dixon (1981, p.256) suggests that these inhibitory effects have two main consequences:

> First, it would heighten awareness of what was beginning to enter awareness—a sharpening and development of figure, coupled with a receding of ground. Second, it would exert inhibitory influences upon inflow that was irrelevant to or unsupportive of the current conscious perceptual hypothesis. The overall effect might be described as the perceptual equivalence of cognitive dissonance. Once a perceptual hypothesis has been formed, all dissonant information, whether sensory or primed in unconscious long-term memory, becomes excluded from subjective experience.

Some process similar to this may be involved in the rigid and absolutistic thinking, and the exclusive focus on their own deficiencies, which Beck et al. (1979) also describe as characteristic of depressives. In this case, excessive conscious processing of a narrow range of experiences (in other words, rumination) may result in the failure to generate contradictory thoughts and ideas of a more positive nature.

A final issue concerns the possibility of attaining awareness of the products of these nonconscious processes. Dixon (1981) argues that such awareness occurs typically in dreams, in other altered states of consciousness, and in extreme circumstances involving stress, deprivation of sensory experience, etc. Under these conditions thoughts are characterized by a richness of associations, and by the failure to inhibit ideas that, although loosely related, appear illogical or contradictory. Such thinking is also characteristic of many schizophrenic experiences, such as delusions and hallucinations, which seem to involve the intrusion of loosely associated thoughts and ideas. This excessive stimulus generalization may be based on a breakdown of the ordinary inhibitory mechanisms that prevent the products of preconscious cognitive processes from becoming conscious (Frith, 1979).

Are such products ever directly accessible in normal states of consciousness? It is plausible that intuitive thinking, which tends to take the form of an implicit perception of the total problem, with little if any awareness of the logical steps involved (Neisser, 1963), is based on fleeting access to the output of preconscious processing. Similarly, the studies of subliminal perception indicate that guesses, hunches, and the like may be informed by stimuli processed out of awareness. Many forms of psychoanalytic therapy, however, assume that information of which the person is unaware, such as a forgotten memory with its associated emotions, can be brought fully and permanently into consciousness. Cognitive therapies also aim to bring to light the underlying rules which, unknown to the individuals involved, govern their information processing. At this time, though, we simply do not know whether such experiences as intuitions and hunches, and the insights obtained in the course of therapy, represent the undistorted output of nonconscious information processing, inferences based on what we can consciously perceive and remember, or some combination of the two.

## COGNITION AND ACTION: REGULATED VERSUS UNREGULATED BEHAVIOUR

The existence of two cognitive systems raises the question of their relative importance in mediating behaviour. For many years behaviourists have argued that people's actions are shaped by environmental events through processes such as operant and classical conditioning, and that conscious beliefs and feelings are "epiphenomenal" by-products of these processes rather than causal influences in their own right. These conclusions derived much of their conviction from the study of pathological behaviours over which individuals could exert little conscious control. As we have seen above, there is ample evidence from many other sources that conscious thought is not a necessary determinant of behaviour. This fact does not, of course, say anything about whether conscious thought *may* (sometimes) determine behaviour, and under what conditions, or whether conscious thought merely predicts behaviour on those occasions in which its content is an accurate reflection of the content of underlying, nonconscious cognitions.

At this point it will be helpful to return to our consideration of the limitations of self-reports. We have noted that these limitations apply mainly to accounts of past actions and events and to complex inferences, whereas there is little reason to doubt the validity of reports dealing with information currently held in short-term memory, such as that concerning intentions, goals, strategies, etc. According to social learning theory (Bandura, 1977a), these conscious goals and plans are among the most important influences on the self-regulation of behaviour (see Chapter 8 for a more detailed discussion of goal-setting). Once aware of their next goal, people adopt what they believe to be the most effective means of achieving it, and adjust these strategies in a flexible way in line with their relative success or failure. Social learning theory is here espousing the commonsense view that people's actions are not wholly determined by past experiences but are in the service of a being with aims and purposes. It is the fact that behaviour is so often simply a means to an end, and not an end in itself, which permits the great variety and capacity for innovation that characterizes human action.

The differences between the social learning and behaviourist views have been considered by some to reflect a different philosophical position concerning the nature of man, and to amount to little more than a resuscitation of the free will versus determinism debate in a new but no more satisfactory guise. Certainly the behaviourist position that all conscious experience is in some way a product of past learning and has no direct role to play in behaviour mediation is difficult to disprove, but its heuristic value in accounting for complex human behaviour is extremely limited. It is more fruitful to regard the two approaches as having developed to provide an explanation for qualitatively different kinds of behaviour, which we may call regulated and unregulated. The latter is often relatively stereotyped, and occurs in response to well-defined environmental circumstances. If asked, individuals are unlikely to be able to provide a good account of why they are behaving in exactly this way. Indeed, they may be unaware of these actions, or may even report that they performed them against their own volition. Regulated behaviour, on the other hand, is flexible and adaptable to changing circumstances. Individuals typically find no difficulty in accounting for their actions, and are likely to invoke some kind of objective, whether immediate or distant.

The distinction between regulated and unregulated actions is illustrated by research on facial expression. At least five basic emotions (happiness, sadness, fear, anger, disgust) are associated with expressions that are recognized across many different cultures, which suggests that there is an unregulated, evolutionarily-determined component involved in their production. Equally, it has been found that facial expression is more often regulated than body cues or tone of voice (Ekman & Friesen, 1974; Zuckerman, Lawrence, Spiegel, & Klorman, 1981), and is subject to cultural display rules that dictate when emotions should be expressed and when they should be concealed. When asked to dissimulate their feelings individuals usually modify their facial expressions rather than postural or vocal cues and, similarly, when people anticipate deception they are most likely to discount facial expression as an accurate index of the other's real attitude. To quote Ekman (1986, p.123):

The true, felt expressions of emotion occur because facial actions can be produced involuntarily, without thought or intention. The false ones happen because there is voluntary control over the face, allowing people to interfere with the felt and assume the false. The face is a dual system, including expressions that are deliberately chosen and those that occur spontaneously, sometimes without the person even aware of what emerges on his own face.

Ekman (1986) argues that different groups of muscles are involved in the production of spontaneous, unregulated expressions and contrived, regulated ones. He has shown that whereas most people cannot distinguish between "false" smiles deliberately put on to please and spontaneous "felt" smiles of pleasure, it is possible to train them to do so by careful observation of the muscles involved in the smile. Spontaneous feelings may also "leak", for example in the form of micro-expressions. Mary, a 42-year-old housewife with a history of suicide attempts, was filmed telling a hospital doctor that she was feeling much better and would like a weekend pass. Before receiving the pass, however, she confessed that she had been lying and still desperately wanted to kill herself. Close examination of the film in slow motion revealed that, when asked about her plans for the future, a fleeting expression of despair, too brief to be noticed in ordinary conversation, had crossed Mary's face. Micro-expressions typically last for less than one quarter of a second, and are then covered by a different expression. But Ekman suggests that experienced clinicians may be able to spot these clues to people's true feelings, and that even the inexperienced can come to recognize them with an hour's intensive practice.

Returning once again to the issue of the accuracy of verbal reports, we can predict that there should generally be good agreement between reports involving short-term intentions and regulated behaviour, since both are under the person's control and could most easily be made consistent. This agreement should be weaker when the reports concern, for example, beliefs about underlying mental states such as emotions or preferences. Verbal reports will only agree with unregulated behaviour to the extent that they represent relatively accurate guesses at these states. In support of these ideas Wilson, Lassiter, and Stone (1984) found that subjects' reported preferences for moderately versus extremely similar others predicted their regulated social behaviours (facial expression, body inclination, and talking time) in the presence of a preferred versus non-preferred other, but did not predict the subjects' unregulated social behaviours (interpersonal distance, eye contact, and body orientation).

We have distinguished so far two broad categories of behaviour, that which is regulated by conscious thought and that which is under the control of an automatic, nonconscious information processing system. In practice, of course, behaviour is usually controlled by a combination of the two systems. The skilled tennis player intends to play certain shots or to adopt certain tactics, but cannot specify the exact combination of movements necessary to achieve them and at times is forced to play strokes about which no prior deliberation is possible. What of the person with psychiatric symptoms? He or she may be experiencing a variety of disturbances in thought, mood, or behaviour that have arisen automatically in the absence of conscious volition. At the same time he or she will be attempting, more or less successfully, to cope with these experiences using the resources of the conscious, self-regulatory system. The outcome will depend on how flexible, imaginative, appropriate, and persistent the person's self-regulatory responses are. In later chapters we will be examining how people actually cope with adversity, what factors determine how persistent and successful they will be, and how psychotherapists attempt to remove symptoms by providing new inputs to one or both of their patients' two cognitive systems.

## THE FREUDIAN CONCEPTION OF THE UNCONSCIOUS

So far we have discussed the evidence that people have restricted access to their internal mental states, and that behaviour can be influenced, in ways that the individual cannot report, both by external stimuli and by internalized rule systems. Thus the argument that there are important cognitive processes of which the individual is unconscious, i.e. unaware, is hardly contentious any longer. But to what extent do these experiments constitute evidence for the psychoanalytic, and specifically the Freudian, view of the unconscious mind?

Freud, in common with many before him, recognized that there must be many mental events of which the individual is unaware, but in his account went considerably beyond this position. He suggested that the mind could usefully be thought of in terms of three regions. In addition to the conscious part, which was highly selective and had a limited capacity, there was the preconscious. This contained ideas that the person was not currently attending to but that could potentially enter awareness, either spontaneously or following an effort at retrieval. The part he called the unconscious contained, in addition to memories of early childhood experiences, ideas and impulses that were *inadmissible* to consciousness and sometimes associated with powerful affects. This notion of the unconscious was intimately connected with *repression*, the process by which ideas are thought to be prevented from ever becoming conscious. (Repression should be distinguished from *suppression*, the deliberate, knowing rejection of a disturbing or unpleasant idea.)

In his initial formulations, Freud argued that unconscious ideas have to pass through the preconscious, which acts as a censor or gatekeeper, if they are to become conscious. At this stage ideas that would be unacceptable because of the psychic pain they would produce (typically ideas with a sexual or aggressive component) are turned away. This process would manifest itself during psychoanalysis as resistance, and the purpose of the analysis was to allow the individual to experience these repressed ideas consciously together with their associated emotions. In his later writings Freud considered in detail the relation of these three regions of consciousness to the other tripartite division between the id, the ego, and the superego. For the present, however, we will confine ourselves to an evaluation of these earlier notions of the unconscious. Its two distinguishing features are that it is a *dynamic* system of ideas, i.e., one that influences a person's behaviour and mental life, and that it involves ideas that have been *repressed*.

Freud based this position on several types of evidence. First, there were clinical observations of patients in dissociative states of various kinds. Charcot had investigated patients suffering from symptoms such as paralysis of a limb, selective anaesthesia, or blindness, for which no organic cause could be found and that were therefore labelled as hysterical. When some of these patients were hypnotized, the symptoms could be made to disappear and reappear by suggestion. Furthermore, patients could be given orders while hypnotized that they subsequently performed while in a waking state, despite having no memory of the original instruction. One example of such post-hypnotic suggestions given by Freud was that of a patient who was hypnotized and told to open an umbrella, indoors, when a particular signal was given. When asked later why he had opened the umbrella, the patient replied that the hypnotist would want it open before venturing outside into the rain.

Breuer and Freud, and also Janet, recognized that hysterical symptoms could be the result of traumatic experiences, the memory of which was normally inaccessible to the patient but which could under certain circumstances be recalled. Bringing to light the original event and having the patient re-experience it as vividly as possible could have beneficial results. Janet and Freud differed, however, in their explanation of why the memory became inaccessible (e.g., Perry & Laurence, 1984). Whereas the latter took the view that the memories were forcefully excluded from consciousness because of their threatening nature, Janet believed that there was a weakening of the ego's ability to integrate and synthesize information, such that certain ideas became dissociated or detached from the main stream of consciousness. This reaction was likely to occur in genetically predisposed individuals, and especially in the context of energy-draining events such as serious physical illness or emotional stressors. This simpler formulation also proposed a dynamic role for ideas of which the person was not aware, but made do without the concept of repression.

A second source of evidence for Freud's conception of the unconscious was the interpretation of dreams. He proposed that dreams were the vehicle for wishes and desires that would be unacceptable in the conscious, waking state, but which could emerge in disguised form during sleep. The latent, unacceptable content was transformed via such processes as condensation (the combining of different ideas into a smaller number of images) or displacement (the detachment of meaning or emotion from the objects to which they belonged and their attachment to other objects), so that sleep would not be disturbed. Freud also found evidence for unconscious processes in his analysis of parapraxes, errors, and mistakes such as slips of the tongue and of the pen. He suggested that these were not random and could sometimes be traced to an origin in unconscious wishes and conflicts.

The evidence that so impressed Freud arose largely out of clinical material and out of intensive investigation of individual experiences. Inevitably it is hard to assess at second or third hand the quality of these data and the extent to which they could be explained by alternative hypotheses. The studies of hysteria convinced Janet, Freud, and many others of the presence of a dynamic unconscious and, as we have seen, this conclusion is in accord with many other lines of evidence that indicate that stimuli of which the person is not aware can influence behaviour. The evidence for repression is much more ambiguous, however, and susceptible to alternative interpretation. Rather than traumatic memories being forcefully excluded from awareness, it is possible that the emotional arousal accompanying the trauma may have affected the registration and storage of the event. It is known, for instance, that anxiety reduces short-term storage capacity and impairs long-term memory, and Eysenck (1984) has suggested that it reduces the elaborateness or extensiveness of processing. We will therefore briefly examine some attempts to verify the existence of repression using experimental rather than clinical methods. For a more detailed review the reader should consult Dixon (1981) or Kline (1981).

The most widely cited evidence for the existence of repression comes from studies of "perceptual defence," a term coined by Bruner and Postman (1947) to account for their finding that words of an emotionally disturbing character were more difficult to recognize than were emotionally neutral words. Perceptual defence, like repression, refers to an assumed mechanism whereby the emotional character of ideas affects their entry into consciousness. It is hard to produce convincing evidence of such a process using a word recognition paradigm, however, and instead some researchers investigated whether a person's perceptual thresholds would be raised in response to threatening stimuli. In a series of studies Dixon

(1958; Dixon & Haider, 1961) examined the effect on one eye's visual threshold of emotional and neutral material presented subliminally to the other eye. Visual threshold was assessed by determining how bright a spot of light had to be in order to be just visible to the subject. The presentation of emotional stimuli such as "whore" or "cancer" produced higher thresholds than did neutral stimuli such as "weave" or "recant". Hardy and Legge (1968) gave subjects the task of trying to detect a faint auditory stimulus while watching a screen upon which neutral and emotional stimuli were presented below the threshold of conscious awareness. They reported that the auditory threshold was higher when emotional stimuli were presented on the screen than when the neutral stimuli were presented, and that this reflected a reduction in sensitivity to stimulation.'

In spite of the technical difficulties involved in demonstrating perceptual defence, these studies provide impressive evidence for the idea that emotional stimuli can reduce the sensitivity of a person's sensory apparatus. Since no verbal response was required, and the subjects were unaware of the nature of the stimuli, the results clearly cannot be explained in terms of a conscious suppression of responding. These findings are extremely important in demonstrating the presence of clinically relevant unconscious processes, but they are still only an analogue of repression as Freud described it in his patients. The raising of a perceptual threshold is still a long way from the complete absence of a memory for a traumatic event, although it is reassuring to know that there is a precedent for a psychological mechanism of this type, and that there are a variety of neural pathways that could mediate these effects (Dixon, 1981). Ideally one would want evidence that experimental repression occurred with stimuli more closely linked to psychoanalytic theory, and that a certain stimulus incurred repression only in individuals with an appropriate life history.

The studies of Silverman go some way towards meeting these aims. He developed a method known as subliminal psychodynamic activation, employing stimuli derived from psychodynamic theory such as a picture of a snarling man holding a dagger or messages such as "Cannibal eats person" and "Fuck Mommy". These stimuli are presented to patients or experimental subjects in a tachistoscope below the threshold of conscious recognition, and their effects on the person's feelings or behaviour are compared with the effects of neutral stimuli. In a recent review of such studies Silverman (1983) reported that thirteen samples of schizophrenic patients have shown increases in pathological thinking and/or nonverbal behaviour after being exposed to slides with an oral–aggressive content. In depressed samples an increase in negative mood followed exposure to similar slides and also to the stimulus "Leaving Mom is wrong". The same techniques have been employed in an attempt to achieve therapeutic improvements, typically by exposing subjects to the subliminal stimulus

"Mommy and I are one". Positive results have been reported with groups as diverse as schizophrenic patients, alcoholics, and the overweight.

In addition to summarizing the results of a large number of studies investigating increases and reductions in pathology following exposure to such stimuli, Silverman (1983) addressed the alternative hypothesis that it was the negative affective quality of the stimuli that produced increases in pathology rather than the specific psychoanalytic content. He was able to cite two studies in which there was negative content that did not intensify one kind of pathology but did intensify another, suggesting that the effects of the negative stimuli may have been specific. Support for the idea that it is inadmissible conflicts that are repressed comes from the additional finding that these same subliminal stimuli typically do not influence pathology levels when they are presented supraliminally. Silverman's work is extremely unusual in providing experimental evidence for the ability of psychodynamically-relevant stimuli, operating out of conscious awareness, to influence people's mood and behaviour. But some of his findings, for example that an Oedipal stimulus, "Beating Dad is wrong", can worsen male students' performance on a competitive dart-throwing task, have proved difficult to replicate (e.g., Fisher, Glenwick, & Blumenthal, 1986).

## CONCLUSIONS

Clinical inferences about the existence of nonconscious processes determining patients' thinking and behaviour have received strong support from the experimental studies described in this chapter. It appears that people do have the ability to detect and respond to stimuli of which they are not consciously aware, either because the stimuli are too weak to be perceived or because they are not recognized as being salient. Experimental demonstrations of priming and automatic-attention effects indicate that prior knowledge and experience can influence many kinds of judgement and decision-making in ways that the person is not aware of. Recent research (e.g., Smith & Lerner, 1986) shows that these effects are not confined to verbal stimuli but include social judgements as well. There is also preliminary evidence that evaluations or affects can be automatically activated and influence subsequent judgements (Fazio, Sanbonmatsu, Powell, & Kardes, 1986).

Apart from the support these findings give to the psychoanalytic notion of a dynamic unconscious affecting everyday behaviour, they have important implications for any kind of clinical practice. They suggest that verbal reports of feelings and accounts of cause-effect relations may be unreliable and amount to little more than plausible inferences, dependent on the availability of appropriate information in memory. On the other hand, as the experiments of Broadbent and colleagues show, people can learn and demonstrate their knowledge in other ways, such as in their actions. This means, effectively, that the knowledge clinicians want to make their formulations, knowledge about the patient's early experience and attitudes towards self and others, may have to be inferred from what patients do as well as from what they say. In some cases the information obtained from the two sources may be contradictory, implying the presence of discrepant internal models of the world containing different end-points or goals. Such a possibility has been considered by many psychoanalytically-inclined writers such as Bowlby (1973) as well as by cognitive psychologists such as Broadbent et al. (1986) and Johnson-Laird (1983). It is discussed further in Chapters 8 and 9.

The dissociation between verbal behaviour and performance is one line of evidence supporting the existence of two cognitive systems, one concerned with the automatic processing of information and one with conscious experience, each having a different knowledge base as well as independent effects on behaviour. Ekman's (1973) research on "microexpressions" illustrates how one type of facial expression may be briefly and automatically produced while a person is consciously trying to put on a quite different expression. A similar explanation may be offered to account for patients who feel fear and avoid certain situations in spite of consciously believing them not to be in any way dangerous. The role of conscious beliefs in phobias and human conditioning is one of the subjects of the next chapter. A similar analysis in terms of conflict between the nonconscious, automatic influences on behaviour and the conscious, self-regulatory ones will be central to the discussion of therapy in Chapter 10.

# 3 Cognition and Conditioning

Any discussion of psychological theorizing in clinical practice must consider the role of learning theory, and particularly the phenomenon of conditioning, which over the years have provided an enormously productive way of thinking about the genesis of fears and phobias. Indeed, at times learning theory seems to have been thought the only broad-ranging psychological theory capable of explaining the nature of such problems and their treatment. Rather unfortunately, the phenomenon of conditioning has also become inextricably linked in people's minds with *behaviourism*, a set of loosely related ideas and precepts about the purpose and scope of psychological enquiry, and with *behaviour therapy*, a set of procedures for eliminating or reducing symptoms and unwanted behaviours. Contrary to popular belief, conditioning effects provide neither unequivocal evidence for a behaviourist view of learning nor an adequate account of successful behaviour therapy, although they are interesting and important in their own right.

In this chapter I discuss the relation between cognition and conditioning theories of neurosis, and in so doing I shall examine traditional conditioning theories from three perspectives. The first concerns the nature of the mechanisms underlying conditioning, and I shall review some recent experiments that demonstrate the involvement of cognitions in human and animal conditioning. The second perspective concerns the ability of conditioning theory to explain the clinical presentation of those disorders (anxiety, phobias, and the like) that are its main focus. Both of these topics have been quite widely discussed and consideration of them has led both to a more sophisticated understanding of conditioning phenomena and to revisions in the conditioning account of neurosis. Finally I shall put forward a critique of this account that emphasizes the role of conscious cognitive processes and the self-regulation of behaviour. This will also give me an opportunity to outline the case for the broader theoretical perspective adopted in this book, and to explain why conditioning theories, however sophisticated, will only ever be of limited use to practitioners.

## MECHANISMS OF CONDITIONING

Why do people develop fears of heights, dogs, spiders, supermarkets, and of many other objects and situations that do not in reality pose a substantial threat? The traditional conditioning model of neurosis regarded such fears as conditioned emotional reactions of the sort demonstrated experimentally in animals and occasionally in young children. According to this model, people and animals acquire neurotic reactions by a process of classical conditioning: neutral stimuli that were present when the organism encountered a stressor (the unconditioned stimulus or UCS), and experienced fear or pain (the unconditioned response or UCR) come to be associated with the stressful situation (i.e., become conditioned stimuli or CS's) and become able themselves to elicit a similar fearful response (the conditioned response or CR). In other words the neutral stimulus, and other stimuli similar to it, become conditioned stimuli for fear. Thus, having been bitten by one dog, individuals are likely to become fearful in the presence of other dogs, the intensity of their reaction tending to diminish as the similarity to the original animal decreases.

The behaviourist explanation of this process is that an association has been formed between the stimulus and the fearful response, so that future presentations of the stimulus automatically come to elicit the response (S-R learning). The strength of the association may vary, however, depending on a number of factors such as the intensity of the initial unconditioned stimulus, the degree of temporal contiguity between the original unconditioned and conditioned stimuli, the number of UCS-CS pairings, etc. Cognitive theories, in contrast, propose that the organism has acquired knowledge of the UCS-CS association (S-S learning). Rather than having learnt that it must respond in a particular way to the CS, it has learnt that the CS heralds the arrival of some UCS. In information-processing terms, the CS activates an internal representation of the UCS that in turn directs subsequent behaviour.

Both these views about what is being learnt during conditioning have a long history, the behaviourist view being particularly associated with Hull and Skinner and the cognitive view with Pavlov and Tolman. From the clinical standpoint, it is important to know which of these two is correct, or whether both types of learning may be represented in phobias and obsessions. Should treatment be aimed at eliminating a fixed response pattern or at changing expectations about the occurrence of frightening or painful events? And what basis do conditioning experiments in animals provide for designing interventions with human beings?

## Animal Conditioning

The question of S-S versus S-R learning has been vigorously pursued in animal experiments. It has been demonstrated using techniques such as the reinforcer revaluation procedure that animals can acquire knowledge of S-S relationships (e.g., Holland & Rescorla, 1975). In one classical conditioning version of this procedure a CS is first paired with food so that the CS alone comes to elicit appetitive behaviour characteristic of an animal in the presence of food. The palatability of the food is subsequently altered by causing the animal to become ill after consuming it. The interest centres on the animal's response if it is now re-presented with the CS. If it has learnt an association between the CS and appetitive behaviour (S-R) it should continue to respond equally strongly to the CS because the CS has never been associated directly with the devalued food. If, on the other hand, it has learnt to associate the CS with the original food UCS (S-S), the internal representation of the appetizing food should have altered and responding to the CS should be diminished. A number of studies have found that reinforcer revaluation does affect the animals' responding, supporting the view that what is being learnt is knowledge about the relationship between CS and UCS. There are exceptions to this finding, however, to which we will return later.

The acquisition of this kind of associative knowledge is now recognized to be a much more complex affair than simple exposure to the temporal and spatial pairing of two events or stimuli (Dickinson, 1980, 1987; Mackintosh, 1983). For example, animals are sensitive to the overall correlation or contingency between events rather than to the number of times they occur together (Rescorla, 1968), which means that they must process information about the times that a UCS and a CS do not occur together as readily as information about the times when they do. No matter how many times a UCS and a CS are paired, if the CS is also frequently presented in the absence of the UCS then conditioning is unlikely to result. Animals are also less likely to learn of the relationship between a new stimulus and a reinforcer if such pairings occur in the presence of an existing CS that is already an efficient signal of the reinforcer. This is Kamin's (1969) "blocking" effect. Mackintosh (1973) has also shown animals to be capable of learning that a stimulus and a reinforcer are unrelated. This knowledge ("learned irrelevance") subsequently retards learning when the two are presented again, but this time in a predictive relationship.

Faced with these findings and many like them, animal conditioning has now come to be seen largely in terms of information-processing. Current theories emphasize that what is learnt depends on the amount of processing that a signal or a reinforcer receives, and that this is influenced by such factors as their surprisingness or their predictive value. Conditioning, in other words, usually involves the selection of relevant information and its integration with internal representations of related past events that are stored in memory. The parallels with human information-processing are becoming increasingly compelling, and it has recently been proposed that the perception of contingent relations between events rests, both in humans and in animals, on the interaction between prior expectations about their covariation and current situational information provided by the environment (Alloy & Tabachnik, 1984).

In spite of this trend towards cognitive explanations there have also been findings that cannot be so readily accommodated by them. For example, reinforcer revaluation may not produce the same effect in second-order Pavlovian conditioning as in the first-order case discussed above (Rescorla, 1980). In second-order Pavlovian conditioning a second CS (CS2) is paired with the the original CS, so that CS2 is itself able to elicit the conditioned response. Whereas revaluation of a UCS often produces altered responding to the initial CS, Rescorla has found that responding to CS2 can survive both the revaluation of the UCS and the extinction of conditioning to the first-order signal (CS1). Similarly, Dickinson (1985) reported that if an instrumental response, such as bar pressing for a food reward, is trained on an extended schedule with many response-reward pairings, revaluing the reinforcer has little effect on responding in an extinction test. Dickinson refers to this persistence in responding to a stimulus that no longer signals a reward as "behavioural autonomy." Control over the behaviour appears to be at least partially independent of knowledge about the consequences, and the behaviour may appear as an automatic response to the eliciting stimulus, as proposed by S-R theorists.

From all these experiments conditioning in animals emerges as a much more complex phenomenon than was originally thought, and as one highly sensitive to differences in the procedures employed. At times animals' behaviour appears responsive to new information and at times it appears reflexive and stereotyped. What can be stated with confidence, however, is that the use of animal models does not restrict one to a simple, associationist view of learning or of the genesis of neurotic disorders.

## Human Conditioning

If animal models are to be helpful in understanding neuroses, the first question to ask concerns the similarity of conditioning phenomena in animals and in human beings. Is there any reason to think that similar processes are involved in the acquisition and extinction of defensive reactions, for example? One long-established observation is that the extinction of classically conditioned aversive responses is relatively much more rapid in adult human beings, and this has something to do with their ability to discriminate the moment when the UCS ceases to be reinforced. If they are prevented from making this discrimination, however, the extinction curve is similar to that shown by animals (Spence, 1966). Classical conditioning of reactions such as the eyeblink response to a puff of air on the eyeball, or of autonomic responses such as heart rate or skin conductance, also tends not to occur unless the adult human subject is aware of, and can verbalize, the contingent CS-UCS relations. This is illustrated by a number of studies, many of which are reviewed by Davey (1983, 1987). It appears that conditioned responding in humans can be spontaneously acquired or eliminated by informing subjects that a CS will or will not be followed by a UCS. Furthermore, providing false information about the CS-UCS relationship can lead to responding appropriate to the false information rather than appropriate to the contingencies actually experienced by the subject.

A recent study (Davey, Gordon, & Smith, 1986) shows the effect of instructions, and of subjects' appraisal of their own reactions, on the extinction of conditioned electrodermal responding. Subjects were first given six pairings of a triangle (the CS) with a loud noise (the UCS), then instructed that presentation of the CS would no longer be reinforced. Their electrodermal responses to the CS during extinction were subsequently monitored under several different conditions. One group were given false feedback of their skin conductance levels, which apparently showed that they were continuing to respond strongly to the CS. Relative to other subjects not given this suggestion, the actual electrodermal responses of this group took longer to extinguish and they reported less confidence in the extinction instructions.

Many studies of this kind demonstrate that conditioned responding in humans, whether of the Pavlovian or operant variety, is very different from the gradual increments and decrements in response strength observed in animals. The most straightforward explanation is that adult human beings' conscious awareness or expectations of the CS-UCS contingency, and their ability to express this relation in a verbal summary, permit them to generate self-instructions that then influence their responding. In support of this idea, it has been found that pre-verbal children's acquisition and extinction of conditioned reactions is much more similar to that shown by animals than to that shown by adult humans (Lowe, 1983).

This means that the responding observed in conditioning experiments is a product both of the experimenter's externally arranged contingencies and of the subject's internally generated instructions. But whereas it makes good sense to suppose that people can instruct themselves to make or withhold a voluntary response such as pressing a key or praising their daughter for her achievements, it is not so obvious that they can voluntarily control their heart rate, skin conductance, or the other variables typically measured in classical conditioning experiments. In fact, people do have a surprising degree of control over these responses that were once considered to be involuntary. To cite only one example, subjects who are told to try and suppress conditioned responding while continuing to be presented with CS-UCS pairings are frequently able to reduce the magnitude of skin conductance levels (Grings & Dawson, 1973).

For some years there has been a major debate about whether conscious awareness of the relevant contingencies is *essential* for conditioning to take place in human beings. In their reviews of electrodermal conditioning studies Grings and Dawson (1973) and Dawson and Schell (1987) describe several studies that have examined whether conditioning takes place when the CS-UCS contingency is concealed from subjects, for example by using a masking task to distract them from the real purpose of the experiment. These studies have produced inconsistent results, those that have measured awareness by requiring subjects to recall the CS-UCS contingency often "succeeding" in showing conditioning without awareness, and those that have measured awareness with a more stringent forced-choice recognition task generally "failing" to do so. The two reviews come to the conclusion that on the basis of present evidence awareness is necessary in adults, but in view of the fact that conditioning can be demonstrated in pre-verbal children it would perhaps be unwise to rule out all possibility of demonstrating conditioning without awareness in the future.

What is well-established, however, is that previously acquired conditioned responses may be performed in the absence of corresponding conscious cognitions. For example, conditioned responses sometimes persist even after conscious expectancies of the UCS occurring have been extinguished by the appropriate instructions or by giving a series of extinction trials. Conditioned responses may also occur when the CS is presented subliminally. These observations accord with the clinical experience that patients are often rather vague about the situations in which they feel anxious. They may initially complain of simply feeling tense, only on careful questioning being able to narrow down the source of their anxiety to a more specific situation such as being criticized for inferior work by a particular individual. Alternatively, as we have seen in this chapter and in Chapter 2, they may actually have formed quite erroneous ideas about the situations that make them respond in a particular way.

A final question that needs to be asked about these laboratory experiments is how they relate to conditioning experiences reported by patients. The major difference is that in real life the conditioned reactions are much stronger. Sometimes this is because the UCS is much more intense and elicits a strong CR, often after a single CS-UCS pairing. Patients' environments may also permit many more CS-UCS pairings than occur in the laboratory, perhaps continuing over a period of many years. The conditioned reactions are much more resistant to extinction and, unlike the laboratory case, instructions have little effect. That is, individuals may themselves be convinced that their fear is irrational, but no amount of reassurance that the contingencies have changed is able to reduce their level of fear. In many ways, then, phobic individuals fail to show the characteristics that differentiate human conditioning in the laboratory from that of pre-verbal children or animals.

These differences between clinic and laboratory have been explained in two main ways. One is to postulate that there are two separate laws of learning, which have been termed the "Rule of Sequence" and the "Rule of Consequence" (Martin & Levey, 1985). The "Rule of Consequence" involves the registration of single, isolated events that are associated with immediate and significant consequences for the individual. This type of evaluative learning (i.e., learning what is harmful or beneficial) is assumed not to be mediated by internal cognitive representations or by an individual's awareness of contingencies, but to consist of a simple and highly robust association between a stimulus and an appetitive or defensive response. The "Rule of Sequence" is involved in learning about a series of similar events, and creating an internal cognitive summary of the order in which they occur. This summary or "script" may readily be influenced by new information, and departures from an expected orderly sequence of events produce orienting behaviour. Most clinical phobias are thought to result from evaluative conditioning following a single traumatic experience, and hence to be resistant to most kinds of new information short of prolonged exposure to the unreinforced CS. However, it is also possible that defensive reactions are based on cognitive summaries of repeated events, and under these circumstances they would be expected to respond to a broader range of interventions, including purely verbal ones.

The other explanation for clinic-laboratory differences relies on a single law of learning, but proposes instead that it is the primary association formed between the CS, UCS, and UCR that is crucial (Davey, 1983;

Mackintosh, 1983). According to this view the CS will be primarily associated with the most salient feature of the situation, which might be an internal event (the UCR) or an external event (the UCS). Responding will then be influenced by information that is relevant to the particular association formed. In the laboratory, where the UCR's are typically weak (and sometimes not discriminable at all by the subject), and the subject is paying careful attention to the sequence of stimuli, he or she will tend to form a primary association between the CS and the UCS (S-S learning). Under these circumstances, in which presentation of the CS first elicits some internal representation of the UCS, information provided by revaluation of the UCS, or by extinction instructions, should have an effect. In the case of a clinical phobia, however, where the individual's reaction (the UCR) is likely to be much stronger, perhaps involving choking sensations, panic, and fear of dying, the primary association is likely to be of an S-R kind. Under these circumstances presentation of the CS will first elicit the full CR, which will be relatively unaffected by new information involving the UCS or the CS-UCS contingency.

There are a number of unexplored possibilities to account for the failure of conditioned fear reactions to extinguish. Perhaps the information necessary for extinction must be presented in a similar form to the acquisition phase. Fear reactions that were acquired through direct experience and without conscious knowledge of the CS-UCS contingency (for example, because the individual was too young at the time) may not respond to verbal persuasion or modelling but only to further experience, this time of the unreinforced CS. On the other hand, it is not the case that phobic patients who *do* recall the critical contingency necessarily respond to cognitive methods alone.

What is potentially useful clinically is the distinction between the two types of conditioned fear reaction, one based on conscious or nonconscious knowledge of stimulus contingencies and one based on a direct association with a frightening stimulus or situation. If this analysis is correct, a direct S-R link, leading to "behavioural autonomy", is more likely when there is an intense CR or extended experience with the CS-UCS contingency. A knowledge-based fear reaction is more likely when there have been a small number of non-traumatic exposures to the CS-UCS contingency, perhaps arising from verbal instructions or vicarious learning. Only the latter would be expected to respond to the therapist's verbal persuasion or extinction instructions alone. At present, however, there are no empirical tests of this hypothesis, and it remains to be seen whether conditioned fear reactions can usefully be classified in this way or whether the majority are based on a combination of both types of learning.

# CONDITIONING MODELS OF NEUROSIS

Just as our views of conditioning have changed a great deal, conditioning models of neurosis have undergone extensive revision over the years. In the 1950s the conditioning account of fear acquisition, in which neutral stimuli come to elicit conditioned emotional reactions by virtue of their association with painful or unpleasant stimuli, was extended to provide an explanation of avoidance behaviour in what has come to be known as the Miller–Mowrer model. According to this view individuals who are exposed to the relevant classically conditioned stimuli try to reduce the unpleasant experience of fear, either by passively avoiding fear-eliciting situations or by actively performing certain actions that have been associated with escape from pain or fear in the past. These two strategies have been thought to correspond to the neurotic phenomena of phobic avoidance and obsessional behaviour respectively (Eysenck & Rachman, 1965). Reduction of fear was also held to act as a powerful reinforcer, leading to the persistence of successful avoidance responses. The Miller–Mowrer model has been extremely influential, and was particularly so in the early days of behaviour therapy, but is now of largely historical interest owing to the many empirical data that it cannot accommodate.

One difficulty faced by this conditioning theory of neurosis is the non-random distribution of phobias. In the Pavlovian view of conditioning, on which the Miller–Mowrer model was based, any neutral stimulus may become a conditioned stimulus, and in the laboratory a wide range of neutral stimuli such as tones and lights have been made conditioned stimuli for fear and have come to elicit avoidance behaviour. Clinical phobias, however, are largely restricted to insects, snakes, small furry animals, heights, water, crowds, enclosed spaces, and social situations. People do not tend to have phobias about bicycles and electric sockets, in spite of the fact that they are in reality more likely to be associated with unpleasant experiences. This observation has led to the concept of biological "preparedness", according to which evolutionary pressures have produced a greater readiness in people to develop fear responses to certain stimuli that have been dangerous in mankind's history (Seligman, 1971).

It would of course be simpler to regard fear of snakes, heights, and so on as innate, which would account more satisfactorily for another observation at variance with conditioning theory, the fact that phobias tend to develop at particular ages (Gray, 1979). But to call such fears innate does not help to explain why only a proportion of individuals fear these stimuli, and fewer still develop phobias. "Preparedness" does therefore seem to be a useful concept theoretically: in spite of circularity in its definition (there is at present no independent way of establishing exactly which stimuli are prepared and which are not), it draws attention to a distinction between fears that may be biologically pre-programmed and fears of neutral stimuli adventitiously acquired.

In practical terms, however, the value of the distinction is less clear. The work of Öhman (e.g., Öhman, Dimberg, & Öst, 1985; Öhman, Frederickson, & Hugdahl, 1978) shows that in the laboratory people do not always develop consistently faster conditioned electrodermal responses to "fear-relevant" stimuli depicting rats and spiders than they do to "fear-irrelevant" stimuli. On the other hand, once such conditioned responses have been acquired, they do tend to be more resistant to extinction and to be less influenced by verbal instructions that the shock will not occur when the stimuli are fear-relevant. The finding of greater resistance to extinction for these stimuli has recently been replicated by Cook, Hodes, and Lang (1986), who also obtained some new evidence for a preparedness effect. Only those subjects whom they presented with fear-relevant stimuli showed conditioned heart rate acceleration, a response that is generally considered to be a defensive reaction in the presence of threat.

It ought to follow, therefore, that phobias about "relevant" or "prepared" stimuli would be more difficult to treat clinically, but a retrospective study of behaviour therapy cases failed to find any evidence that this was the case (de Silva, Rachman, & Seligman, 1977). One reason may be that the findings obtained by Öhman et al. are restricted to the particular unconditioned stimulus used by them (mild electric shock). Cook et al. failed to get similar results using loud noise instead of shock as the UCS. They also reported that the differential electrodermal conditioning effects were not particularly robust, and they were unable to confirm the finding that reactions conditioned to fear-relevant stimuli are less affected by instructed extinction. Thus the clinical significance of these interesting experiments remains to be established.

Another difficulty encountered by conditioning theories of neurosis lies in individuals' reports that they have sometimes never encountered the object or situation of which they are afraid. Somewhere between 40–80% of individuals with fears or phobias typically cannot recall any traumatic experience associated with onset. It was therefore suggested that fears and phobias might be acquired vicariously from observations of others as well as from direct experience (e.g., Bandura, 1977a; Rachman, 1977). The most convincing demonstration of such a process comes from a series of studies that have exposed laboratory-reared monkeys not initially afraid of snakes (the observers) to the sight of wild-reared monkeys (the models) behaving fearfully with snakes and non-fearfully with other objects (Mineka, 1987). One conclusion from these studies is that monkeys can readily acquire fear vicariously, and that this fear generalizes to other situations and persists for long periods of time. Moreover, the degree of disturbance exhibited by the fearful model in the presence of the snake is very highly correlated with the degree of disturbance subsequently shown by the observer monkey exposed to a snake.

Mineka (1987) also discusses the possible mechanisms that might underlie such observational learning. Are the observer monkeys simply responding to the distress of another by becoming distressed themselves, or is some kind of inferential process taking place in which the observer learns to attribute the model's distress to the snake? Mineka and her co-workers reasoned that in the former case the observers should display similar levels of distress whether or not they could see what the model was reacting to. If the latter were true, however, observers who could also see the object provoking the distress should display more fear than observers who saw only the model. What they found was that initially observers showed similar levels of distress in the two conditions, but that whereas this distress continued unabated when the snake was also visible, observers who could only see the model soon ceased to show signs of fear. In cognitive terms, observers who could only see the model learnt to attribute the distress they observed to a characteristic of the model rather than to a characteristic of the environment. In further experiments, however, it was shown that observer monkeys only acquired fear in this manner when the stimuli were "relevant" (e.g., snakes) and not when they were "irrelevant" stimuli such as flowers. Thus the cognitive inferential process appears in this species to operate within biologically defined boundaries.

These experiments provide a sound basis for the speculation that human fears and phobias can be acquired vicariously through the social transmission of information. Other experiments in the series reveal that the acquisition of fear can be blocked by exposing observer monkeys to a prior "immunization" treatment in which they watch models behaving non-fearfully with snakes. In human beings it has been demonstrated similarly that exposing phobic patients to non-fearful models reduces levels of fear (Bandura, 1971), and that children can be to a certain extent immunized against the fears attendant on hospitalization by exposing them to a filmed model coping successfully with a related situation (Melamed & Siegel, 1975). There are thus additional grounds for emphasizing the importance of cognitive or informational factors in the acquisition and reduction of fear and for being cautious about the utility of a conditioning model relying on the idea of simple associations formed by direct experience.

Another element of the Miller–Mowrer model that has been contradicted by the evidence is the assertion that avoidance behaviour is motivated by a reduction in the fear produced by the conditioned stimulus. Although fear reduction is probably important initially in establishing avoidance behaviour, in the laboratory fear soon seems to disappear altogether once an effective avoidance response has been learnt. The problem is that both animals and human beings tend to persist with avoidance responses, often for long periods of time, in spite of the apparent absence of fear. What, then, causes this behaviour to continue? Among the many possibilities suggested are that it is maintained by secondary rewarding stimuli ("safety signals") that accompany the successful avoidance of punishment (Gray, 1971), and that the behaviour becomes so well practised as to be elicited "automatically" in certain situations without the need for direct motivational antecedents (Kimble & Perlmuter, 1970).

Avoidance learning in the laboratory has been extensively discussed by behaviour therapists because its persistence appears analogous to the persistence of neurotic conditions such as phobias and compulsions. While it may provide a useful model of some clinical states, it is dissimilar to most in that, as mentioned previously, well-established avoidance behaviour tends to occur in the absence of fear. Similarly, in the laboratory, emotional reactions that have been conditioned to neutral stimuli extinguish quite quickly when those stimuli are presented unreinforced, i.e., without the shock or loud noise that originally accompanied them. Patients who attend clinics, on the other hand, typically experience moderate or high levels of anxiety that may persist for years, despite the fact that they are no longer being exposed to the combination of the original conditioned and unconditioned stimuli. Nor is the Miller–Mowrer theory able to explain why anxiety sometimes increases with repeated exposure to a phobic object or situation, with the result that the eventual conditioned response of anxiety is considerably more severe than the original unconditioned response (Eysenck, 1987).

Recent conditioning theories of neurosis (e.g., Eysenck, 1979, 1987) have attempted to respond to these various criticisms while still maintaining that a process of Pavlovian conditioning is central to this group of disorders. Revisions have been extensive, including an acceptance that conditioning cannot be regarded as a simple associative phenomenon, agreement that "rational" fears may be acquired through alternative channels such as the verbal transmission of information, and rejection of the idea of "equipotentiality" of stimuli in favour of biological "preparedness" influencing the selection of those stimuli that become conditioned. The focus of the approach has been narrowed to concentrate on persistent, maladaptive behaviours recognized to be irrational by the individual concerned, thus specifically excluding "rational" fears, adjustment to severe environmental stressors, and other types of emotional reaction commonly presenting in clinical settings.

Eysenck has also proposed a mechanism to account for the persistence of neurotic anxiety and for its liability to increase over time. As we have noted, classical conditioning theory predicts that a conditioned reaction will extinguish if the person or animal is repeatedly exposed to the conditioned stimulus in the absence of the original UCS. Eysenck argues that, unlike a CS signalling food, a CS signalling an unpleasant UCS such as shock (and itself eliciting fear) may be experienced by the person or animal as having an effect equivalent to the original UCS. In other words, the subject's or patient's reaction to the CS is virtually identical to their reaction to the UCS. In this case it is not really possible from the subjects' point of view (as opposed to the experimenter's) to expose them to an "unreinforced" CS, i.e., the CS without the UCS, since the experience will be very similar in either case. Repeated presentations of the CS alone will therefore still tend to be aversive, and Eysenck argues that under certain conditions (primarily a strong conditioned response and a short CS exposure time) *incubation* or strengthening of the conditioned response of anxiety will result. With a weaker conditioned response and a longer CS exposure, on the other hand, the CR will tend to extinguish.

The theory of incubation provides a neat way of accounting for the observation that levels of fear fluctuate over time. It is still controversial, however, and in need of more empirical support (see commentaries accompanying Eysenck, 1979). Alternative explanations exist based on phenomena such as "reinstatement" (Rescorla & Heth, 1975). "Reinstatement" refers to the finding that, following extinction of a fear CR, exposure to a traumatic UCS alone can have the effect of eliciting the CR even though no further CS–UCS pairings have occurred. This raises the possibility that fears may persist because they are reawakened through subsequent, unrelated aversive experiences.

In addition a number of criticisms may be made of conditioning theories of neurosis, even in their most recent form. Marks (1977), for instance, has consistently drawn attention to the lack of any comprehensive account of the different forms that neurotic phenomena may take, i.e., why some people develop phobias, others rituals or obsessional thoughts, and why panic is a feature of some disorders and not others. Another set of criticisms have been made by cognitively-oriented theorists, and some of these are reviewed in the next section.

## A COGNITIVE CRITIQUE OF CONDITIONING THEORIES OF NEUROSIS

As we have seen, recent conditioning theories of neurosis accept that classical conditioning involves the processing of information about environmental contingencies, in particular information signalling the probability of reward and punishment. This information, theorists are generally agreed, may come from a variety of sources including direct experience, observations of the experiences of others and, in the case of human beings, oral and written accounts. The role of cognitive processes does not end here, however. The acquisition and extinction of fear also appears to depend on the perception of information about the predictability and controllability of the environment, and on perceptions of the availability of successful avoidance responses.

Mineka (e.g., Mineka & Kihlstrom, 1978) has been one of several writers who have documented how in animals levels of fear depend to a considerable degree on instrumental contingencies such as the availability of a successful avoidance response (control) and on informational contingencies such as the presence of stimuli signalling the onset and offset of shock (prediction). These variables appear to be important determinants of reactions both to aversive UCSs (stressors) and to the conditioned stimuli that have been associated with them. For example, animals are less fearful when they can predict the occurrence of an aversive UCS. They also tend to acquire more fear when shocks are inescapable than when they are escapable, and fear extinction tends to proceed more rapidly when the animal can perform an avoidance response than when it cannot. In other words, there is more to fear acquisition than the perception of a contingency between a neutral stimulus and an aversive UCS. A wide range of information appears relevant to the eventual outcome.

In human beings, too, both self-report and physiological measures of emotion are affected by the degree of control over an aversive event (Gatchel, 1980). What appears to be important is not the actual instrumental contingencies present, however, but subjects' consciously-held perceptions of control. In one experiment Geer, Davison, and Gatchel (1970) began by giving all their subjects a series of painful six-second electric shocks, followed by a series of shorter, three-second shocks. Half the subjects were simply told when they could expect the briefer shocks, whereas the other half were led to believe that it was their own improved performance that was reducing shock duration. Geer et al. found that the electrodermal component of autonomic arousal was significantly reduced in this latter perceived control group. Other studies have found that nonveridical perceived control can lead to decreased physiological reactivity and less impaired task performance in the presence of an aversive event or events.

The significance of these studies derives from the fact that the instrumental contingencies and causal influences operating in real life are immensely more complex than they are in the laboratory, where the relations between response and reinforcement are typically straightforward. Few responses are available there, and a response will either succeed or not succeed in terminating an unpleasant state of affairs devized by the experimenter. Outside this sheltered world people are often unclear about the cause of their problems and have available a large number of response options whose effectiveness is hard to predict, particularly where long-term outcome is concerned. They may be exposed to other opinions about what they should do and what will work best, and can draw on their own memories of how successfully they behaved in related situations. This large pool of potentially relevant information means that there will usually be scope for great variation, and frequently error, in individuals' conscious beliefs about the availability of an effective escape, avoidance, or other coping response. These judgments, whether accurate or inaccurate, nevertheless appear likely from the results of the above experiments to influence the acquisition and extinction of fear.

On the basis of this kind of evidence many theorists (e.g., Bandura, 1977b; Gatchel, 1980; Lazarus, 1966; Seligman, 1975) have proposed that the course of fear and anxiety is dependent on perceptions of control versus helplessness in the face of an aversive situation, and that therapeutic interventions are effective or ineffective by virtue of their ability or inability to increase perceived control on the part of the patient. One of the most comprehensive statements of this position has been made by Bandura (1977b), who proposes that a person's level of fear is primarily determined by their perceived "self-efficacy", i.e., their ability to escape from or master aversive situations. In support of this he cites evidence showing, for instance, that behaviour with a feared object such as a snake is better predicted by reported self-efficacy than it is by reported levels of fear. Clearly, this result is difficult for conditioning theory to explain.

This is not the place to discuss in detail the alternative proposals made by Lazarus, Bandura, and others. The assumptions that typify their critique of the conditioning model will recur throughout this book, and the empirical support for the alternative cognitive theories is addressed in detail at numerous points. Lazarus' arguments are outlined in Chapter 4, for instance, whereas Chapter 6 contains a discussion of how fear may be exacerbated by the way in which people label their experiences. In Chapter 7 the evidence for Bandura's self-efficacy theory is considered in detail.

It is worth bearing in mind, however, that the cognitive critique comes in two parts, concerned with nonconscious and conscious processes respectively. The first demands that conditioning phenomena be recognized as depending on a complex synthesis of information about the probability of reward and punishment in different situations, their predictability, the availability of effective avoidance responses, etc. These processes can be demonstrated equally well in animals and in human beings and require relatively minor modifications to a traditional conditioning account of neurosis. One obvious change is that human beings are influenced by symbolic information in the form of words or pictures. Fear and avoidance are still seen as being produced by environmental events acting on the organism, albeit in a more complicated way that takes into account attentional factors, interactions with prior events in memory, etc.

The second part of the critique, logically distinct from the first, holds that in human beings conscious beliefs also affect the acquisition and extinction of fear by virtue of the human capability to create to some extent one's own environment. Human beings are considered to be active agents who try to comprehend themselves and their situation and, guided by their thoughts, to regulate their own behaviour, initiate plans, and achieve their consciously-held goals (e.g., Bandura, 1977a). Men and women have the option of deliberately frightening themselves, or of avoiding most sources of fear, by manipulating the activities they perform, the people they mix with, the risks or precautions they take, the topics they choose to think about, and so on. This philosophical position, that people are to some extent at least the architects of their own environment, is obviously at variance with the determinism enshrined in the conditioning account, and with the view that people react passively to circumstances.

Fortunately it is not necessary to put all one's money on either one of these possibilities. As so often in science, the different theories have developed in order to explain different kinds of phenomena. A conditioning or information-processing account based on nonconscious processes is necessary to explain why people carry out certain behaviours that they know consciously to be irrational and even damaging. As we saw in the previous chapter, behaviour can frequently be demonstrated to be under the control of contingencies of which the person is not aware. Equally, a theory that assigns a role to conscious thought processes is necessary to explain how people can alternately frighten and reassure themselves by thinking different thoughts, test out a variety of different coping responses, set goals and reward or punish themselves depending on the outcome, etc. One of the reasons that neuroses are so fascinating is precisely because this interplay between conscious and nonconscious influences is acted out in such a readily observable way.

## CONCLUSIONS

Laboratory demonstrations of conditioning in animals, for so long the favoured analogue of clinical phobias, have turned out to be complex phenomena dependent in large measure on the integration of many sorts of information. As has been pointed out by several authors, conditioning shares many features with the process of attribution described by social psychologists. Both involve attempts to learn about the cause–effect relations present in the environment, and both are strongly influenced by the covariation between events, and by the primacy, contiguity, and salience of stimuli. We will return to this issue in Chapter 6. Conditioning in adult humans is strongly influenced by conscious awareness of the CS–UCS contingency, and for this reason does not correspond very closely to clinical phobias. This may be because in the typical human experiment the UCS is weaker, or the number of trials is fewer, than that occurring in real life. It has been suggested that the type of learning that occurs in the presence of an intense or traumatic stimulus is qualitatively different from the registration of sequences of less intense stimuli.

Conditioning models of neurosis have also changed considerably since the Miller–Mowrer model of the 1950s. They now take account of the non-random distribution of phobias, and of the transmission of fear through observation or symbolic channels. As models of psychopathology they still have many shortcomings, however, and need to be supplemented in various ways if they are to provide an adequate account of the clinical phenomena. One aspect that needs to be elaborated is the role of people's conscious appraisal of their coping resources and degree of helplessness. Another suggestion is that the learning that takes place in infancy, before the maturation of neural systems involving the hippocampus, has different characteristics from later learning. Under stress residues of early experience are thought to be reinstated and incorporated into the adult memory, where they may exercise some control over the person's behaviour (Jacobs & Nadel, 1985). Yet another approach, to be described in the next chapter, seeks to understand phobias in terms of a more general model of the formation and subsequent processing of emotional memories.

# 4 Cognition and Affect

The term "affect" is a broad one, and has been taken by psychologists to include more specific experiences such as moods, feelings, attitudes, preferences, evaluations, and emotions. All these experiences may vary in intensity and in duration, but emotions tend to be regarded as relatively intense and of short duration, whereas the term "mood" tends to be used for less intense but longer-lasting states. Affective judgements are involved, for example, when we decide that a certain person makes us nervous or that we disapprove of a particular point of view. Although in psychiatric terminology "affective disorders" refer mainly to depression and mania, many problems with which clinicians are faced have a disturbance of affect (in its broader sense) as one of their defining characteristics. These may involve strong positive feelings (cravings) towards harmful substances or inappropriate sexual objects. Sometimes there are strong negative affects, such as hate, guilt, or jealousy. Both depression and anxiety, which are prominent features of most psychological disorders, have a large affective component.

Clinical psychology is therefore in need of theories that can give an account of how affective states, and in particular distressing emotions, come about and how they may be altered. In the previous chapter we examined the origins of one particular type of affective response, conditioned fear, and concluded that there was strong evidence for the involvement of cognitive processes. We will now consider more general theories of emotion and the role that they assign to cognition. Because the literature on cognition and affect is extensive, we will focus on four topic areas of direct relevance to clinical practice. The first is concerned with cognitive theories of emotion, i.e., theories that emphasize the importance of a person's cognitions in determining the nature of the emotional response. An opposing perspective, namely that affective judgments often occur prior to cognitive operations, forms the second topic. The third concerns the influence of transient emotional states on cognitive processes, particularly memory. The fourth deals with emotional reactions to major stressors from the point of view of imagery and memory processes, and includes an account of how emotional memories may be altered by exposure to corrective information. By this point we shall be in a better position to discuss the complex nature of the relationship between cognition and affect.

## COGNITIVE THEORIES OF EMOTION

Cognitive processes such as attention, recognition, and forgetting should in theory be able to occur with little, if any, accompanying affect, so long as the material being processed has no particular emotional significance for the individual. To ask a person to identify the capital cities of the countries of South America may be assumed to be a fairly affect-free task, unless that person has pleasant or unpleasant memories from a previous visit. Cognitive theories of emotion assume that a stimulus or a situation must first be attended to, recognized or classified, and related to previous experiences stored in memory before it can be evaluated or can arouse an emotional response. A small number of "basic" emotional responses have been identified, and it has been suggested that other emotions are made up of a blend of these. The five most commonly cited are happiness, anger, fear, sadness, and disgust, although, using the criterion that the facial expression associated with a basic emotion should be recognized all over the world, Ekman (1973) has argued that surprise should be included. Three influential proponents of cognitive theories of emotion are Schachter (1964), Lazarus (1966), and Weiner (1986).

### Schachter's Theory

This two-factor theory of emotion has been extremely influential. According to Schachter, the experience of emotion is dependent on the conjunction of two elements, the perception of peripheral physiological arousal and the label that such arousal is given. The experience of physiological arousal, such as churning of the stomach or rapid beating of the heart, is considered to be relatively nonspecific, i.e., it does not take distinct forms corresponding to different emotional states. Emotional specificity is provided by cognitive appraisal of the source of the arousal. In most instances arousal will be attributed automatically to the stimulus or situation that elicits it, probably on the basis of the temporal contiguity of stimulus and reaction (see Chapter 6 for a discussion of attributional determinants). The knowledge that we have stored in long-term memory about appropriate emotional responses will automatically generate an appropriate label, so that we have the experience of fear when a large dog is leaping up at us and growling, but the experience of anger on discovering that our home has been broken into during our absence.

Considerable attention has been devoted to the special case in which individuals perceive that they are physiologically aroused but have no immediate explanation of why this should be. Schachter suggested that the experience of arousal would trigger a search for an appropriate cause, an emotion only being experienced if suitable cues were present to account for the arousal. A famous experiment was designed (Schachter & Singer, 1962) in which physiological arousal was induced in some subjects by injecting them with adrenaline whereas other subjects were injected with a placebo. Some of the adrenaline group were then given accurate information about the accompanying sensations of arousal, whereas others were given no information or were misinformed. Finally, contextual cues were manipulated to suggest to subjects that they were feeling either happy or angry. It was predicted that the experience of emotion should be strongest in the two groups who were least able to attribute their sensations of arousal to the effect of the adrenaline injection.

The results were broadly in agreement with Schachter and Singer's predictions, but there were also several anomalous results. For example, the mean emotional self-reports of all the experimental groups fell on the "happy" side of the neutral point, indicating that the "anger" cues had not succeeded in inducing a corresponding subjective emotional state. The emotion ratings of the placebo group also tended to be as extreme as those of the subjects given adrenaline, casting doubt on the assertion that physiological arousal is a necessary condition for the experience of emotion. Since then a number of studies have attempted to replicate these findings and to provide support for the two-factor model. Many of these studies are reviewed by Manstead and Wagner (1981) and Reisenzein (1983). Briefly, it has proved very difficult to show that individuals' emotional experiences in ambiguous situations are a product of physiological arousal plus cognitive appraisal. Several reports indicate that unexplained arousal tends to be experienced as unpleasant, even when there are contextual cues signalling happiness. Results using behavioural measures are also generally inconsistent with self-report emotional ratings.

Part of the problem is that all these experiments are extremely complex and have technical deficiencies that leave their results open to doubt. As Reisenzein notes, the experiments have to succeed both in manipulating level of arousal, and in getting subjects to attribute their arousal to the cues present in the situation, before valid conclusions can be drawn. This has hardly ever been achieved, partly because of the difficulty in supplying emotional cues that are sufficiently plausible to account for sensations of arousal but do not directly produce arousal themselves. Inevitably the experimental situations turn out to be highly artificial. There is also the criticism that peripheral physiological arousal is unnecessary for the experience of emotion. One basis for this is that it takes time for such peripheral changes to occur, whereas our experience of emotion is sometimes very swift. Second, there is no consistent evidence that the experience of emotion is reduced when awareness of physiological arousal is restricted through spinal cord injury or the ingestion of adrenergic receptor blocking agents.

## Lazarus' Theory

Lazarus (1966; Lazarus, Kanner, & Folkman, 1980) has proposed a more wide-ranging theory to account for everyday emotional states. According to Lazarus et al. (1980, p.192), "A cognitive theory of emotion, at its bottom line, assumes that emotion arises from how a person construes the outcome, actual or anticipated, of a transaction or bit of commerce with the environment." Their central construct is that of cognitive appraisal, a series of related processes that mediate a person's response to any environmental event. *Primary appraisal* results in the event being evaluated as irrelevant to well-being, as benign–positive, or as stressful. They distinguish three forms of stressful evaluation, harm–loss (related to injuries that have already occurred), threat (related to anticipated injuries), and challenge (related to a potential for mastery or positive gain). *Secondary appraisal* involves evaluation of the resources, both personal and environmental, that are available to deal with the situation. Finally, primary and secondary appraisals may be modified by constant *reappraisal* of the success of coping efforts and of the continuing impact of the event on the person.

Negatively-toned emotions arise when an event is appraised as harmful or threatening and when the available coping resources are perceived as inadequate or of doubtful efficacy. Lazarus also proposes that coping behaviours, whether intrapsychic ones such as denial or direct attempts to alter the environment, also mediate the relationship between an event and an accompanying emotional response. In contrast to the more static Schachterian view, emotions are regarded by Lazarus et al. as changing reactions that are continually influenced by what a person thinks and does. In turn, the experience of an emotion may interrupt ongoing behaviour patterns and signal to an individual that adaptive efforts are required to deal with a threat. Emotions are thought of as complex, organized states consisting of cognitive appraisals, action impulses, and patterned somatic reactions. This last suggestion, that each emotion is associated with a particular physiological response profile, is controversial and also departs from the position taken by Schachter. But support for Lazarus has come from a recent study of autonomic nervous system changes associated with reliving different emotions and adopting different facial expressions of emotion (Ekman, Levenson, & Friesen, 1983).

Experimental evidence for the importance of cognitive appraisal processes comes from a series of well-known studies by Lazarus and his colleagues (reviewed by Lazarus, Averill, & Opton, 1970) in which subjects were required to watch stressful films. One film involved a rite of passage among Australian aborigines during which there were crude operations on the penis and scrotum of adolescent boys. Three sound tracks were created for the film, one focussing in a traumatic way on the threatening events in the film (the trauma passage), one characterizing the procedures as harmless and non-distressing (the denial passage), and one communicating intellectual detachment from the events (the intellectualization passage). The trauma sound track was found to increase subjective and autonomic indices of anxiety relative to a control condition, whereas both the denial and intellectualization sound tracks reduced anxiety, thereby illustrating how emotions are influenced by the subjective interpretation of external events.

The ideas of Lazarus and his colleagues have arisen primarily from a consideration of the unpleasant emotions associated with stressful experiences. Their focus on real-life problems has led them to a more complex view of the determinants of emotion and a concern to account for individual differences in reactions to events. Along with this greater breadth, however, has gone a rather general level of description. Although they acknowledge that many of these experiences produce negative emotions such as guilt, envy, and jealousy, their theory is not on the whole concerned with the antecedents of specific emotional states. Nor do they attempt a formal account of the nature of appraisal processes other than by including within the term such cognitions as beliefs, values, expectancies, and attributions. In contrast, Weiner (1985a, 1986) has proposed that a number of specific emotional states can be linked to prior causal attributions.

## Weiner's Theory

According to Weiner, there is a general tendency for positive outcomes to produce positive affective responses such as happiness, and for negative outcomes to produce negative affective responses such as dissatisfaction or frustration. These "outcome–dependent affects" depend for their strength on the perceived pleasantness or unpleasantness of the event. Greater emotional differentiation is provided by more complex cognitions such as the attribution made for the cause of the event. For example, when the self is perceived to be the cause of a positive outcome, pride is typically experienced in addition to happiness. This link between pride (an emotion related to self-esteem) and the locus of perceived causality can be found in children as young as six years old. Graham, Doubleday, and Guarino (1984) asked children to describe an incident in which they had felt pride and found that the causes of these events were predominantly internal to the child, the association growing with age. Similarly, self-attribution of a negative outcome has been linked to emotions such as guilt and shame. This cognition–emotion link is commonly assumed to underlie the "self-serving bias" whereby individuals tend to make internal attributions for success and external attributions for failure (Bradley, 1978).

Feelings of guilt and shame are also thought to be related to attributions of controllability, guilt being generally experienced in the context of negative, personally controllable outcomes. This association has been reported among children aged nine to twelve years, but among six and seven year-olds there were frequent reports of guilt even though the outcome was accidental (Graham et al., 1984). Weiner suggests that whereas guilt tends to occur when a person has been negligent or has not tried hard, shame tends to be experienced when an attribution is made to an internal and stable cause such as lack of ability or absence of physical attractiveness. Shame and guilt differ in other important ways, however. Guilt tends to occur when personal standards are not lived up to, whereas shame is more closely connected with the breaking of society's rules and conventions. Shame also requires an audience, either real or imagined, whereas guilt does not.

Attributions for the controllability of an outcome are also thought to underlie social emotions such as pity and anger (see Chapter 9 for a more extended discussion). Typically anger is experienced when another person behaves badly and the attribution, maybe to their carelessness or selfishness, is to a controllable cause. Pity is a response to an uncontrollable negative outcome experienced by someone else, such as being born with a disfigurement. The more stable or permanent the cause, the more pity and anger tend to be amplified. A recent study by Weiner, Amirkhan, Folkes, and Verette (1987) investigated occasions when social contracts were broken and the reasons that were offered or withheld. Withheld reasons were primarily internal and controllable ("I did not want to go"), and were expected to be greeted with more anger than the reasons actually given, which tended to be external and uncontrollable ("My car broke down").

An overview of Weiner's (1985a, 1986) complete model of motivation and emotion is given in Chapter 6. Although he does not claim to provide a comprehensive theory of emotion, Weiner does draw attention to the way in which many emotional states seem to depend on a specific type of appraisal, namely a causal attribution for an event. Such principles help to explain why human beings seem to experience a more differentiated set of emotions than do other animals. This point is elaborated on by Lazarus et al. (1980, p.198):

> We are saying that not only do emotions arise as the result of evaluation of the transaction or encounter, but the ongoing appraisals are themselves an integral and intrinsic component of the emotion. Anger, for example, includes the attribution of blame for a particular kind of injury or threat, and guilt also involves such attribution of blame to oneself, with the further implication that one has not only done harm but has acted badly in accordance with personal standards of behavior. These attributions are forms of cognitive appraisal that are more than initial evaluations; they become an ongoing and critical dynamic in the experience of anger and guilt.

## THE PRIMACY OF AFFECT

It has been argued by Zajonc (1980, p.169) that it is incorrect to think of affect as exclusively post-cognitive, i.e., as occurring only after such operations as recognition and classification. He characterizes affective responses, in contrast to cognitions, as being "effortless, inescapable, irrevocable, holistic, more difficult to verbalise, yet easy to communicate and understand." He notes that it is possible to fail to notice the hair colour of someone we have just met, although we usually have an impression of an agreeable or disagreeable person. In support of his thesis, he cites a number of experiments in which, for example, subjects are presented with a series of pictures or melodies. If this is done either for very brief periods or when subjects are engaged in another task, they are often unable to say whether they have previously seen the picture or heard the melody. But if the subjects are asked which of these same pictures or melodies they *prefer*, and are given a choice of some that are new and some that they have already encountered, they are more likely to choose the stimuli with which they are familiar.

Zajonc cites many other examples in which processing of the affective aspects of a stimulus appears to lead to better recognition or recall than processing of its physical features. He suggests that it may therefore be more useful to think in terms of parallel and partially independent systems for processing cognition and affect, so that affective responses accompany all cognitions, albeit sometimes weakly and vaguely. The gist of his argument is that the evaluation of stimuli, and the adoption of a positive or negative attitude towards them, is a very basic process that occurs at least as early as, and separately from, the more cognitive operations of recognition and classification.

Notwithstanding the fact that the evidence discussed by Zajonc came exclusively from laboratory studies involving preferences and other weak evaluative reactions, his ideas were related by Rachman (1981) to the observation that clinical patients often show strong emotional reactions to stimuli even though they "know" them to be objectively harmless. This is an example of the "desynchrony" between physiological, subjective, and behavioural responses to phobic stimuli noted by Rachman and Hodgson (1974), which would be expected if cognitive and affective responses are processed relatively independently. Rachman argued further that cognitive psychotherapies might be mistaken in their assumption that affective responses are post-cognitive and can therefore be modified by altering a person's cognitions: If affect is largely independent of cognition it might be more profitable to adopt other treatment approaches such as direct modification of unwanted emotional reactions.

The position taken up by Zajonc has been criticized on a number of grounds. First, the evidence he discusses relates to *conscious* recognition and affective judgements and does not rule out the possibility, considered plausible by many (e.g., Isen, 1984; Lazarus, 1982), that affect depends on some degree of *preconscious* cognitive processing. Zajonc has not produced evidence that affective judgements are independent of this aspect of cognition, which, as discussed in Chapter 2, does occur rapidly and automatically. Lazarus (1982) also feels that Zajonc misrepresents cognitive theories of emotion. He points out that emotion is not generally seen as an eventual reaction that occurs only after extensive perceptual and cognitive processing. Emotional reactions may occur almost immediately to very incomplete information, and then be modified as it is appraised or as more information becomes available. For Lazarus, emotions and cognitions are not separable, because he regards cognitive appraisal as being part of the emotional reaction itself. It must also be emphasized that Zajonc's arguments are concerned with fairly superficial judgements made about unfamiliar and often meaningless stimuli. It is far from clear that they are relevant to the emotional reactions seen in clinical practice, which are generally concerned with familiar or highly meaningful situations, are themselves the subject of considerable cognitive processing, and which with time may wax, wane, or change in character.

## THE INFLUENCE OF AFFECT ON COGNITION:
## MOOD AND MEMORY

Although the argument is hard to sustain that affective processing of a stimulus occurs prior to *any* form of cognitive processing, it is generally accepted that affective changes can influence a person's cognitive processes.

This gives credence to the position that affect and cognition are at least partially independent, if often interlinked. Mood states have been found to affect a number of cognitive variables, such as free associations and interpretations of ambiguous events (Bower, 1981), but their influence has been most extensively documented by investigating memory processes after the experimental induction of elated or depressed moods. Among the several forms that this influence may take, it is possible to distinguish a state-dependent learning effect, and mood congruity effects operating during encoding and recall.

"State-dependent learning" refers to the well-established tendency for material to be recalled best when there is a close match between the conditions in which it was originally learnt and the conditions in which the person tries to remember it. This has been demonstrated using alcohol and marijuana to produce drug-induced states and also, in one or two studies, by manipulating mood. Bower, Monteiro, and Gilligan (1978; Study 3) induced happy and sad moods in hypnotized subjects and had them learn two lists of words, one while in each state. Free recall of these lists was selectively facilitated when subjects were once again placed in the corresponding mood state. Bower et al.'s results have been replicated by Schare, Lisman, and Spear (1984; Study 3), using a different mood induction technique, but on the whole state-dependent learning effects have been hard to obtain except under rather specific experimental conditions (Blaney, 1986), and even then have not always been replicated (Bower & Mayer, 1985).

"Mood congruity" effects, unlike state-dependent learning effects, depend on a similarity between the mood and the nature of the material that is being learned or remembered. Blaney (1986) reviewed over thirty such studies, using any one of six different methods of inducing mood, and concluded that recall is usually superior when there is a match between the affective valence of the material and the mood in which the material is recalled. In a series of studies, Teasdale and his colleagues (e.g., Teasdale, Taylor, & Fogarty, 1980) induced elated and depressed moods and had subjects retrieve autobiographical memories of pleasant and unpleasant past experiences. They showed that subjects in elated mood recalled more pleasant memories than when in a depressed mood, but recalled more unpleasant memories when depressed than when elated.

Such effects have also been demonstrated with positive and negative verbal material. Isen et al. (1978) reported that positive personality trait words were more likely to be remembered following success on a computer game than following failure, although there were no differences in the recall of neutral or negative trait words. Their finding for positive trait words was replicated by Teasdale and Russell (1983) using a different mood induction procedure; in depressed mood, Teasdale and Russell's subjects also recalled more negative than positive trait words. However, Bower et al. (1978) failed to demonstrate any congruence between mood at recall and the number of positive and negative abstract nouns remembered, a finding attributed by Teasdale and Russell to the nature of the verbal material. Consistent with this view, Clark and Teasdale (1985) found the predicted interaction between mood and word pleasantness for trait descriptors but not for abstract nouns.

The significance of Clark and Teasdale's (1985) finding is in the suggestion that mood congruence effects are not simply related to the affective valence of the material but also to its association with the individual's past experience. Specifically, they argue that trait words are more likely than abstract nouns to have been associated with actual past instances of depressed and elated mood. Among their other findings was that mood congruent recall of trait words was restricted to women subjects, and this enabled them to test the hypothesis that the phenomenon was somehow related to personal experience. In a second study they found that women were more likely than men to use these particular trait words in everyday life. Moreover, among their women subjects, the frequency with which the word was used was positively correlated with the likelihood that the word would be preferentially recalled in a congruent mood state.

Reports of mood congruence are also common in studies that, rather than manipulate elation and depression, investigate groups of subjects with naturally occurring differences in mood. Both mildly depressed college students and clinically depressed patients tend to overestimate number of past failures relative to successes, and to show a recall bias favouring the retrieval of negative rather than positive verbal material (Blaney, 1986). These studies, too, indicate that recall bias is most pronounced when subjects are asked to focus on the applicability of the material to themselves rather than to other people. Bradley and Mathews (1983), for example, found that depressed patients, relative to non-psychiatric controls, recalled more negative than positive self-referent adjectives. When asked to focus on the applicability of these words to others, however, they showed the normal positive recall bias. Other similar studies are discussed in Chapter 5 in the context of current theories of depression. For the present it is sufficient to note that in those instances where mood congruent recall has not been shown, this may have been because the material used, like the abstract nouns in the Clark and Teasdale (1985) study, did not lead to many associations with subjects' own experiences or self-perceptions.

The finding that depressed individuals selectively recall more negative material could simply be a reflection of having had a greater number of negative life experiences, were it not for the mood induction studies that assigned subjects randomly to the different experimental conditions.

Another study that is important in illustrating that memory biases are more than indices of life experiences was carried out by Clark and Teasdale (1982). They selected patients with pronounced diurnal mood variations and tested each of them on two separate occasions, once when they were relatively depressed and once when they were relatively non-depressed. On both occasions patients were asked to retrieve autobiographical memories in response to a series of cue words. These memories were more often of happy than unhappy events when the patients were less depressed, but more often concerned experiences that had been unhappy rather than happy when they were more depressed. Mood also influenced patients' ratings of how positive or negative the events seemed now, looking back, and Clark and Teasdale concluded that "mood has two separate effects: It influences the selection of emotional material for entry into consciousness and it also affects how pleasing or upsetting that material will be, once it has entered consciousness".

## Associative Network Theory

Bower (1981) has proposed that the effects of mood on cognitive processes can be incorporated within a general associative network theory of long-term memory (e.g., Anderson & Bower, 1974; Collins & Loftus, 1975). According to this theory of memory, concepts are represented by individual "nodes" that have associative connections of varying strength depending on the individual's personal experience. For example, the concept "white" is likely to have strong links to concepts such as "black" and "house," but weaker links to concepts such as "swan" and "gold." Activation of the concept "white," perhaps while reading a book or in conversation, will in turn tend to activate associated concepts, beginning with those with the strongest links. If the activation level exceeds some threshold these concepts, in the form of thoughts or images, will enter consciousness. Bower sums up the assimilation of new experiences to the network as follows (1981, p.134):

> Human memory can be modeled in terms of an associative network of semantic concepts and schemata that are used to describe events. An event is represented in memory by a cluster of descriptive propositions. These are recorded in memory by establishing new associative connections among instances of the concepts used in describing the event ... Activation presumably spreads from one concept to another, or from one proposition to another, by associative linkages between them.

Bower suggests that distinct emotions such as joy, fear, and depression, have their own node or unit in memory. Linked associatively to each of these nodes will be information about autonomic reactions, facial expressions and gestures, verbal labels for the emotion, typical situations likely to elicit the emotion, and actual situations in which the emotion has been experienced. Emotion nodes can be activated by any of these related events or phenomena, and if the activation is sufficiently strong they transmit excitation to units that produce the corresponding patterns of autonomic arousal, facial expression, etc. In addition activation of the emotion node makes thoughts, beliefs, and situational memories that are associated with it more accessible to consciousness. At the same time emotions of opposing quality, and the concepts and propositions with which they are associated, may be inhibited.

During the acquisition phase of state-dependent learning the material to be learned is thought to become associated with a particular emotion node or unit representing a particular internal state. At recall the reactivation of this node will in turn activate the associated material and thus make it more accessible. Attempts to recall the material in a different emotional state will not benefit from this activation process, however, and there may be interference from other material that *is* associated with this second emotion. As Bower notes, the associative links between the material and mood during acquisition are likely to be fairly weak. This means that state-dependent effects will be more common in free recall, where minimal cues are given for the retrieval of target words, than in a recognition task where the existing cues are much stronger. Mood congruity effects at recall can similarly be explained by postulating that being in a certain emotional state automatically activates semantically-related concepts and autobiographical events in which the emotion was experienced, thus making both more likely than competing concepts or events to enter consciousness.

It is worth noting, however, that many instances of depressive mood induction seem to have reduced the accessibility of positive memories rather than increased the accessibility of negative memories (e.g., Isen et al., 1978; Teasdale et al., 1980). Similarly, the autobiographical memories of clinically depressed patients are often affectively neutral rather than being negative in absolute terms (e.g., Clark & Teasdale, 1982). A recent illustration of this point is provided by Williams and Broadbent (1986), who investigated the autobiographical memories produced to cue words by people who had recently attempted suicide by overdose. Relative to controls, suicide attempters had more difficulty in retrieving memories to positive cue words, and took longer to do so, whereas there were no group differences in the retrieval of memories to negative cue words. As the authors point out, this is surprising given the typical increased incidence of negative life events preceding attempted suicide. Williams and Broadbent also reported that, even though instructed to produce memories of specific events, their overdose group tended to produce inappropriately general memories. This was particularly the case for memories to positive cue words.

Such findings are difficult for associative network theory to explain. The fact that they occur with clinical samples means that they cannot be attributed to the weakness of any depressive affect produced by the typical mood induction procedure. Although network theory does postulate that activation of one emotion node may inhibit other emotion nodes of an opposing quality, it would not be predicted that such inhibition should have a greater effect than the original activation. Nor does it address the issue of the generality versus specificity of retrieved memories. A final problem with simply interpreting the mood and memory findings in terms of "depression nodes" is that memory biases may also be associated with stable individual differences such as neuroticism (Martin, Ward, & Clark, 1983) and with dysfunctional attitudes (Kuiper, Olinger, MacDonald, & Shaw, 1985). The latter study found that mood–congruity effects were not shown by depressed individuals unless there was also evidence of negativity in their reported attitudes.

## MEMORY, IMAGERY, AND THE EMOTIONAL PROCESSING OF FEAR

The close connection between memory and psychopathology is evident in the effects of severe real-life traumas. Such events also remind us that fear, anger etc. are not just brief, situation-specific responses but, particularly when provoked by extremely stressful events, may last for quite long periods of time, fluctuate considerably in intensity, and sometimes return quite unexpectedly. This is graphically illustrated by a report in *The Sunday Times* dated 14 September 1986 and describing the experiences of survivors of the Manchester Airport disaster. In August 1985 fifty-five people had died in a fire after an engine exploded on a Boeing 737 that was waiting to take off. "It didn't sink in for days", said one of the survivors. "Then I started turning the whole thing over and over again in my mind. Some nights I couldn't sleep and when I did I dreamt about the plane and the fire. I was moody and I became irritable for no reason". The smell of any sort of smoke reminded survivors about the pungent fumes from the burning aircraft. Bad dreams and fits of irritability were triggered by sounds, pictures, and by the coroner's inquest. The following year four of the survivors were travelling by coach in the South of France when they passed a forest fire. One of them recounted his experience as follows: "I remembered the black smoke, the pitch darkness and I thought I was going to die again". Another said: "When the coach stopped moving because of a traffic jam I felt trapped. There were bushes on either side of the road and I kept thinking that if the fire got closer there would be nowhere to run".

This account includes a description both of unconditioned emotional reactions immediately following the fire, and of conditioned reactions to associated stimuli (such as smoke) that occurred considerably later. The pattern is typical of what the American Psychiatric Association's (1980) *Diagnostic and Statistical Manual of Mental Disorders (DSM III)* has termed "post-traumatic stress disorder" (PTSD). This syndrome is frequently observed in war veterans, in the victims of civil disasters such as fires, terrorist bombings, and earthquakes, and as a frequent accompaniment of severe individual stressors such as assault, rape, and accidental injury. In addition to re-experiencing the trauma and sensitivity to stimuli reminiscent of it, other characteristic features are numbing of responsiveness or reduced involvement with the external world, along with hyperalertness and disturbances of sleep and concentration.

After the two world wars sufferers from "combat neurosis", as this form of PTSD was sometimes called, were frequently treated by means of "abreaction". This refers to procedures, sometimes involving hypnosis, for inducing intense emotion accompanied by a revival of traumatic memories. Such procedures were derived from early psychoanalytic writing (e.g., Breuer & Freud, 1893), which described how psychopathological symptoms were sometimes linked to affect-laden memories. In the famous case of Anna O., Breuer and Freud recount the apparent origin of a drinking phobia. Under hypnosis Anna recalled having entered the room of her much disliked governess and finding the governess' dog drinking out of a glass. She had not expressed her disgust at the time, but now asked Breuer with a great deal of anger for a drink of water. She then came out of the hypnotic state while holding the glass and was not subsequently bothered by this symptom. Marks (1987) also notes several instances in which patients have retrieved forgotten memories during behaviour therapy. For example, a woman with a phobia about firemen's helmets suddenly recalled during exposure that her fear had originated with seeing a fireman falling to his death many years previously.

Many of these examples have the common feature that the normal emotional response to the traumatic incident may have been inhibited by circumstances, such as the inappropriateness of showing fear overtly on a battlefield. If the trauma is sufficiently severe, however, there are likely to be prolonged emotional consequences whether emotional expression is initially inhibited or not. Clinical studies indicate that abreaction is often followed by symptomatic improvement, although this is by no means always the case. There is disagreement over whether it is simply the discharge of emotion that is therapeutic, or whether it is the conscious association of the emotion with the traumatic memory (Marks, 1987). Some of the intriguing questions that these observations raise, however, concern the process by which emotional memories are lost, and whether emotional arousal is essential for these memories to be therapeutically neutralized. These issues have recently been addressed under the heading of "emotional processing".

Rachman (1980) has suggested that it may be useful to think of people as either successfully or unsuccessfully processing or absorbing their emotional reactions to stressful events. According to this view, conditioned fear reactions are only one of many signs that an event has not been successfully processed emotionally. Other direct signs are disturbing dreams, unpleasant intrusive thoughts, some hallucinatory experiences (for example, involving someone who has recently died), disruptions of behaviour, inappropriate expressions of distress, and the sudden return of fear. Fatigue, insomnia, restlessness, irritability, and interference with concentration may also be indirect signs of unsatisfactory emotional processing. The potential value of this perspective is that it links together a wide range of signs and symptoms, and suggests a common process underlying both post-traumatic stress disorders and other problems, such as phobic disorders, that are sometimes of traumatic origin but may not be presented for treatment until much later in life. The reappearance of fear after it has diminished in intensity is a phenomenon that has been particularly hard to encompass within traditional theories of conditioning. Rachman also discusses the factors that might facilitate or impede emotional processing of stressful stimuli. Many of these, such as personality attributes and the stimulus attributes of intensity, unpredictability, and uncontrollability, have a substantial cognitive component and have already been considered in the context of conditioning.

A consistent feature of many of these accounts of emotional reactions to major stressors is that victims experience affect-laden memories, often in the form of visual images. These images may intrude in the waking state or occur in the form of dreams and hallucinations. Images are also, of course, deliberately employed in therapeutic techniques such as desensitization, which involves instructing patients to imagine themselves in a series of frightening situations while remaining calm and relaxed. Lang (1977, 1979) has addressed himself to the question of how images and affect are connected, and how the ability of images to evoke emotional responses can be altered. He suggested that images should not be thought of as faithful visual representations of past experience, like photographs that can simply be retrieved from a library, but rather as representations constructed from information stored in memory in propositional form. This view that images are stored in the form of sets of related propositions is particularly associated with Pylyshyn (1973) and is, by design, highly compatible with the associative network model previously encountered in the context of experiments on memory for events and verbal material (e.g., Bower, 1981).

Lang suggested that emotional images are constructed from three main classes of propositional unit, one concerned with stimulus information, one concerned with response information, and one concerned with information about the meaning of the situation. The first contains details about the location and physical characteristics of the stimulus or situation, such as an expression on someone's face or the appearance of a particular type of animal. The second contains details about verbal, physiological, and behavioural responses occurring in the situation, such as signs of autonomic arousal or avoidance behaviour. The third contains an interpretation of the stimulus and response elements and of their significance (positive or negative) for the individual. Underlying the emotional response of fear, Lang proposed, is a prototype fear image stored in long-term memory. This prototype is available as a model against which new events and situations are tested: If they correspond sufficiently closely to it, the stored memory with its response components becomes activated and fear is experienced. Emotional images should therefore be regarded as programmes, sometimes available to consciousness but not necessarily so, whose function is not only to recognize and interpret certain stimuli but also to respond appropriately to them.

These ideas have been further developed by Foa and Kozak (1986), who describe how emotional images may be altered or "processed", whether naturally or in the course of therapy. The two conditions they think to be necessary are, first, that fear-relevant information must be made available in such a way that the memory structure is activated. This can be achieved by exposure to the actual feared situation or by other means, such as visual displays and verbal descriptions, providing they are sufficiently similar to the prototype image. Activation can be inferred from increased self-reports of fear and from increased physiological responsiveness. Second, if fear is to decrease, new information must be available to be integrated with this structure that is inconsistent with that in memory. To use Foa and Kozak's example, a dog phobic's repeated exposure to dogs without being bitten constitutes information that the probability of being bitten by a dog is quite low. This will presumably contradict erroneous propositions in memory about the likelihood of threat. Within therapy the presence of emotional processing can be inferred from habituation to feared stimuli occurring within and between sessions.

Foa and Kozak go on to describe in more detail the hypothesized changes that take place when fear is modified (1986, p.27):

When physiological responses decrease during confrontation with feared situations, interoceptive information about the absence of physiological arousal is generated. This information is available for encoding as response propositions that are inconsistent with those of the structure, thereby weakening the preexisting links between stimulus and response elements. The resultant less "unitized" configuration of elements is less readily evoked by information that matches only some of the elements in the structure.

As they note, and as we have seen from the discussion of false feedback studies in Chapter 3, this also applies to *beliefs* about physiological reactions that may not be veridical. New information is also likely to alter representations of the probability of threat and of its meaning, such as the belief that panic will lead to insanity or cardiac failure. This dissociation between the stimulus, response, and meaning elements of a fear structure is illustrated in Fig. 4.1.

The idea that a relevant memory structure must be activated for change to occur is clearly consistent with earlier notions that psychopathology is related to emotions being blocked off and their expression inhibited. Just as dog phobics remain calm (but also remain phobic) by avoiding their feared object, traditional psychoanalytic theory proposes that individuals avoid anxiety-provoking thoughts and memories through the use of defence mechanisms that prevent their entry into consciousness (see Wachtel, 1977, and the discussion of perceptual defence in Chapter 2). It is often stated by psychoanalytic writers that change is dependent on these ideas being readmitted into conscious awareness *with the appropriate affect* (this is sometimes known as "emotional" rather than "intellectual" insight). The emphasis placed by such writers on attending to the affective accompaniments of patients' statements appears consistent with the suggestion that information may be of little value unless it makes contact with the appropriate structure in memory. The importance of providing new information that contradicts patients' expectations is also a feature of many kinds of psychotherapy. A particular example is the psychoanalytic concept of a "corrective emotional experience", in which the patient has his or her expectations of other people revealed and disconfirmed in the therapeutic relationship

## CONCLUSIONS

Affect and cognition are related in a number of different ways. In novel situations affective judgements may occur very rapidly in association with preconscious cognitive processes. Such processes are good candidates for explaining the acquisition of conditioned emotional reactions and the fact that fear reactions can be almost instantly elicited by situations that are reminiscent of an earlier traumatic experience. The alteration of such reactions can also usefully be seen in terms of the introduction of modifications to a memory structure that is not itself available to conscious awareness, even though it is capable of integrating consciously-held information and beliefs. Emotional experience is not confined to these relatively

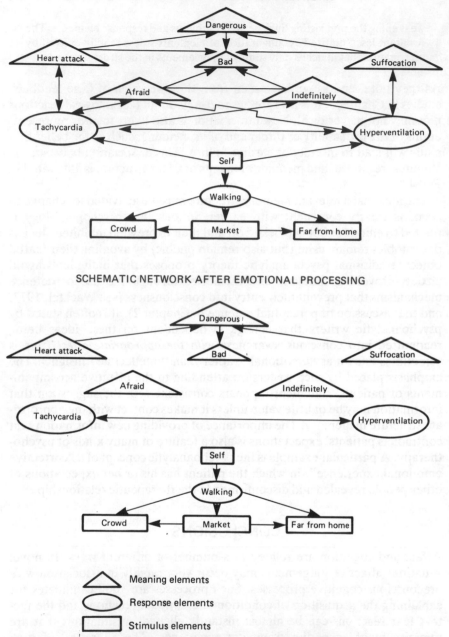

**SCHEMATIC AGORAPHOBIC FEAR NETWORK**

**SCHEMATIC NETWORK AFTER EMOTIONAL PROCESSING**

△ Meaning elements

○ Response elements

▢ Stimulus elements

**FIG. 4.1** Fear network before and after emotional processing, illustrating that successful therapy disintegrates this fear structure into three clusters of stimulus, response, and meaning elements. Connecting vectors suggest directions for the various conceptual relations among the elements, e.g., tachycardia causes heart attack, heart attack brings tachycardia, self is walking in the market (Foa & Kozak, 1986). Copyright by the American Psychological Association. Reprinted by permission of the author.

rapid reactions, however, but also depends to some degree on conscious appraisal of the threatening nature of a situation, of the availability of coping resources, and of the causes that have led to the situation. These conscious cognitions lead to a further differentiation of emotional states, forming an integral part of the experience of emotions such as pride and guilt. Nevertheless, they are not so integral that manipulation of such appraisal cannot produce emotional change. Such manipulation may be practised by therapists or, through the operation of deliberate mood-maintenance and mood-repair strategies, by individuals themselves.

A sophisticated contemporary view of emotion that incorporates and elaborates these ideas is the perceptual-motor theory of Leventhal (1984). He proposes that within the central nervous system there is a hierarchical system with at least three levels for the construction of emotional reactions. Each of these levels is involved in any emotional response, but to different degrees on different occasions. The first and most basic level consists of an expressive-motor mechanism, which includes an innate set of programmes for generating a distinctive set of expressive reactions and feelings in response to well-defined situations. This system is operative at birth and provides infants with their first, relatively undifferentiated, emotional experiences. The second level is an automatic processing system that codes emotional experiences in the form of schemata in long-term memory. This system makes a record of stimuli associated with emotional experiences as well as coding accompanying subjective feelings, autonomic reactions, and instrumental responses. Its main functions are to integrate experience and to provide a basis for the rapid, automatic appraisal of new events and situations. Like the emotional memories described by Lang (1977) and Foa and Kozak (1986), which were based on associations between different nodes in a network rather than on a unified schema whose components are stored in a common physical location, emotional schemata are thought to shape our experience without awareness of their activity. The third level consists of a conscious conceptual system that contains propositions or rules about emotional experience. These rules, for example concerning what emotions are appropriate in different circumstances, may be culturally transmitted or derived from observations of one's own feelings and behaviour. They depend on the drawing of inferences and, as has been discussed in Chapter 2, have certain limitations. The conceptual system forms the basis for attempts to voluntarily modify one's own emotional reactions.

According to current thinking, then, immediate affective responses are intimately connected with preconscious cognitions. Conscious appraisal may amplify or reduce these responses, and determine the quality of the eventual emotional state. This emotional state may in turn exert an influence on conscious and preconscious cognitive processes, for example by increasing the accessibility of certain kinds of material in memory. Most theorists would agree with this view that cognition and affect are reciprocally related. At the same time, the fact that a thought or an image can be experienced with relatively more or less affect at different times means that they must also be partially independent. In the following chapter many of these ideas will reappear as the basis for theoretical models of clinical anxiety and depression.

# 5 Information-Processing, Anxiety, and Depression

In the previous chapter conditioned emotional reactions to specific stress-ful events were explained in terms of prototypical "fear memories", which could be activated by stimuli sufficiently similar to the stimulus elements of the memory. Post-traumatic stress reactions and phobic reactions of this kind are of course extremely common in the general population, and are rarely so disruptive as to require professional attention. A minority of individuals, however, described as suffering from panic disorder, anxiety state, generalized anxiety disorder or agoraphobia, experience fear that is not linked with any one situation. Sometimes no specific stimuli can be found that elicit these episodes of anxiety or panic, but more often they are found to be precipitated by a fairly extensive class of situations, such as those involving evaluation by other people. Agoraphobia *is* relatively situation-specific in the sense that individuals have a marked fear of being alone, or of being in public places from which escape might be difficult or help not available in case of sudden incapacitation (DSM III: American Psychiatric Association, 1980). Nevertheless, because of the variety of eliciting stimuli and the severity of the condition, agoraphobia is more often regarded as similar to the anxiety states than to simple phobic disorders (e.g., Turner, McCann, Beidel, & Mezzich, 1986).

Depression can also be thought of as a generalized mood disorder because it typically involves altered reactions, not just to one situation, but to many aspects of the person's life. Beck (1967) has captured this in his description of the depressive "cognitive triad", which consists of negative views of oneself, of the rest of the world, and of the future. Among the most typical depressive cognitions are hopelessness, and the belief that any reverse or disappointment is characteristic of lack of ability or of a *general* tendency to fail (e.g. Carver, Ganellen, & Bihar-Mitrani, 1985). The central problem with these more generalized disorders is to explain why the emotional memories presumed to underlie them have not been corrected by experience, i.e., why they have not responded to new information disconfirming the expectation of threat or disappointment. In the case of simple phobics it is reasonable to suppose that the emotional memories may remain intact if the person is careful to avoid any prolonged contact with the feared object or situation. But it is unlikely that the person with a generalized mood disorder can avoid all the situations that contain potentially relevant information.

How is it, then, that these disorders can last for months and sometimes years? In some cases there must be a persistence of objectively threatening or disappointing circumstances, providing information consistent with that already in memory. For women with young children, for example, recovery from long-term depression is associated with an independently assessed prior reduction in a chronic social difficulty (Brown, Adler, & Bifulco, in press). Interestingly, Brown et al. also found recovery to be associated with the occurrence of "fresh start" events, such as the reversal of a previous sterilization in a woman very much wanting a child. Although this particular example leaves open the possibility that clinical improvement precedes and makes possible such a "fresh start", in other cases these events appear to have been independent and to have occurred prior to any improvement.

However, the fact that difficulty reduction or "fresh starts" do not invariably occur, and that depressive beliefs tend not to be confined to a particular situation, suggests the involvement of an additional personal factor. One influential proposal (Beck, 1967) is that certain individuals have systematic biases in the way they process incoming information. The presence of these biases means that not all information is attended to equally or given equal weight, with the result that only certain information has full access to the schemas (also known as "schemata") or other structures that comprise long-term memory. If the bias is for information about the presence of threat or disappointment to be registered, one would expect the corresponding schemas to be more easily strengthened by confirmatory evidence than weakened by conflicting evidence. In other words, the informational value of new experiences depends on how they are processed by the individual. In this chapter we examine such information-processing models of anxiety and depression. There is at present considerable overlap between them, reflecting not only the recent arrival of these theories but also the difficulty of finding groups of "pure" depressives who do not also experience marked anxiety.

# ANXIETY

According to one recent account (Beck & Emery, 1985), the structures ("schemas") that comprise long-term memory contain propositional information that may be thought of as rules, assumptions or formulas. Schemas are not simply the repositories of different kinds of information, however, but play an active role in organizing the constant inflow of new information. When a schema is activated it influences the subsequent selection of stimuli to be attended to, facilitates the recall of relevant material from memory, and determines the overall significance to the individual. In the words of Beck and Emery (1985, p.56):

> When a threat is perceived the relevant cognitive schemas are activated; these are used to evaluate and assign a meaning to the event....There occur a series of adjustments to 'fit' appropriate schemas to a specific threat. One's final interpretation is the result of interaction between the event and the schemas.

Schemas are thought to be further organized into constellations or sub-systems ("modes") that correspond to broad motivational concerns. There are many kinds of mode, such as depressive, hostile, erotic, and fear or danger modes. Beck and Emery suggest that the particular cognitive schema that is activated depends not only on objective features of the person's current situation but also on which mode is currently dominant. In generalized anxiety disorders the fear or danger mode appears to be overactive, not being switched off when threats are no longer present. This leads to the indiscriminate interpretation of new environmental events as dangers, and to excessive mobilization of the somatic and autonomic nervous systems. The reasons for the persistent dominance of one mode are unknown, although Beck and Emery speculate that fatigue or the presence of certain neurochemical disturbances might have a role to play.

Mathews and Eysenck (1987) and Mathews and MacLeod (1985) have also suggested that generalized anxiety is associated with a bias in processing information related to personal threat. Individuals are presumed to possess "danger schemata" in memory, some of which are innately "prepared" and some of which are acquired through actual and vicarious experiences with threatening stimuli or situations. A preconscious or pre-attentive bias to register stimuli corresponding to the contents of these schemata could result in such stimuli capturing the individual's attention. Information about such stimuli would then be preferentially processed, and encoded into memory, while more reassuring information might be ignored. The end result might be the creation of highly elaborated schemata in memory that would be readily accessed when the individual was faced with making judgements about ambiguous situations (see section entitled Labelling and Interpretation in Chapter 6).

The idea that threatening stimuli might capture the attention or processing resources of anxious patients was tested by Mathews and MacLeod (1985) using a version of the Stroop test. In this task subjects are presented with words written in different coloured inks and are required to name the colour of the ink as quickly as they can. Certain types of word, such as the names of colours not matching the ink, typically interfere with subjects' performance and decrease speed of colour-naming. Mathews and MacLeod found that the performance of anxious patients, but not that of controls, was selectively retarded when the words had a threatening content, such as "cancer" or "lonely." They then divided their anxious group into those whose worries predominantly concerned their physical health and those who were most worried about social relationships. The colour-naming of both these groups was equally retarded by words suggesting a social threat ("pathetic", "inadequate"), but only the group complaining of physical health worries were slowed down by words suggesting a physical threat ("coronary", "deathbed"). The authors note that there are at least two explanations of their results. First, extra processing resources may have been immediately allocated by the anxious patients to the threatening stimuli, fewer resources therefore being available for naming the correct colour. Alternatively, it may have been the emotional arousal arising from the perception of relevant words that indirectly interfered with colour-naming.

Two subsequent studies confirm the salience of threat stimuli for anxious patients. MacLeod, Mathews, and Tata (1986) investigated the distribution of visual attention by presenting subjects with two words on a VDU screen. Immediately after presentation a small dot sometimes appeared in place of one of the words and the subjects were required to register this by pressing a button as quickly as possible. On the trials of interest one of the words had a threatening content. Distribution of attention was inferred from a comparison of the time taken to respond to the dot when it appeared in place of the threatening word with the time taken when it appeared in place of the non-threatening word. Anxious patients, but not controls, responded faster when the dot appeared in place of the threatening word, indicating that such words had been receiving more of their attention. Evidence for the claim that the selective processing of threat cues occurs outside conscious awareness was obtained by Mathews and MacLeod (1986). In a dichotic listening experiment anxious patients and controls wore headphones and were exposed to subliminal threat and non-threat words on one channel while shadowing neutral stories on the attended channel. The impact of the unattended words was assessed by means of a simultaneous reaction time task. Although none of the subjects were able to identify the words on the unattended channel, Mathews and MacLeod found that the anxious patients' reaction times were significantly slower when they were being exposed to words with a threatening rather than non-threatening content. In contrast, controls' reaction times were unaffected by the emotional significance of the unattended words.

As far as the initial stages of information-processing are concerned, these experiments offer good evidence for the tendency of threatening stimuli to capture the attention of anxious patients. There is less evidence that threatening stimuli are preferentially encoded into or retrieved from memory, however. One study (Nunn, Stevenson, & Whalan, 1984) found that agoraphobic patients were more likely than controls to remember prose passages with a potentially phobic content, e.g., about shopping, and words such as "travel" and "crowd". Other studies (Mathews & MacLeod, 1985; Mogg, Mathews, & Weinman, 1987) have found no recall or recognition bias in favour of supposedly negative or threatening words. Among the possible explanations one could point to are differences in the stimuli used by Nunn et al., which were very specific to agoraphobic symptoms and which also allowed for personal elaboration and interpretation, and those used by Mathews and his colleagues, which were threatening in a more general way. Since high levels of trait anxiety have also been found to be associated with the preferential recall of negative self-related words (Martin et al., 1983), it is probably premature to draw any conclusions about the presence of memory biases in anxiety. If such biases do prove hard to establish, however, it will be difficult for information-processing theories to account for the persistence and generalization of anxiety.

Other important questions about the role of information-processing biases need to be answered. For example, are such biases still present after successful therapy? Although there are no data for generalized anxiety disorders, Watts et al. (1986) have studied the changes brought about by the desensitization of spider phobias. Prior to treatment spider phobics showed retarded colour-naming relative to controls on a Stroop test using spider related stimulus words. There were no differences between the groups in the interference produced by words that were generally threatening, however. Compared to no treatment, successful desensitization led to a significantly greater reduction in interference with the colour-naming of spider-related words, indicating that these attentional processes can be modified in therapy.

As far as the origin of these biases is concerned, it is possible that biological differences are important. Inherited characteristics might influence the threshold of activation of neurophysiological systems underlying anxiety, such as Gray's (1982) behavioural inhibition system. A lower threshold could result in the occurrence of a greater number of significant emotional experiences to be coded into memory. Alternatively, a higher incidence of stressful external events, the existence of highly anxious "models" in the family, or the occurrence of interpersonal reactions that exacerbated rather than alleviated anxiety, could have the same effect. In all these cases there is an assumption that a greater number of anxious or fearful experiences could lead to more readily accessible emotional schemas. There are many other possibilities, however. For example, as discussed in Chapter 3, when an aversive event occurs it is likely to be the most salient stimuli that come to be associated with the accompanying emotional reaction. In the absence of clearly identifiable environmental cues much vaguer stimuli, such as internal physical sensations or feelings of anger, may come to be coded as part of the memory for the event. Thus the generalizability of emotional reactions may depend on the particular situational cues that were available during previous emotional episodes.

# DEPRESSION

## Information-processing Theories of Depression

As described in the previous chapter, Bower (1981) has outlined an associative network model of memory that incorporates emotional states such as depression. Each emotion has a corresponding "node" in memory and associative links are formed between such nodes and propositional representations of past experience. In this model it is assumed that there will be large individual differences in the number of episodes and experiences that are associated with previous depressed mood, and in the strength of those associations. Generalization of depression can thus be accounted for in at least two ways. First, the presence of more and stronger depressive associations would mean that similar experiences in the future would be more likely to correspond to a critical internal representation and trigger activation of the depression node. Second, once the depression node had been activated, there would be a greater tendency for recollections of similar experiences to enter consciousness. The larger the number of such memories that became accessible, the more likely feelings of hopelessness and worthlessness would be to generalize rather than remaining specific to a particular situation.

This model has been further developed by Teasdale (1983) and Ingram (1984). Teasdale reviewed the evidence that cognitions affect depressive mood and mood in turn affects cognitions, and suggested that these two processes might combine to form a vicious cycle maintaining depression. Depressed mood produces greater accessibility of past negative experiences. If there were many such experiences stored in memory, depressed people would be more likely to remember past failures, think negative thoughts about themselves, and feel more hopeless about the possibility of changing their situation. These negative thoughts would in themselves be depressing and would tend to prolong or exacerbate the disturbed mood, while the sense of hopelessness would undermine active coping.

Ingram (1984) has similarly suggested that the maintenance of depression can be accounted for by the activation of negative memories that enter consciousness, absorb the individual's attention, and recycle activation back to the depression node in a continuous loop. Phenomenologically, this process is experienced as the constant presence of thoughts or images related to the disappointment or loss that triggered the episode. Activation recycles automatically through the depression node until either it eventually decays with time, new and incompatible information becomes available, or the person succeeds in interrupting the process. Ingram also suggests that this preoccupation with depressing thoughts uses much of the individual's capacity for conscious information-processing and can account for many other symptoms of depression such as sleep disturbance, delusions, cognitive and motor slowing, and lack of motivation.

Beck's theory of depression (e.g., Beck, 1967; Beck et al., 1979) is similar to his model of anxiety described above. Previous negative events are thought to be coded in the form of schemas that are activated when similar events are subsequently experienced, and that influence the interpretation of those events. Depressive schemas contain propositional information ("basic assumptions") indicating that the self is defective, the external world composed of insuperable difficulties, and the future hopeless. Activation of these schemas has two main effects. First, some of this information enters consciousness involuntarily in the form of negative automatic thoughts such as "Nobody loves me" or "There's no point in going on". The second effect of depressive schematic thinking, argues Beck, lies in the logical errors made by the depressed in appraising their situation: they make *arbitrary inferences* on the basis of inadequate or contradictory evidence; *selectively abstract* details out of context rather than considering the total picture; *over-generalize* from isolated or unrepresentative incidents; *magnify and minimize* the significance of events in an unrealistic way; *personalize* events inappropriately; and *dichotomize* events into opposite and extreme categories.

The automatic thoughts and systematic logical errors lead to negative evaluations of self, world, and future, and the contents of consciousness become increasingly gloomy and self-critical. This in turn helps to depress mood still further. When a person is only mildly depressed such thoughts may be viewed with some objectivity, but in severe depressions patients are thought to lose much of their voluntary control over their thinking processes, to become dominated by negative automatic thoughts, and to rely increasingly on schematic processing of new information.

Whereas theories of anxiety have emphasized the acquisition of knowledge about dangerous situations, theories of depression have repeatedly drawn attention to the self-concept, which may be thought of as a system of knowledge or beliefs about one's own nature. For example, in Oatley and

Bolton's (1985) social–cognitive theory of depression, it is proposed that certain life events are stressful because they pose a threat to selfhood, where the sense of self is realized in a role or roles. A role, such as being a good mother or breadwinner, "provides an identity and is bound up with personal goals, plans, and expectations" (p. 377). Oatley and Bolton suggest that the onset of depression depends on the relationship between a person's role expectations and the fulfilment of those expectations by others who take part in important role relationships. The loss of one of these others, or any other situation that makes it impossible to enact a role central to one's self-definition, will provoke depression. Vulnerability, on the other hand, they see as the lack of subsidiary or potential roles through which self-definition goals can be pursued in the event of a loss.

Kuiper and his colleagues (e.g., Kuiper, MacDonald, & Derry, 1983) have made the self-schema the focus of their model of depression, which is an extension of Beck's. This conception emphasizes the more stable aspects of knowledge about the self, whereas the concept of role emphasizes the actions that are taken to sustain such knowledge. Based on their research Kuiper et al. suggest that in the non-depressed individual positive information about the self is processed more efficiently than negative information, leading to a recall bias for positive information. At mild levels of depression individuals begin to incorporate more negative information into their self-schema. This is thought to abolish the bias for positive information and to lead to decreases in processing efficiency, since new input must be compared with a self-schema whose content has a degree of internal inconsistency. In more severe cases of depression the self-schema is predominantly negative and processing efficiency is regained, but this time for negative information. At this point it may be helpful to consider how a self-schema might be organized and to review the evidence that information consistent with a self-schema is processed differently from information that is inconsistent.

## Mental Representations of the Self

It has been assumed that the overt expressions of low self-esteem that often accompany depression reflect internally represented knowledge that one is unloved, unworthy, incompetent, and so on. This approach is compatible with the distinction made by William James between the self as knower, i.e., the part that is invested with consciousness, and the self as the object of knowledge (also known as the phenomenal self). The quality of the phenomenal self is normally assumed to depend on social interaction with others and to reflect their opinions of and behaviour towards one (Chapter 9 contains a developmental account of this process from the perspective of attachment theory). This aspect of self may be thought of as a concept that, like any other concept, is stored in memory as a knowledge structure and is part of the individual's wider knowledge about objects and events in the social world. It is a high-order concept that provides a way of organizing personal experiences within the context provided by one's knowledge of the world and of other people. For a more detailed description of how self-knowledge may be organized, see Epstein (1983) and Kihlstrom and Cantor (1984).

As in the case of information about dangerous situations, information about the self may be organized in various ways, for example as part of an associative network or in the form of schemata, memory structures incorporating conceptually or empirically related elements. This view of the self as a system of schemata is elaborated by Markus and Sentis (1982), who note that schemata provide categories for organizing and reducing the enormous quantities of incoming information, and also enable individuals to fill in the gaps when information is inadequate or ambiguous. The concept of a schema implies both a *structure* containing certain kinds of information and also a *process* engaged in selection and interpretation. Schemata are both elicited by incoming information ("bottom-up" or "event-driven" processing) and act to fit incoming data to internalized models or expectations ("top-down" or "schema-driven" processing). The relative balance of these two forms of processing depends on the novelty of the situation and the accessibility of conceptually relevant schemata.

Markus (1977) had subjects rate a number of personality traits for the degree of self-descriptiveness and importance to their self-concept. From these ratings she was able to divide subjects into those who were schematic for a variety of traits such as dependence and independence, i.e., they saw these traits as characteristic of themselves, and those who were aschematic, i.e., did not characterize themselves along this dimension. When these individuals were presented with new, but related, trait adjectives, those who were schematic for dependence took less time to decide that "dependent" words such as "conforming" and "obliging" were characteristic of them than they did to characterize themselves as "individualistic" or "assertive". Subjects who were schematic for independence showed the opposite pattern, describing themselves more rapidly in terms of the "independent" than the "dependent" adjectives. There were no differences, however, in the time taken by the aschematics to describe themselves in terms of these two sets of words. Markus and Sentis (1982) review evidence showing that schematic subjects, relative to aschematics, are also more able to supply examples of episodes in the past when they have shown the relevant behaviour, are more resistant to information that conflicts with their view of themselves, and are more likely to recognize schema-relevant than schema-irrelevant material. They argue that these findings are consistent with the idea of stable cognitive structures that lead to the selective processing of new information.

This evidence suggests that certain schemata central to the self-concept are easily accessible and may be involved in the analysis of stimuli at an automatic, nonconscious level. This possibility was investigated in a study by Bargh (1982) using a dichotic listening paradigm in which subjects had to repeat out loud the words played to one ear while ignoring the words played to the other ear. Subjects were divided, using Markus' criteria, into those who were or were not schematic for independence. One of the channels consisted of a list of nouns and the other a list of adjectives, some of which were related to independence. At intervals during this task a light would go on and subjects had to respond as quickly as possible. It was assumed that their reaction time to this stimulus would be an indirect measure of how much attentional capacity was being used by the main task. As predicted, subjects schematic for independence responded faster to the light than aschematics when they were attending to and repeating ("shadowing") the independent adjectives. This was thought to be because such adjectives received a degree of automatic processing in the schematic group that reduced attentional requirements. When subjects were shadowing the list of nouns and the independent adjectives were presented in the unattended channel, however, the schematics took longer to react to the light than the aschematics, presumably because a greater amount of conscious attention had to be allocated to the nouns in order to keep the independent adjectives from consciousness.

The results of this complex experiment indicate that stimuli related to a person's self-concept may be registered and receive some automatic processing even when they never enter consciousness. Subjects in the Bargh (1982) study were completely unaware of the presence of the "independent" adjectives in the unattended channel while they were shadowing the nouns. And when the unattended adjectives were unrelated to independence, the two groups did not differ in the time taken to respond to the light. In addition to these effects of which the person is never conscious, it has been shown that more rapid decisions may be made about stimuli related to the self-concept, and that memory for such stimuli is enhanced. The variety of findings suggest that some account in terms of a mental representation of the self is warranted and could help to bring order to the various observations. The findings also provide an empirical basis for theorizing about the role of information-processing in depression.

## Evidence for Schematic Processing in Depression

A major source of support for the existence of schematic or schema-driven processing derives from the studies of mood and memory described in the previous chapter. There it was noted that depressed mood may be associated both with increased accessibility of negative experiences and with decreased accessibility of positive experiences. In addition, these differing patterns of recall are largely confined to material that has been encoded in relation to the self. Considered together with the self-schema studies reviewed above, these findings are consistent with the theoretical notion of a depressive self-schema that contains relatively less positive information and relatively more negative information than the non-depressive self-schema. As a number of authors have suggested, differences in the accessibility of such information should also affect conscious judgements made under conditions of uncertainty. Such judgements depend heavily on the information most readily brought to mind (the "availability heuristic" of Tversky and Kahneman, 1974), and so the presence of systematic differences between depressed and non-depressed could be taken as indirect evidence for the presence of schema-driven processing.

The relative accessibility of different kinds of memory ought to affect such judgements as causal attributions and expectations about the future, greater numbers of negative memories increasing the tendency to blame oneself for failure and to have lower expectations. Clinical observations of greater self-blame or greater hopelessness do not constitute acceptable evidence for schema-driven processing, however, since they may simply reflect different experiences and environmental opportunities. The same limitation applies to studies showing that the depressed are more hopeless or endorse more dysfunctional attitudes (see Segal & Shaw, 1986, for a review). A more appropriate test is to compare judgements about standardized situations, and here there is considerable evidence that the judgements of the depressed do differ from those of the non-depressed. For example, the depressed are more likely to attribute hypothetical negative outcomes to causal factors that are internal to themselves, affect many areas of their lives, and are relatively long-lasting, whereas the non-depressed are more likely to blame external, specific, and temporary causes (Sweeney, Anderson, & Bailey, 1986; see also Chapter 6). The depressed estimate that negative events such as accidents and illnesses are more likely to happen to them (Pietromonaco & Markus, 1985) and, given the same set of information with which to make predictions, the depressed are also more pessimistic about the likelihood of success than the non-depressed (Alloy & Ahrens, 1987).

These studies, and many others, indicate that situations are evaluated differently by the depressed and the non-depressed, and the findings are consistent with the idea of different kinds of information being retrieved from memory. It should be noted, though, that schema-driven processing is not synonymous with *biased* processing. According to Beck (1967), depressive schemas are maladaptive and give rise to distortions in the way information is registered and evaluated. This cannot be inferred simply from the presence of depressed–non-depressed differences, since the non-depressed may also demonstrate processing biases. The three main possibilities to be distinguished are that the depressed alone show biases and the non-depressed are accurate, that both groups show biases but in opposite directions, and that the non-depressed show biases whereas the depressed are accurate. This is known as the issue of "depressive realism".

Depressive realism in the context of judgements of contingency has been investigated in a series of studies by Alloy, Abramson, and their colleagues (e.g., Alloy & Abramson, 1979, 1982). Studies of contingency judgement have the advantage that subjects' estimates can be compared with the objective contingencies set by the experimenter. Thus the judgements of both depressed and non-depressed can be evaluated for the presence of biases. In these studies subjects, usually non-depressed or mildly depressed college students, are given a number of trials on a simple task and provided with feedback about their success after each trial. When the task is over they have to estimate the degree of contingency between their responses (usually choosing whether or not to press a button) and the outcomes (i.e., the success feedback). These estimates can be compared with the actual response–outcome contingency that has been set by the experimenter. This may vary anywhere between 0% (feedback is completely unrelated to the subjects' response) to 100% (feedback is completely determined by their response).

Whereas all subjects are fairly accurate when the contingency is set at 25%, 50%, or 75%, the groups differ in their ability to detect objective non-contingency (0%). Mildly depressed subjects are more consistently accurate than non-depressed subjects, who are likely to overestimate the degree of contingency and whose estimates are much more likely to be influenced by extraneous factors such as the rate of reinforcement, the presence of financial rewards and penalties, or pretreatment with uncontrollable noise. These results have been taken by some to mean that depressives are more "realistic" than non-depressives. Certainly, they indicate that the non-depressed are sometimes inaccurate and tend to overestimate their degree of control in objectively non-contingent situations (this phenomenon is well-established and is referred to as the "illusion of control" by Langer, 1975). Caution is needed in the interpretation of the findings for the depressed group, however, since their apparent superiority has only been demonstrated under conditions of objective non-contingency. In any case none, or very few, of the subjects were severely depressed. A final caveat is that the tasks were not aimed at important self-evaluative concerns, with the result that critical schemata were unlikely to have been activated.

This last point has been addressed by Vazquez (1987). Instead of the success feedback consisting of a neutral outcome such as the onset of a light, he arranged that the feedback would be a short sentence flashed on a screen. Some of these sentences contained positive and some negative content, referring either to the self or to other people. An example of a negative self-referent statement was "My problems are unsolvable", its other-referent equivalent being "Problems of human beings will never be solved". Vazquez found that when the outcomes produced by subjects' responses were negative self-referent statements and the actual contingency was 0%, depressed students lost their customary accuracy and exhibited an illusion of control. Thus "depressive realism" in contingency judgements may be limited to certain very specific circumstances; when the outcome concerns negative self-related material, biases consistent with schema-driven processing become apparent.

The presence of biases in information processing has also been investigated by asking subjects to recall the number of reinforcements actually received on an experimental task. Several studies have showed that depressed students underestimate reinforcement frequency. DeMonbreun and Craighead (1977) found that depressed psychiatric outpatients recalled receiving less positive feedback on a laboratory task than either non-depressed psychiatric patients or medical patients. Gotlib (1983) also showed that depressed patients, relative to psychiatric and non-psychiatric controls, rated the interpersonal feedback they received as being less favourable. Their subsequent recall of this feedback was distorted in a negative direction, whereas the recall of the non-depressed groups was relatively accurate. In contrast to these studies, Nelson and Craighead (1977) reported that depressed students were more accurate than the non-depressed in their recall of punishment received. There is also evidence that, when asked to rate their own social performance, depressed people's negative appraisals may be quite realistic and more in agreement with independent judges than the over-optimistic appraisals of the non-depressed (Lewinsohn, Mischel, Chaplin, & Barton, 1980).

To summarize the evidence so far, depressed and non-depressed individuals show differences in recall of positive and negative material, in contingency judgements, and in their past and future evaluations. This is support for the idea that the contents of memory, and in particular internal representations of the self, differ too in systematic ways. Non-depressed individuals often show an illusion of control when making contingency judgements, overestimate their social performance, and are more self-serving when making predictions or attributions. That is, they are more likely to be optimistic about their own outcomes than other people's outcomes, and more likely to make internal attributions for success than for failure (Alloy & Ahrens, 1987; Bradley, 1978). In comparison the depressed tend to make more accurate contingency judgements, and to be more even-handed in their predictions and attributions, although they tend to underestimate the occurrence of positive reinforcement. To date, then, the evidence that the non-depressed have a positivistic bias is rather stronger than the evidence that the depressed have a negativistic bias.

To what extent do these ambiguous findings challenge or support Beck's hypothesis that depression is characterized by negative schemas that introduce distortions into the processing of new information and lead to faulty inferences? First, the tasks that have been used to assess biases may often not have been sensitive enough or may not have used the right stimuli. The results of Vazquez (1987) illustrate this. In addition, there has been little attempt to ensure that the task contents are relevant to the subjects' concerns. If the tasks employed stimuli individually tailored to the experience of the depressed person, they might be better able to confirm clinical observations and detect the presence of consistent biases. Another important point has been made by Power and Champion (1986), who note that it is misleading to think of the depressed as being the only ones who make logical errors in thinking. Rather, because of their more negative model of the world, the depressed are likely to be more accurate than the non-depressed in evaluating negative information that is true and positive information that is false. However, they are likely to be less accurate than the non-depressed when they are evaluating positive information that is true and negative information that is false. Clinically, therefore, it would seem unwise for a therapist to assume that depressed patients' accounts of their circumstances are always unrealistically gloomy. Their assessments of the negative aspects may indeed be quite realistic, although hopeful signs and positive opportunities are likely to be given insufficient weight.

## Self-schemas and Vulnerability

Having decoupled the question of depressive realism from the issue of schematic processing, and discussed the evidence that the content of depressed people's self-schema differs from that of the non-depressed, it is time to consider whether self-schema differences are simply a reflection of current emotional state or whether, as Beck and others suggest, they could be implicated in vulnerability to depression. This has been investigated in prospective studies and in several comparisons of recovered depressed patients with non-depressed controls.

At present there is considerable controversy about whether patients' reported dysfunctional attitudes and attributions return to normal when the depressive episode is over. The finding of persistent dysfunctional attitudes in the absence of any remaining symptoms would encourage cognitive vulnerability theorists to look for long-term differences in information-processing. As Segal and Shaw (1986) note, of the available studies all find some degree of improvement in attitudes with symptomatic recovery, but they are roughly equally divided on the issue of whether these attitudes improve to a level where they are comparable to those of normal controls. Deficiencies in these studies, particularly in ascertaining that patients are fully recovered and have no residual symptoms, mean that the question cannot be answered at this time. There are studies, however, that have examined information-processing differences directly using a similar design.

Bradley & Mathews (1987) investigated whether the pattern of recall of positive and negative material shown by recovered depressed patients would be more similar to that of currently depressed patients or that of non-depressed controls. Whereas their group of currently depressed showed the predicted negative recall bias for material that had been encoded in relation to themselves, the recovered group were similar to the controls in favouring positive self-referent material. Unexpectedly, the recovered depressed were unlike both the other groups in recalling less positive material that had been encoded in relation to an unfamiliar other person. Another unexpected finding was that currently depressed patients who were not eligible for entry into the study, either because they had had a previous manic episode or because they had received cognitive therapy, did not show a negative self-referent recall bias and were similar to the recovered and non-depressed groups. Both these findings need to be replicated on larger samples, however.

In a similar study to that of Bradley and Mathews, Teasdale and Dent (1987) compared the recall of recovered depressed and never depressed individuals, finding that the former remembered fewer positive adjectives than the latter, although both groups recalled equivalent numbers of negative adjectives. The authors also tested what they termed the "differential activation" hypothesis, according to which some negative self-schemas may remain latent until the person is actually in a depressed mood. They therefore went on to compare recall after inducing mild depressed mood in their two groups. Under these conditions the recovered depressed remembered more self-descriptive negative words than did the never depressed. Teasdale and Dent's findings are not as clear as one might wish because it was not possible to test the critical hypothesis that recall differences between the groups would be significantly greater in the induced depressed mood than in normal mood. Their recovered group were also slightly more depressed in the week prior to testing than were the controls, leaving open the possibility that the results could be accounted for by differences in current emotional state. A third study, this time with college students, found that the recall of positive and negative personal memories by the recovered depressed was more similar to that of the non-depressed than to that of the currently depressed (Hammen, Marks, deMayo, & Mayol, 1985). It would therefore seem that further research is necessary before any conclusions can be drawn about the presence of maladaptive self-schemas in the recovered depressed.

Hammen et al. (1985) also investigated whether self-referent recall biases would predict future depression in their student sample. In fact future depression was predicted only by initial depression and not by the presence of a negative recall bias, even in interaction with the number of life events students had experienced. The authors commented that vulnerability may be linked to more specific schemas rather than to general negativity in relation to the self. In a study reported separately (Hammen, Marks, Mayol, & deMayo, 1985) they therefore had subjects recall as many incidents as they could in which they had felt either good or bad about themselves. Subjects were then divided into those who recalled more interpersonal events ("dependent schematics") and those who recalled more achievement-oriented events ("self-critical schematics"). The authors followed up all subjects and measured levels of depression over the next four months, recording as well the incidence of any life events. During this period dependent schematics showed significantly stronger associations between depression and schema-relevant interpersonal events than between depression and schema-irrelevant negative achievement events. Self-critical schematics tended to show the opposite pattern, with stronger associations between depression and achievement events than between depression and interpersonal events, but this was less often statistically significant.

This study therefore confirms that recall measures suggestive of important underlying cognitive structures might be an index of cognitive vulnerability. Although the measures used by Hammen et al. do not tell us much about the kind of information contained in these putative schemas, we can speculate that it was of emotional significance and may have corresponded to the individuals' major goals (see Chapter 8). Obviously, prospective studies of this kind are essential if the notion of cognitive vulnerability is to prove useful, and once again these preliminary findings need to be replicated and extended. But support for the idea that vulnerable individuals can be identified comes from research into the onset of depression among working-class women with children (Brown et al., 1986). These investigators reported that low self-esteem acted as a vulnerability factor to increase the likelihood that women experiencing a stressful provoking agent would subsequently become depressed. Low self-esteem was also related to the absence of social support, however, and the study suggests that there is a complex interaction between self-esteem, support, and depression. This is a timely reminder that an emphasis on self-schemas and information-processing should not lead to a neglect of social variables.

# CONCLUSIONS

The studies reviewed indicate that generalized anxiety is characterized by attentional biases favouring stimuli that signal threat or danger. Some of these biases appear to be preconscious and to operate completely outside awareness. Similarly, research on the self-concept confirms that stimuli related to a person's habitual self-definition can absorb attentional capacity even if that person is not consciously aware of them. As yet few published studies have investigated such fully automatic processes in depression. There is considerable evidence from research on mood and memory, though, that preconscious processes are involved in selecting material for entry into consciousness, and that in depression positive experiences are relatively less accessible whereas negative experiences are relatively more accessible. This differential accessibility is consistent with the more negative expectations of the depressed and with their greater accuracy, relative to the non-depressed, in recognizing unfavourable environmental contingencies.

Such studies, in addition to many reviewed earlier in this book, confirm clinical observations of thoughts and feelings that occur without conscious volition. It is clear that there are large individual differences in how new information is monitored, evaluated and remembered, and this could potentially account for the fact that anxiety and depression persist and generalize in some people but not in others. There is thus a pressing need for a theory of how information is internally represented, and how such representations interact with mood and with new information. Among the most influential suggestions have been that knowledge is stored in the form of associative networks, in which activation spreads passively between different nodes, or in the form of schemas, more molar units ("packages") of information that are activated when one of their constituent parts is encountered.

There are a number of possible ways in which these internal representations might affect mood. Beck (1967; Beck et al., 1979) suggested that past experience is represented in the form of permanent schemas that, if they contain negative content, constitute a form of cognitive vulnerability. These remain latent until activated by a similar experience, when they influence the interpretation of that event and its consequences. This kind of schema is clearly event-related, one implication being that individuals are vulnerable only to particular kinds of event and not others. Oatley and Bolton's (1985) model conceives of internal representations of goals, plans, and expectations, which together make up a sense of self. Vulnerability exists when selfhood is defined in terms of a narrow range of goals, and depression occurs when an event makes it impossible to pursue goals central to one's self-definition.

In contrast to these models of depression onset, Teasdale (1983) and Ingram (1984) emphasized the role of cognitions in depression maintenance. In their view, once an event has activated the postulated depression node, a wide variety of negative experiences that may have little connection with the provoking agent become more accessible to consciousness. The greater the number of such experiences, and the stronger their links to the depression node, the more likely they will be to enter consciousness and retard the recovery process. At present, as we have seen, the evidence that such mood-dependent effects exist is stronger than the evidence for more permanent cognitive vulnerability in depression. But we should also note that self-schema studies in the non-depressed have demonstrated selective processing of stimuli used to define the self. These effects were not mood-dependent, and suggest that application of similar methods might reveal the presence of permanent, highly accessible schemas in the depressed.

The idea that knowledge is represented in the form of associative networks or schemas has been useful in stimulating research, but it has also been criticized by Power and Champion (1986) both on empirical grounds and for being inadequate to deal with the complexities of experience. One problem with associative networks is that there are many different kinds of link between nodes, representing different kinds of relations such as "means the same as" or "occurs in conjunction with." At present the theoretical status of all these kinds of link is equivalent, even though in practice they may have a very different significance. Quite what schemas look like, and how information is organized within them, is also very vague. Power and Champion suggest that a more sophisticated account of internal representations is necessary, such as that provided by the theory of mental models (Johnson-Laird, 1983). Among other advantages this theory makes provision for people to have models of what others believe as well as of what they themselves believe, and allows models to contain inconsistent information. Such a theory is probably superfluous when representing information about the simple contingency between two events (as in the case of specific phobias). It may, however, have considerable advantages when trying to explain the underlying representation of the more complex beliefs encountered in depression or in relationship problems.

Some of these more complex beliefs appear to involve mental representations of the self. It would be wrong, however, to associate negative self-schemas exclusively with depression. Although depression does often involve negative self-perceptions, this is not always the case. In sufferers from chronic physical disorders such as arthritis and Parkinson's disease, for example, it is characterized by hopelessness, decreased drive, and increased concern with health, but not by cognitions involving guilt, self-blame, or worthlessness (Gotham, Brown, & Marsden, 1986). The findings about self-related information processing reviewed above may therefore only be relevant to a subset of depressions. It should also be remembered that many anxious patients, particularly social phobics, perceive themselves in negative terms, although it is not known whether these perceptions are as global and all-encompassing as in a typical depression. Negative self-schemas may accompany any psychiatric or physical disorder, although depressed patients are probably unique in their conscious acceptance of a negative view of themselves. More commonly, individuals attempt in various ways to combat negative thoughts. This is discussed in more detail in the section on self-esteem maintenance in Chapter 8.

Information-processing models have received considerable support to date, and they offer the possibility for the future of a unified theoretical approach that could encompass such traditionally psychoanalytic concerns as unconscious fears, goals and mechanisms of defence. It appears that one of the functions of automatic processes operating outside awareness is to influence the entry of different kinds of material into consciousness. By this means they have the potential to influence people's conscious appraisal of their environment and the actions that then follow. Of particular concern to clinicians is how people appraise threatening, demanding and challenging situations, and the next two chapters give an account of two of the most important types of appraisal, involving explanations and expectancies.

# 6
## Explanation and Attribution

In recent years social psychologists have become very interested in how people explain the events they observe or that happen to them, and in the consequences of such explanations. According to attribution theorists, for instance, human beings have an in-built desire to explain their world in order to exercise a greater degree of control over it. Causal explanations are particularly noticeable when anything unusual, unwanted, or unpleasant occurs (Weiner, 1985b), which is of course precisely the situation of most people who consult clinical psychologists. A concern to know the cause of their predicament has been noted, for example, in accident victims (Bulman & Wortman, 1977) and in cancer sufferers (Taylor, Lichtman, & Wood, 1984). It is in fact rare to come across any patients who have not thought, often at considerable length, about the origin of their problems or symptoms, and this has led to numerous attempts to apply attribution theory to clinical problems (e.g., Antaki & Brewin, 1982).

Given that people do try to explain why misfortune has befallen them, this chapter will explore whether these explanations have an impact on how the person then thinks, feels, and behaves. One important point to note is that real-world events are often extremely complex, leaving plenty of scope for misunderstanding or only partial appreciation of the causal factors involved. Information about the causes and consequences of different illnesses is often lacking, either because it has not been offered or not remembered. People may have all sorts of misconceptions about the general frequency of the upsetting events they experience, and about causal elements such as their own abilities and others' motives. We can therefore take it for granted that people's explanations are unlikely to be all the same.

We shall begin by examining in more detail the different functions that people's explanations serve and whether certain kinds of explanation are more likely to lead to successful personal adjustment in the face of adversity. At least four separate functions can be distinguished: labelling and interpretation, in which people decide on the nature and meaning of a particular event; causal attribution, in which the responsible causal factors are identified; moral judgement, in which people's actions are evaluated against standards of right and wrong; and self-presentation, in which explanations are selected in order to put across a particular view of oneself. All these functions are evident in the explanations patients produce for their illnesses and misfortunes.

## LABELLING AND INTERPRETATION

In the search for explanation we often have first to describe or label an experience that is ambiguous. For instance, before we can say why we are feeling terrible, we have to decide whether we are depressed, have flu, are tired, or have a hangover. In the same way patients who develop a pain, lump, or other unusual symptom consult a doctor in order to reassure themselves that the symptom can be labelled as harmless. Often it is difficult to discriminate between two experiences, such as indigestion and a heart attack, one of which has an extremely threatening label whereas the other is not at all threatening. Labelling involves categorizing experiences according to the knowledge that we have available, either using our existing categories or creating a new category that can be defined in terms of the existing ones. Each category or label will be associated with its own set of information concerning the frequency of the problem, the likely outcome, and so on, information that may be accurate, inaccurate, or simply missing.

In many cases, therefore, understanding *why* appears to be intimately connected with knowing *what* an experience consists of. The label may then supply useful information about the likely cause. There is an interesting parallel here with Schachter's (1964) theory of the emotions, which, as we have seen in Chapter 4, claimed that emotional experience consists of an undifferentiated state of physiological arousal that is then assigned a specific label such as anger or fear according to the way in which environmental stimuli are appraised. There have been a number of experiments that have attempted to use this principle and achieve some therapeutic benefit by getting people to relabel their experiences in a more helpful way. In a well-known example of this "misattribution" approach Storms and Nisbett (1970) gave people suffering from insomnia a pill to take at bedtime. Although the pills were inert, Storms and Nisbett told half the subjects that the pills would calm them down and the other half that the pills would produce feelings similar to those of high physiological arousal. Their reasoning was that insomnia sufferers tend to be tense and highly aroused, which would lead them to worry about the cause of the arousal and so find it more difficult to get to sleep. By providing a new and emotionally neutral label for these feelings, i.e., side-effects of the pills, sufferers should worry less about them and so fall asleep more easily. Consistent with this prediction, the group who were told that the pills would produce symptoms of arousal reported falling asleep faster than the group who were told that the pills would have a calming effect.

The findings of the "misattribution" studies will not be evaluated in detail here as this has been done elsewhere (Brewin & Antaki, 1982; Harvey & Galvin, 1984). Suffice it to say that their results have been difficult to replicate and that clinically significant effects have not been established. In part this must be because of the inherent implausibility of many of the manipulations, in which subjects were presented with novel environmental stimuli and expected to relabel fairly familiar experiences. It is hardly surprising that subjects were loath to abandon their original (and presumably plausible) categories in favour of new and untested ones. In principle, however, there is no reason why people who have wrongly or unhelpfully categorized their experiences should not benefit from having them reassigned to a less threatening category. An example of an appropriate and powerful use of relabelling comes from recent work on the treatment of panic attacks.

It has often been noted that the effects of over-breathing or hyperventilation are similar to the experience of a panic attack. In both conditions the person has an intense feeling of apprehension or impending doom accompanied by distressing physical sensations such as vertigo, blurred vision, palpitations, numbness, tingling in the hands and feet, and breathlessness. According to a recent model of panic attacks (Clark, Salkovskis, & Chalkley, 1985; Salkovskis & Clark, 1986) some individuals increase their respiratory ventilation and over-breathe when under stress, which produces a range of these unpleasant sensations. These are then labelled by the patient as symptoms of a heart attack or other medical emergency, or as indications that the patient is going mad. The frightening consequences of these labels lead to further apprehension, to further increases in ventilation, and so on in a vicious cycle. Their treatment consists of helping patients to relabel their sensations as symptoms of hyperventilation rather than of some more catastrophic condition. Patients first practise voluntary over-breathing, then introspect on their sensations and compare them to those experienced during panic attacks. The therapist then gives an explanation of how over-breathing can induce panic attacks and trains them in a pattern of slow breathing that is incompatible with hyperventilation. Although this treatment contains a number of disparate elements, so that improvement need not be the result of relabelling, Salkovskis and Clark argue that the extremely rapid initial reduction in panic attack frequency and self-reported anxiety points to the importance of the cognitive element.

Just as patients may have difficulty in labelling internal sensations, observers may not know whether to label behaviour as an intentional act, as a symptom of a disease, as a drug side-effect, and so on. To take one example, husbands and wives may have great difficulty in correctly labelling the early symptoms of schizophrenia as being a product of mental illness. Yarrow, Schwartz, Murphy, and Deasy (1956) describe how wives cannot generally pinpoint the time when their husband's problem emerged. The subjective beginnings are seldom localized in a single strange or disturbing incident, but only after an accumulation of odd behaviour and reactions. At first, these odd behaviours may be denied or normalized, and assimilated into existing expectations. Early interpretations of them may shift back and forth a good deal, and are often couched in terms of physical difficulties, character problems, or environmental distress. Although the progressive disruption produced by the symptoms usually leads to an explanation in terms of mental illness, some wives maintain the same explanation throughout, either within or outside a psychiatric framework. Another example of the difficulty in labelling others' behaviour comes from studies of children referred to psychiatric clinics for "deviancy" (Lobitz & Johnson, 1975; Rickard et al., 1981). In contrast to what might be expected, these children do not always differ from non-referred controls on behavioural measures. A more reliable distinguishing feature is that their parents label their behaviour as "deviant", even when it appears to be similar to that of children in general.

There seems no reason not to recognize relabelling as a powerful clinical tool, providing the new label is less threatening and is supplied in a convincing way. The process is probably widely applicable and should not be thought of as synonymous with the more restricted "misattribution" studies, which struggled under the self-imposed requirement to mislead people rather than to enlighten them. Before leaving the topic of labelling, it should be noted that sociologists have written extensively about the effect on patients of the labels that society uses for their behaviour (e.g., Field, 1976). Part of the knowledge one has about the world includes expectations about the effects of such diseases as epilepsy, diabetes, and schizophrenia, and it has been argued that patients tend to respond to social pressures and act in conformity with the public stereotypes associated with a particular label (the concept of "secondary deviance"). So people with epilepsy may come to regard themselves as unreliable and even dangerous if consistently treated in this way by others.

# CAUSAL ATTRIBUTION

The studies reviewed above illustrate the frequent difficulties encountered in labelling and interpreting events and symptoms. Despite this, the sort of explanation with which psychologists have been most concerned assumes that the nature of the event is clearly understood. Causal attribution describes the process whereby people decide what causal factors have produced a given event or outcome. In this research the focus of interest is on the terms in which causes are most commonly described, how people arrive at their causal attributions, and what effect those attributions have on their subsequent behaviour. Theories that are concerned with the consequences of these causal perceptions are sometimes called "attributional" theories to distinguish them from the "attribution" theories that concentrate on the antecedents of causal judgements. In this section we shall have most to say about the attributional theories, but first a few words are in order about how people make attributions. The important point to note is that this is a complex process, open to error and bias, that often affords only a partial or distorted view of the world.

## The Formation of Attributions

Following Fritz Heider's *The Psychology of Interpersonal Relations*, published in 1958, a distinction has been drawn between causes that reside within the person (internal) and those causes to do with other people, luck, or circumstances (external). Most events, whether becoming ill, getting promotion, or being run over by a car, can be attributed to internal or to external causes, or to a mixture of the two. Becoming ill might be attributed to the external cause of exposure to another person's germs, for instance, or to the internal cause of not taking enough care of oneself and becoming run down. What cause we actually subscribe to depends on a number of factors.

A great deal of research has been carried out on the antecedents of causal attributions (see Kelley & Michela, 1980). Apart from the influence of the "fundamental attribution error" (the tendency to underestimate situational causes of behaviour), and of the motivational concerns discussed later in this chapter, the antecedents can be roughly divided between those that are based on past experience and those that represent current situational information. Causal beliefs (or causal schemata) are suppositions or expectations about cause–effect relations that are based on past experience and that can be called upon to analyze complex or ambiguous situations. These expectations may contain some specific content, for example that people in authority want to repress those under them or that men are invariably unfaithful, and may result in rapid interpretations being made of behavioural instances that appear to fit the particular pattern.

Explanations based on such causal beliefs may come to mind instantly and may be subjectively quite compelling, so that the person may not stop to consider alternative explanations and may sometimes angrily reject evidence that is contrary to it.

Three types of current situational information relevant to the formation of attributions have been discussed in some detail. Kelley (1967) suggested that for many events the most common causal factors are persons (P), stimuli (S), and occasions or times (T). The attribution of a given P's response to a certain S on a particular occasion (T) depends on the perception of the degree of its consensus with other P's responses to S, its consistency with this P's response to S on other occasions, and its distinctiveness from P's response to other Ss. Particular patterns of information are thought to lead to particular attributions. For example, behaviour that is low in consensus, high in consistency, and low in distinctiveness tends to produce person attributions, whereas behaviour that is highly consensual, highly consistent, and highly distinctive tends to be attributed to the stimulus.

This analysis has proven very fruitful, although a number of defects have been pointed out and improvements suggested (Hilton & Slugoski, 1986; Jaspars, Hewstone, & Fincham, 1983). It is easy to see how a parent's attribution for a child's misbehaviour with a particular playmate would be influenced by information about how many other children misbehaved with this playmate (consensus), how often the child had misbehaved with this playmate in the past (consistency), and how often the child misbehaved with other playmates (distinctiveness). But many important real-life events, such as accidents, bereavement, or redundancy, do not possess this person–stimulus–occasion structure, with the result that some of this information is unavailable. If the event is only likely to happen once, or if no more then one stimulus is ever likely to be involved, consistency and distinctiveness information may have to be combined to yield a cruder judgement of *how often something similar has happened in the past*. Consensus information about how others would have behaved or about the frequency in the general population of a particular experience can also be extremely hard to come by. In practice the individual trying to explain an event may not have any ready access to this kind of information other than from his or her own memory. These estimates may be affected by current mood, the recall of past negative outcomes being enhanced and the recall of past positive experiences being inhibited when one is depressed (see Chapters 4 and 5).

Most research has treated attribution as a conscious process of inferring causation that is triggered by an unexpected outcome and that proceeds by weighing up how the effect to be explained covaries with a number of potential causal factors. Expected outcomes, it is thought, are processed rapidly and automatically according to pre-existing causal beliefs, so that the person may hardly be aware of the causal inferences he or she is making. But there is some evidence that conscious causal reasoning, too, is affected by automatic cognitive processes, over and above the mood effects already mentioned. This is not so surprising when it is recalled that human beings' capacity to estimate event covariation or correlation is quite limited, at least when they are asked to make a verbal report (Nisbett & Ross, 1980). What, then, does affect the attribution made when there is a complex sequence of events that exceeds that capacity? A reliable finding is that people are more likely to conclude that one event has caused another if it stands out and attracts their attention in some way, or if it occurs in close temporal and spatial proximity. These basic situational features influence attribution both in young children and in adults, just as they influence conditioning in animals. It has therefore been argued that our perceptual apparatus may have an innate, pre-wired tendency to respond to these basic cues as indicative of causal relationships (Kassin & Baron, 1985). These tendencies may have some basis in naturally occurring environmental relationships, but at times they may also be responsible for incorrect causal inferences.

## Consequences of Attributions

Does it make any difference if a person attributes their accident to carelessness, bad luck, or faulty machinery, or attributes their illness to smoking, overwork, too many worries, or some constitutional weakness? It has been suggested that underlying the huge number of causal factors that people may invoke there are a few critical dimensions, along which all causes vary and which have very specific consequences. According to Weiner (1985a, 1986), the perceived causes of an event differ primarily on the three dimensions of internality, stability, and controllability. As we have seen in Chapter 4, the internality and controllability dimensions are thought to be particularly involved in the genesis of esteem-related emotions such as pride and guilt, and interpersonal emotions such as pity and anger. In this model the stability dimension is also linked, by way of intervening expectancies of success and failure, to motivational factors such as the intensity and persistence with which a person performs a particular behaviour. Attributing successful outcomes to stable, unchanging factors leads to raised expectations of future success, and hence to greater persistence in the face of difficulty, whereas attributing unsuccessful outcomes to stable factors leads to lowered expectations of success and a tendency to give up trying.

Weiner's complete model of motivation and emotion, which contains a number of cognitive elements other than attributions, is shown in Fig. 6.1.

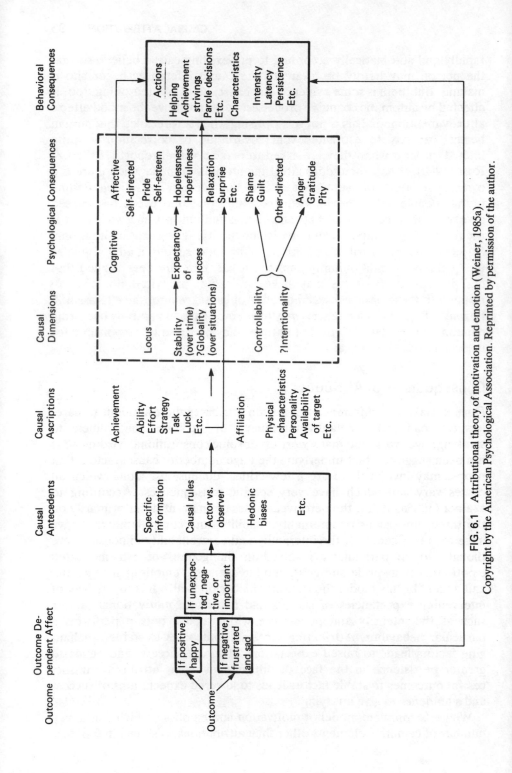

FIG. 6.1  Attributional theory of motivation and emotion (Weiner, 1985a). Copyright by the American Psychological Association. Reprinted by permission of the author.

It is not possible to examine the model in detail here, but it is worth noting that it can be applied to both achievement and interpersonal (affiliative) events, and that attributions are considered to have a wide range of cognitive, affective, and behavioural consequences. Thus it is relevant to understanding many of the feelings and behaviours displayed by patients, their relatives, and professional carers, including low self-esteem, guilt, lack of motivation, and hostile feelings towards others. The interpersonal consequences of attributions are reviewed in Chapter 9, and attempts to manipulate attributions therapeutically in Chapter 10. Here we concentrate on two other areas of enquiry, depression and health behaviour, which have also been influenced by Weiner's research and which illustrate in more detail the relation between patients' causal perceptions, feelings and behaviour.

## Attribution and Depression

In 1978, the current version of learned helplessness theory underwent a radical change of emphasis. Seligman (1975) had proposed that when people or animals experience an event that they cannot control, they develop an expectation of lack of control in similar situations (specifically, they come to expect that there is no relation between their actions and the outcomes they experience). In those situations they then demonstrate a number of "learned helplessness" effects, such as failure to initiate escape responses from an aversive environment and failure to learn from successful escape experiences. Research with human subjects attempted to demonstrate analogous helplessness effects by giving them inescapable noise or an insoluble problem, and then monitoring their performance on a second test task to see if they did worse than subjects who had not been made helpless. But it was found that people often (1) performed better rather than worse after helplessness induction; (2) showed helplessness effects in some situations but not in others; and (3) were affected by instructions about how other subjects had done on the task.

Abramson, Seligman, and Teasdale (1978) therefore proposed that, rather than helplessness automatically following an experience of uncontrollability, a person's response depends on their understanding of why the uncontrollable experience occurred. If the cause is perceived as being stable rather than unstable, then helplessness effects in that particular situation are likely to be long-lasting. If the cause is perceived as influencing many situations rather than just that one situation (a "global" rather than a "specific" cause in Abramson et al.'s terms), then helplessness effects are likely to generalize to other situations. Finally, if the cause is perceived as being internal ("personal helplessness") rather than external ("universal helplessness"), then that person is likely to suffer a loss of self-esteem.

Let us illustrate these ideas with an example. A woman is criticized for a piece of work by her boss. If she attributes this to an unstable cause such as her boss being temporarily in a bad mood, she should be less likely to experience helplessness than if she attributes it to a stable cause such as her inability to handle this type of work. If she attributes it to a specific cause such as difficulty with this particular superior, any helplessness she experiences will generalize less to other situations than if she had attributed it to a global cause such as difficulty in relationships with all superiors. Finally, if she attributes it to an internal cause, based for example on a consensus judgement such as "My boss is only critical of me", she will experience lower self-esteem than if she makes an external attribution based on the judgement "My boss is critical of all the women who work for her".

As with previous versions of the theory, it has been proposed that the reformulation provides a model for certain instances of depression. Although Abramson and her colleagues recognized that depression may have a number of causes (e.g., biochemical ones), they suggested that there is a substantial subset of "helplessness" depressions in which the expectation of uncontrollability plays an important role. They viewed depression as a complex disorder made up of at least four classes of deficits: motivational (reduced initiation of voluntary responding); cognitive (impaired learning of the association between a person's actions and contingent events); self-esteem; and affective (sadness). Depressed affect comes about when a person loses something highly desirable, or experiences something very unpleasant. The importance of this event will influence the intensity of their emotion, as will the strength or certainty of their belief that the event is uncontrollable. The more stable their attribution for the event, the longer-lasting the depressive deficits will be, and the more global the attribution, the more generalized the deficits will be. According to the model people may become depressed whether their attributions are internal or external, but internal attributions (personal helplessness) will lead to the specific depressive deficit of low self-esteem.

This model emphasizes the potential role of attributions in the *onset* of a depressive episode. A number of other attribution–depression relationships are possible, however (Brewin, 1985), and these are shown in Fig. 6.2. Peterson and Seligman (1984), for example, have suggested that certain individuals have a "vulnerable attributional style", in other words a set of reasonably permanent causal beliefs leading them to attribute their positive experiences to external, unstable, and specific factors, such as good luck, while attributing their negative experiences to internal, stable, and global factors, such as incompetence or lack of intelligence. Peterson and Seligman suggest that when people with such a vulnerable style have a failure or setback, they will be more likely to make an internal, stable, and global attribution and to suffer a more severe depressive reaction. The fact that women are less likely than men to take credit for success and are more likely to blame themselves for failure has also been put forward as an explanation for why women have higher rates of depression than do men (Dweck & Reppucci, 1973; Ickes & Layden, 1978).

In addition to this *vulnerability* model it is possible to outline at least three additional models. The *recovery* model does not require that attributions be involved in the onset of depression, but holds that people who make internal, stable, and global attributions will take longer to recover from the depressed state. The *coping* model makes even fewer assumptions, predicting simply that the depressive attributional pattern will be associated with lower resistance to depression, whether or not the person is depressed to start with. Note that neither the recovery nor the coping model requires the person to have necessarily experienced any major negative event. Instead, specific attributions or a more permanent attributional style are thought to determine how people respond to the symptoms of depression themselves. Finally, the *symptom* model, the only one to be completely incompatible with learned helplessness theory, holds that depressive attributions are a symptom of the clinical state of depression and play no causal role either in its onset or maintenance.

## Critique of Attributional Theories of Depression

In spite of a large research effort put into testing the reformulated learned helplessness model of depression, empirical support for the theory is equivocal. On the one hand, depressed people do seem to make greater numbers of attributions for failure than the non-depressed (Kammer, 1984). If the results of many studies are put together, small to moderate correlations are found between the predicted attributional patterns and depression (Sweeney et al., 1986). Clinical studies also indicate that the attributions made by depressed patients about real-life difficulties change in the predicted direction as they get better (Firth-Cozens & Brewin, 1988). But these designs do not exclude the possibility that it is depressed mood that influences a person's attributions (the symptom model) rather than the other way round, and so do not provide an adequate test of the theory.

When evidence for the five models shown in Fig. 6.2 is examined separately (Brewin, 1985), there appears to be little or no support for the onset and vulnerability models. In part, this is undoubtedly because these two models make the largest number of assumptions and so are most difficult to test. Recently, however, the vulnerability model was examined in four groups of working-class women, those who had and had not experienced a major stressor and those who were and were not depressed (Parry & Brewin, 1988). Contrary to the vulnerability model, which claims that both environmental stress and maladaptive attributions are necessary

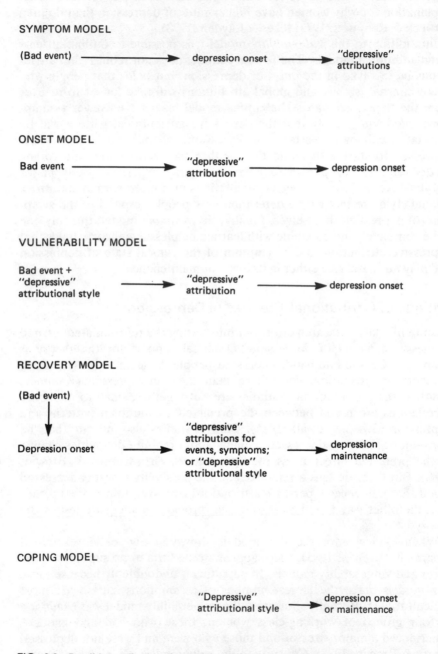

**FIG. 6.2** Possible attribution–depression relationships (Brewin, 1985). Copyright by the American Psychological Association. Reprinted by permission of the author.

for (helplessness) depression, the highest levels of self-blame were found among women who had become depressed in the *absence* of a stressful event. In contrast to the lack of support for these two models, there is evidence that people's mood affects their causal judgements (the symptom model), attributions for negative events being more internal, stable, and global during a depressive episode and becoming more "normal" after the episode is over. There is also encouraging evidence for the recovery and coping models. Attributions help to predict who will be more depressed weeks and months later, even when it is taken into account that not everyone is equally depressed to start with.

It does seem, then, that the depressive pattern of attributions is associated with weakened resistance to, and poorer recovery from, depression. But there has been little support for models in which the occurrence of an uncontrollable aversive event was a necessary part. It is possible, therefore, that the account provided by the reformulated model to explain depressive onset is erroneous or only seldom applicable. This may be because cognitions about the triggering event are irrelevant or because the wrong cognitions have been measured.

The reformulated model is rooted in laboratory situations in which aversive experiences can be controlled and repeated (e.g., electric shocks, loud noise, or failure on an insoluble task). Attributions are assumed to be important because, in the case of recurrent events, the attribution is closely linked to expectations of successful performance next time the situation is encountered. Are these the kind of experiences that normally precede clinical depression? The work of Brown and Harris (1978) particularly identifies such experiences as being characterized by moderate or severe long-term threat, i.e., bad consequences lasting longer than one week. These events, such as bereavement, redundancy, or an unpleasant revelation about a loved one, usually involve loss or disappointment and tend in the short term to be non-recurring. With this sort of event, causal attributions are unlikely to be so closely related to future adjustment. For example, attributions about the cause of a close friend's death may be less relevant to adjustment than one's expectations of being able to cope without him or her.

We have been arguing that some events may have such a major impact on their own account that causal cognitions are relatively unimportant. There are two possible counter-arguments here. First, epidemiological studies such as that of Brown and Harris may only have identified major events preceding depression. It may be that numerous cases of depression are precipitated by a series of more minor events, such as family rows, but that such events have not shown up in the large-scale studies because they are only significant to some individuals and not to others. Alternatively, loss events such as divorce and death may be important because they *do* represent a recurrence of an early experience in a person's life (Brown & Harris reported that women who had lost their mother before the age of twelve were more vulnerable when they experienced a severe event). In both these cases the learned helplessness model, with its emphasis on recurrent events, would appear to be appropriate. At present, however, there is doubt about whether Abramson et al. (1978) are correct in their assumption that an analysis of recurrent events in the laboratory can be used to explain the effects of real-life events that recur seldom if at all.

We have also raised the possibility that, as far as events are concerned, the wrong cognitions are being measured. These might, for instance, be moral or self-evaluative rather than causal perceptions. In other words, people might be more concerned with the adequacy or propriety of their own conduct or character than with the fact that their actions played some part in a causal chain leading to the uncontrollable event. Learned helplessness research tends to confound these two kinds of judgement, not considering that one may make an internal causal attribution without the feeling that one has necessarily acted foolishly, recklessly, or incompetently (Brewin, 1986). In support of this point, some studies (e.g., Janoff–Bulman, 1979) have reported that depressed mood is not related to greater self-blame for one's actions but only to greater self-blame for one's character. Characterological self-blame involves feelings of guilt and deservingness and thus appears to be an evaluative as well as a causal judgement. This analysis of self-blame into causal and evaluative elements may help to explain why some recent studies have linked depressed mood in college students to perceiving negative events as more controllable, another finding which is contrary to learned helplessness theory. Seeing events as more controllable is related to guilt, i.e., to feeling that one has transgressed one's standards of conduct. Thus events may be important in precipitating depression for reasons other than their perceived causal properties.

## Attribution and Health-related Behaviour

We have devoted a great deal of space to examining attributional theories of depression because they have received most attention to date. These theories can be applied just as successfully, probably more successfully, to patients whose disorders are predominantly physical. Whereas with depression attributions for environmental stresses were thought to influence the disorder, in the case of physical medicine researchers have been interested in the impact of attributions for the disorder itself on its future course and on the patient's adjustment to it. Just as in the case of depression, however, patients often experience a single event, the onset of illness, which they do not expect to recur. Even if the illness is one with an expectation of recurrence, as in cancer or heart disease, the causes of the first episode may not be perceived to be the same as those of subsequent episodes. For instance, the probability of future heart disease may be substantially determined by the degree of damage to the heart and arteries sustained in earlier episodes.

Health contexts provide a rich variety of combinations of circumstances, each of which must be individually analyzed. Victims of minor accidental trauma, for instance, usually have to cope with the situation in which their accident originally occurred, whether this be at home, at work, or on the roads. Major trauma such as spinal injury, on the other hand, frequently means that the person's whole environment or way of life changes so that they never encounter that situation again. One would therefore expect causal judgements about minor accidents to be more relevant than judgements about major accidents in predicting future adjustment. Patients with chronic diseases such as diabetes mellitus can make causal attributions both about the onset of their disorder and about recurrent events such as hypoglycaemic episodes that reflect the routine course of the disorder. Once again one would neither expect that these attributions be similar in content nor expect that their consequences would be the same. Attributions about day-to-day events should theoretically stand the best chance of predicting adjustment and health behaviour, and this may explain why some studies of attributions for disease onset have not found the predicted relationship to adjustment (e.g., Taylor et al., 1984).

One much-quoted study that appears to go against this principle is that of Bulman and Wortman (1977). These researchers interviewed accident victims with severe spinal injuries that had left them with varying degrees of paralysis. Patients rated by their therapists as coping most successfully with their condition: (1) tended to blame themselves for their accident; (2) were less likely to blame other people; and (3) believed they were less able to prevent their accident. There are, however, a number of difficulties in interpreting these results. All interviews were carried out at a similar point in time, so we cannot say whether attributions affected adjustment or vice versa. There is also an evident contradiction between holding beliefs (1) and (3) at the same time: if one blames oneself more, one should believe oneself *more* able to prevent the accident, not less able. A subsequent study (Brewin, 1984a) measured the attributions of patients for accidents at work. These were accidents involving minor fractures needing an average of four to five weeks at home before patients returned to work. Upon their return, victims who felt that they had caused the accident reported themselves to be less tense and anxious, and more alert and active. Some evidence about the direction of causation was obtained from the small minority of accidents where there was some clearly identifiable environmental fault or failure that acted as a precipitating agent. Patients who had been involved in this type of accident rated themselves as less causally responsible immediately after the accident, took longer to get back to work, and appeared more poorly adjusted when they did so.

Causal perceptions may be associated with a variety of other behaviours such as choice of treatment. Bradley et al. (1987) investigated the psychological factors that were associated with choice of a new treatment for diabetes, continuous subcutaneous insulin infusion (CSII), versus a more traditional regimen of daily or twice-daily self-injections. CSII treatment involves having an insulin pump strapped to the body that automatically releases insulin throughout the day. Using a set of scales specifically developed to measure patients' attributions of controllability for day-to-day events connected with their diabetes, it was found that choice of CSII was predicted by the perception that medical staff had a greater degree of control over the patient's diabetes. Patients choosing injection regimens, on the other hand, thought they had higher levels of personal control. The scales also predicted how successful patients would be at controlling their diabetes during the following year. In another study (King, 1982) patients were more likely to attend a screening for high blood pressure if they perceived the causes of the condition to be external but controllable.

## MORAL EVALUATION

Understanding and explaining events is not simply a matter of locating a cause, however. When faced with misfortune a person is likely to want to know not only whether his or her actions produced the outcome, but also how reasonable or appropriate those actions were. As we have already seen in our discussion of depressive attributions, it is quite possible to blame oneself in the causal sense but not in the moral sense, as for instance when you make some perfectly understandable error of judgement. It is quite another matter when you try to cut corners, ignore the normal procedures, or take unnecessary risks. Under these circumstances, when disaster subsequently occurs, you know that you ought to have acted differently and the self-recriminations are likely to be painful and prolonged. The essence of this aspect of explanation is the question of what you *ought* to have done, rather than the consequences of what you did do.

To date, few clinically-relevant studies have examined causal and moral attribution separately. One exception is the previously mentioned study of accident victims (Brewin, 1984a). In the sample as a whole greater causal self-blame was associated with victims feeling less tense and anxious, whereas greater moral self-blame was associated with a more rapid return to work. These two effects were quite independent of each other even though, as one might expect, the two kinds of self-blame tended to occur together. In another recent study, Furnham, Hillard, and Brewin (1985) investigated the causal and moral judgements typically made by people with a hard-driving, impatient, coronary-prone (Type A) personality compared with people with a more relaxed, unambitious, and non-coronary-prone (Type B) personality. Both groups were given a questionnaire describing a number of negative experiences, such as not being able to get work done or being accused of gossiping about a friend, which came about through either controllable or uncontrollable circumstances. The major differences between the groups were confined to the uncontrollable negative outcomes: Type A subjects were more likely to feel angry with themselves and to judge that their actions had fallen short of their standards. Even in situations beyond their control, Type A subjects seemed to feel that they ought to have done better, although they did not reveal any more causal self-blame than the Type Bs. Another way of expressing this finding is that the Type A personality sets high standards and makes less allowance for circumstances when evaluating how he or she has done relative to these standards.

Self-evaluation or moral judgement appears to be important in many other clinical contexts, although the research has often been described using the language of attributions. For instance, Storms and McCaul (1976) proposed a common mechanism to account for the exacerbation of a variety of anxiety-related behaviours such as stammering, insomnia, male impotence, shyness, and blushing. This mechanism involves: (a) seeing the cause of unwanted behaviour as one's own negative dispositions or characteristics; (b) an increase in an unpleasant emotional state such as anxiety or depression following from this negative self-evaluation; and (c) a consequent exacerbation of the same unwanted behaviour that gave rise to the initial attribution. They reported evidence that negative self-evaluation is common among stutterers, who often have low self-esteem and experience intense anxiety about speaking.

Storms and McCaul's exacerbation model appears to be describing moral rather than causal judgements because they are describing people who feel that they *ought* not to be displaying the unwanted behaviour, of which they will in many cases be ashamed. Shame is a common reaction to many problems that people bring to psychologists and doctors. Storms and Nisbett (1970) reported anecdotal evidence that people with insomnia were prone to worry about the disorder and view it as a serious personal problem possibly indicative of pathology. In a test of this model, Lowery, Denney, and Storms (1979) compared two types of attributional treatment with a no-treatment control condition. In the "misattribution" treatment subjects were induced to relabel their symptoms of arousal as a drug side-effect, while in the "non-pejorative self-attribution" treatment they were persuaded that their arousal was due to autonomic activity that was somewhat above average but that they were otherwise completely normal.

Lowery et al. found that subjects in both treatment groups said they fell asleep more easily than did the controls, but only the group whose self-evaluation had been manipulated reported that they also fell asleep more quickly. Other examples of the close connection between causal and moral judgements are given in Chapter 9.

## SELF-PRESENTATION

A number of writers have drawn attention to the fact that making explanations is often a public activity and has the function of enhancing how one appears in the eyes of other people. Whether or not they are aware of it, people may also try to enhance their own view of themselves by making self-protective or esteem-enhancing attributions (see Chapter 8). Sportsmen and politicians are noted for their ability to find a face-saving explanation for an unexpected defeat or change of policy, and their pronouncements are often treated with a good deal of scepticism. Should we therefore treat patients' explanations for their problems with a similar degree of scepticism or, alternatively, should we be inclined to believe everything they tell us?

Clearly, the attributions made by patients are unlikely to serve a wholly self-presentational function or else their ability to predict such things as choice of treatment and speed of return to work would be hard to account for. Also, if patients were solely concerned with giving the most socially acceptable explanation there would be very little difference between them. It may be argued that the predictive validity of attributions simply comes down to the predictive validity of different self-presentational strategies rather than of sincerely-held causal beliefs, but this is a weak argument because self-presentation theories make no predictions about subsequent behaviour, whereas attributional theories do. It appears intuitively likely that when attributions serve a largely self-presentational function they will be of little use for prediction, but there is as yet no evidence with which to test this hypothesis.

At first sight, patients' attributions appear to be completely non-defensive. The self-blame reported by accident victims and depressed patients is diametrically opposite to the typical self-serving pattern of taking credit for success and blaming external causes for failure. As Bradley (1978) points out, however, this self-serving pattern is typically encountered when a person is being evaluated on a single occasion; if he or she anticipates future evaluations the person may adopt the "counter-defensive" strategy of appearing cautious and modest so as not to have too positive a self-evaluation publicly invalidated. Tetlock (1980) has shown that this "counter-defensive" strategy can produce more favourable reactions in other people, thus underlining its potential value in achieving optimal self-presentation. Depressive attributional style might then be regarded as a self-presentational device to emphasize incompetence and thereby minimize other people's expectations. This would be a logical tactic for someone who was concerned about being found wanting, since it carries the message that the observer should not be disappointed with a low level of performance, and indeed should expect failure. Under some circumstances it might have the additional advantage of earning marks for modesty. Consistent with this view, House (1983) found that self-effacing attributions were only correlated with depression when they were made in the presence of an observer and not when they were made privately.

Other groups of patients demonstrate more obvious self-serving attributions. King (1983) reported that patients with heart disease commonly cited stress, worry, and rheumatic fever in childhood as causes, while tending to ignore other medically accepted factors such as smoking, overeating, and lack of exercise. As she notes, the emphasis on external causation absolves patients from personal responsibility for their illness. The same tendency to attribute negative outcomes to more external and uncontrollable causes than positive outcomes has been demonstrated in diabetic patients by Bradley et al. (1984).

A final example uses data from a study of naturally-occurring attributions extracted from family therapy sessions (Stratton et al., 1986). Unsolicited attributions demonstrate very clearly that the definition of the event to be explained is an important factor to be taken into consideration. Father: "I know I've got to tell him (son) to wash his hands because if I don't he won't". Here the event to be explained is expressed in the language of compulsion, i.e., "I had to do it". Not only has the speaker already assumed that he had no choice in acting as he did (an attribution that has already taken place), but he assumes that hand-washing is a necessary activity. The causal part of the statement is a claim about the contingent relationship between his actions and his son's actions, one that of course cannot be disproved by the observer. A little later the mother says: "He (son) was two years younger then so obviously you're going to have to tell him and tell him". This use of supposedly shared rules or facts as a warrant for an explanation is another common device (Antaki, 1985). It appears likely that individuals in general use the rhetoric of causal explanation in such a way as to present themselves and their actions in the best possible light, and that patients also do this at least some of the time.

## CONCLUSIONS

In this chapter we have examined some of the major functions of explanation. The act of explaining is common when people are faced with the unexpected, and this seems particularly true when the unexpected involves illness, accidents, or misfortune. Explanations involve the labelling of experience and the attempt to make sense of it in terms of what people already know about themselves and the world around them. When they have determined what sort of event they are dealing with, they can try to attribute it to a cause or to a combination of causes. They will be concerned with whether this cause is internal or external to them, whether it is temporary or permanent, and whether it is controllable or uncontrollable. These judgements are likely to affect their self-esteem and their perceptions of future control in similar circumstances. In addition, their attributions for progress in changing their behaviour will contribute to maintaining that change. They will also be concerned with evaluating their behaviour against their own standards of conduct, and in determining what they ought to have done. Finally, they will in some cases want to portray themselves in a positive light to the outside world, so that the explanations they offer to others may not be the same as they make to themselves.

Many of the people seen by clinical psychologists will have gone through this process, and come to the conclusion that they are exposed to various kinds of threat, that they are relatively powerless to effect changes in their own lives, that they are worthless and responsible for the bad things that happen to them, and that they are unable to live up to certain standards they have set themselves. While some of these views may be veridical, they will sometimes be erroneous by virtue of lack of information, distorted information, or powerful causal beliefs that over-ride what accurate information is available. Whether true or false, these conclusions may have serious consequences.

Although there is now reasonable evidence to suggest that explanations mediate a variety of responses to illness and accidents, their role in determining the specific response of depression following stressful life events is far from clear. There is little reason at present to believe that an attribution about the cause of a specific event will influence whether or not a person suffers a depressive onset following that event. Attributions do appear to be a predictor of subsequent depression, but this effect may occur in the absence of stressful events as much as in their presence. Attributions may help to determine some component of depression, such as its chronicity, the amount of active coping attempted, or the utilization of social support, but this possibility awaits further research.

To sum up, the act of explanation is not a matter of idle armchair reflection. In times of trouble it is an attempt to re-establish control over the world and to determine what changes need to be made. Sometimes the changes will need to be to the person and sometimes to the environment, and sometimes no changes will be possible. Sometimes people may fall back on explanations that relieve them from the burden of taking any action at all. In any event, explanation is almost certain to be an integral part of any reaction to adversity.

# 7 Expectancy and Perceived Control

In the previous chapter it was argued that one way in which causal attributions influence a person's behaviour is through their relation to that person's expectancies about the future. For instance, attributions for some failure or setback to a stable cause will tend to produce lower expectancies of success next time the situation is encountered. According to expectancy-value theories of motivation (see Chapter 1), expectancies are in turn thought to be related to performance, with higher expectations of success leading to greater effort expenditure and persistence at a task (Archibald, 1974; Bandura, 1977b; Feather, 1982; Weiner, 1980). It will be recalled from Chapter 3 that expectancies of control over aversive situations also appear to be related to the acquisition and extinction of fear, both in animals and in human beings. Expectancies, whether conscious or nonconscious, are thus a central construct in contemporary accounts of emotion, motivation, and behaviour.

In this chapter we shall take a closer look at the concept of expectancy, distinguish between several different kinds of expectancy, and critically examine the evidence that expectancies help to determine patients' behaviour and, in some cases, their symptoms. Most attention will be devoted to the expectancy-value theories of motivation, which have been applied to explaining preventive health behaviour, choice of treatment, and the different degrees of enthusiasm and effort with which patients approach therapy or rehabilitation. Why do some patients persist doggedly in the face of daunting obstacles, while others give up almost immediately they encounter disappointment? Most of the theorists in this area seem to have assumed that the important expectancies are conscious ones, and have not considered the possible interplay of conscious and nonconscious expectancies. Later in the chapter I discuss the difficulty in measuring one of these conscious expectancies, self-efficacy beliefs, bearing in mind the limitations on people's ability to report on their beliefs and feelings. The same points could equally well be made in relation to the other conscious cognitions reviewed in this book.

When discussing attributions we noted that it was possible to distinguish attributions for specific events and more generalized attributional styles. In Rotter's (1954) social learning theory there are similarly two main kinds of expectancy, generalized and situation-specific. Briefly, Rotter says that when we assess how successful our actions are going to be we utilize not only our knowledge of that particular situation but also beliefs that have developed through the lifespan concerning more general capabilities, beliefs that summarize a wide range of disparate experiences. Researchers have investigated the influence on patients' behaviour of both these types of expectancy. In particular, they have focussed on expectations of control and mastery.

## GENERALIZED EXPECTANCIES

### Locus of Control

One type of expectancy that has probably attracted a disproportionate amount of research is locus of control or, to give it its full title, generalized expectancies for internal–external control of reinforcement. This construct reflects the degree to which individuals believe that reinforcements, i.e., the good and bad things that happen to them, are under their own control or under the control of external factors such as chance. In the scale that Rotter (1966) devised to measure this construct the subject has to decide which of a series of pairs of statements best fits their beliefs. The scale includes such diverse pairs of items as: "Many of the unhappy things in people's lives are partly due to bad luck" versus "People's misfortunes result from the mistakes they make"; and "Becoming a success is a matter of hard work, luck has little or nothing to do with it" versus "Getting a good job depends mainly on being in the right place at the right time". Each of the pairs of items contains one reflecting a belief in internal control and one a belief in external control, and the subject's score consists of the number of external items he or she has endorsed. Rotter suggests that this kind of measure will be more likely to predict people's behaviour when they are in novel or unfamiliar situations, whereas in familiar situations specific expectancies are more likely to be appropriate.

Strickland (1978) has provided a useful review of studies that have related locus of control to the attitudes and behaviour of people with physical and psychological disorders. The more anxious or depressed a person is, the more external their locus of control tends to be. Furthermore, people usually become more internal as treatment progresses. There is also some evidence that internals respond better to treatments that give them greater control and responsibility, whereas externals prefer treatments with greater structure. A recent study found that external clients had more positive expectations of external therapists, whereas internal clients had more positive expectations of internal therapists (Foon, 1986). This suggests that matching clients and therapists on locus of control may be helpful in maximizing treatment benefits. Strickland concludes her review as follows (1978, p.1205):

> Although results are not altogether as clear, convincing, and as free from conflict as one might hope, the bulk of the research is consistent in implying that when faced with health problems, internal individuals do appear to engage in more generally adaptive responses than do externals. These range from engagement in preventive and precautionary health measures through appropriate remedial strategies when disease or disorder occurs.

In spite of the promising results obtained with locus of control measures, the construct has been criticized on a number of grounds. First, Rotter's (1966) scale has been shown to contain a number of different dimensions. Collins (1974) found four major components of the scale, which he labelled "Belief in a difficult world", "Belief in a just world", "Belief in a predictable world", and "Belief in a politically responsive world". Gurin, Gurin, and Morrison (1978) distinguish a factor of "personal control" and a factor of "ideology about control," but also acknowledge that a variety of factors may emerge depending on the type of factor analysis used and the method of scoring the items.

Second, locus of control scales usually fail to distinguish beliefs about good and bad outcomes. Rotter and others have assumed that if a person took responsibility for their successes, they would also be likely to take responsibility for their failures. In a number of studies, however, beliefs about these two sorts of event have been found to be essentially unrelated. Strickland (1978) pointed out that anxious and depressed individuals usually appear very external on locus of control scales, although one of the symptoms of depression is guilt for causing one's misfortunes. This paradox would be resolved if it turned out that locus of control scales tended to reflect beliefs about positive but not negative outcomes, since it would be appropriate if the depressed felt that good experiences were externally determined but it would be surprising if they thought that way about bad experiences. In a study designed to test this hypothesis, Brewin and Shapiro (1984) developed separate scales measuring responsibility for positive and negative outcomes. As expected, Rotter's locus of control scale correlated with the positive outcome measure but not with the negative outcome measure.

A third problem with early locus of control scales was the notion that all external determinants of reinforcement were equivalent. Levenson (1974) suggested that instead of one internal–external scale there should be three scales measuring the perceived influence of internal factors, chance, and powerful others. This is because the consequences of your life being seen as ruled by chance may be very different from a perception that it is ruled by other people. This distinction was first used in research on political activism and on the views of minority groups about their position in society. It is equally relevant in the clinical context where the "powerful others" will be health professionals. Clearly it may be unwise to lump together beliefs about the influence of chance and beliefs about the influence of doctors on the course of illness, just because both are external factors from the patient's perspective. Wallston, Wallston, and DeVellis (1978) have therefore developed multidimensional health locus of control scales that allow these distinctions to be preserved when investigating general health attitudes.

Fourthly and finally, Weiner (1985a) has criticized the notion of internal–external locus of control because it combines causal dimensions that need to be kept separate. It is possible to have internal causes such as heredity or lack of ability over which a person has little control, and similarly there may be some external causes, such as the actions of friends or relatives, which a person feels are reasonably controllable. Weiner argues that it will often be necessary to measure separately beliefs about locus (internal–external) and beliefs about stability or controllability. As we have seen in Chapters 4 and 6, within his theory these dimensions have separate consequences.

## Helplessness, Hopelessness, and Depression

In Seligman's (1975) learned helplessness theory it was originally thought that the experience of uncontrollability produced a generalized expectancy that outcomes would be independent of the person's or animal's responses. This expectancy then led to the helplessness deficits of failing to initiate new responses and less effective learning of new response–outcome relationships. The attraction of the theory lay in the fact that the experience of uncontrollability in one situation generalized to produce helplessness in a different situation. The theory has now been modified (Abramson et al., 1978) to specify the conditions under which this generalization occurs. As discussed in Chapter 6, generalization of helplessness in humans is thought to depend on the attribution of the uncontrollable outcome to a global cause.

Whereas helplessness is concerned with response–outcome independence, other generalized expectations such as pessimism and hopelessness are concerned with the probability of bad outcomes occurring. It is possible to feel helpless to influence the future without feeling that the future will necessarily be bad. The expressions "Something will turn up" or "It will be all right on the night" are sometimes used to convey the idea that the world is a benevolent place in which it does not matter if we cannot control everything that happens to us. The hopeless person, by contrast, feels certain that the future holds nothing but disaster and disappointment. Thus it is possible to feel helpless without being hopeless, but not vice versa. In Chapter 5 we noted that Beck (1967) has identified hopelessness as a core symptom of depression, and he has suggested that it leads both to paralysis of the will (since any response will be ineffective) and to the desire to escape from an intolerable situation. Suicidal intent appears to be more closely related to these negative expectancies about the future than with depression itself (Minkoff, Bergman, Beck, & Beck, 1973).

Early helplessness theory regarded all depressive symptoms as arising from perceived response–outcome independence, regardless of whether the outcomes were good or bad and of how likely they were to occur. In contrast, the attributional reformulation of helplessness theory (Abramson et al., 1978) proposed that only a subset of cases of expected lack of control, those involving negative expectations about the occurrence of highly valued or important events, would result in depression. People who perceived themselves as helpless to prevent good things happening were no longer expected to become depressed, and neither were people who, although feeling personally helpless to avoid a negative outcome, remained hopeful that other people or fate would intervene on their behalf. This revision brought the learned helplessness model into line with theories, such as Beck's, that emphasized the primary importance of hopelessness. The most recent version of Seligman's original theory (Alloy, Abramson, Metalsky, & Hartlage, 1988) actually replaces the concept of helplessness with that of hopelessness as the cause of a large subset of depressive disorders.

## SPECIFIC EXPECTANCIES

Many criticisms of measures of generalized expectancies such as locus of control have pointed to the failure to distinguish various more specific beliefs. In one sense this criticism is unfair since the scales were designed to tap general expectations that might be expected to influence behaviour when people found themselves in unfamiliar situations. As we have seen, locus of control is related to a very wide range of behaviours, and criticisms should perhaps not be levelled at the scale so much as at the researchers who have not used it appropriately. But the generality of the scales does mean that subjects' scores may reflect any of a number of quite different beliefs, and that results using it are therefore hard to interpret. For these reasons, and in the interests of further improving the prediction of behaviour, it has been found necessary to develop expectancy measures that focus on specific situations with which patients may be familiar and on specific beliefs. The development of health locus of control scales provided one step in this direction, but such measures still cannot be used to predict responses to a particular disorder unless the assumption is made that attitudes to health in general are strongly related to attitudes about specific disorders. This assumption becomes increasingly problematic, the more experience patients have of a disorder and the more they become involved in its treatment.

Bandura (1977b) has reminded us that at least two classes of specific expectancies can be distinguished, outcome expectancies and efficacy expectancies. The former are concerned with people's beliefs about the likely success of a treatment or other course of action, and the latter with their beliefs about their own ability to actually carry out those actions. Thus it is possible to imagine a person who believes flooding to be an effective form of treatment for his phobia (high outcome expectancy) but does not believe himself capable of exposing himself to his most feared situation (low efficacy expectancy). Both these expectancies have been shown to be important in clinical practice.

## Outcome Expectancies and the Placebo Effect

The importance of beliefs about the effectiveness of treatments (outcome expectancies) is amply demonstrated by one of the most reliable psychological phenomena in medicine, the placebo effect. A placebo is traditionally a pharmacologically inert substance that a patient takes in the belief that it is an active drug. When such a substance leads to changes in the patient's state it is said to produce a placebo effect. These effects are so widespread that placebo controls are routinely included in tests of drug action: a drug is four to five times more likely to be reported as effective if there is no placebo control than if there is (Shapiro, 1971). Placebos have been shown to have a beneficial impact on a huge variety of disorders, including dental pain, asthma, multiple sclerosis, the common cold, diabetes, ulcers, and Parkinson's disease. Even surgical procedures may owe some of their efficacy to placebo effects, as has been demonstrated by studies that have compared genuine surgery with a placebo condition in which patients were anaesthetized and an incision made but no further surgery was performed. In one such study (Cobb et al., 1959) patients suffering from angina obtained as much relief from placebo as from genuine surgery, although it should be added that this particular surgical procedure is rarely performed today. Placebos have also been known to be so convincing that their termination produced withdrawal symptoms.

Ross and Olson (1982) note that the proportion of patients responding to placebos varies widely from study to study, and they describe five patterns in the data that contribute to this variability. First, the direction of the placebo effect seems to be related to the drug under study. Placebos have, for instance, been known both to increase and to decrease blood pressure depending on the effect of the active drug with which they were being compared. Second, the strength of the placebo effect is proportional to the strength of the drug effect. A placebo compared to morphine would prove to be more effective in reducing post-operative pain than a placebo compared with aspirin. Third, placebos often provoke side-effects that are similar to those of the active drug being studied. Fourth, placebos may demonstrate similar time–effect curves to active drugs, their effects increasing and decreasing together over time. Fifth, they may show similar dose effects, the effects gradually building up over time with the supposedly increasing concentration of the drug in the body.

These striking effects are generally attributed to patients' expectations about ingesting certain drugs or undergoing certain medical or surgical procedures. Ross and Olson (1982) describe a number of mechanisms that might account for the influence of these expectations. Placebos may, for instance, reassure patients or relax them and thereby improve their condition. This would be a plausible explanation in a number of conditions where it is known that stress or anxiety can exacerbate the problem, e.g., headaches or diabetes, but it would not explain the ability of placebos to act in the opposite direction, e.g., increasing rather than decreasing blood pressure. Another possibility is that placebos may encourage patients to view their symptoms in a more positive light, taking more notice of small improvements and ignoring small exacerbations. It has also been suggested that patients are simply responding to the demands of the situation and telling doctors what they want to hear. These last two explanations are not adequate, however, because placebos do not only influence patients' self-reports but also a variety of physiological indices that are not so readily fakeable.

Some placebo effects may be conditioned responses reflecting previous experience with active medication and elicited by stimuli associated with the administration of the drug. For instance, Hilgard and Hilgard (1975) suggested that some people may obtain immediate relief from pain-killing drugs, before the drugs have had any pharmacological action, by virtue of a conditioned response to them. Again, this mechanism cannot explain the variety of placebo effects, which may occur in the absence of prior experience with a drug. Finally, placebos may be able to induce somatic changes in their own right. It has been suggested that they may trigger the release of endorphins, morphine-like substances in the brain that are thought to influence pain perception. At present, however, this remains an intriguing possibility rather than an established fact.

Outcome expectancies have also been considered important in the design and interpretation of research on psychological therapies, and it has been common to compare treatments such as systematic desensitization with supposedly ineffective placebo treatments to control for these expectations. Unlike drugs, however, whose efficacy cannot be readily assessed by the patient, psychological therapies can be assessed in this way and patients can form views about which are most likely to be effective. Many placebo manipulations have been found to be intrinsically less credible than the "real" treatments with which they were being compared, thus biasing studies in favour of the latter. When treatments such as systematic desensitization are compared with equally credible control procedures, their superiority is reduced and often disappears altogether (Lick & Bootzin, 1975). In their review, these authors also note that procedures for fear reduction are much more effective when they are presented with a therapeutic rationale than when subjects carry out the same procedures under the impression that they are taking part in an experiment on, for instance, visualization.

Not all experiments have demonstrated expectancy effects, however. When people with minor fears are told that they are receiving either a very effective treatment or a not very effective treatment (but in fact receive the same treatment in both cases), no great difference in performance ensues. It is hard to know whether to attribute this to the nature of the subjects, the failure of the expectancy manipulation, or the failure of expectancy to influence performance. Lick and Bootzin concluded after examining evidence from all these different sources that expectancy factors seemed to be important mediators of fear reduction. Among the most plausible reasons for this they suggested that high expectancies might encourage subjects to test the hypothesis "I am cured" by exposing themselves to real-life phobic stimuli. Other possibilities were that subjects might be responding to the demand characteristics of the situation, or that high expectancies might produce reassuring self-talk (such as "I'm really not afraid of heights, I don't have anything to worry about") which would directly reduce anxiety.

Recently a number of writers (e.g., Kirsch, 1978) have questioned whether it still makes sense to talk about "placebo effects" in psychotherapy research. There are two ways in which the term "placebo" is usually employed. One is as an "inert" as compared with an "active" treatment. Note, however, that this means "inert" according to the theory of the researcher designing the experiment. Because there is so much disagreement about how therapies work, even ones whose efficacy is well established, it is quite possible that a procedure considered inert by one person might be considered active by another. And with the constant change in theoretical understanding it is not impossible that yesterday's placebo becomes today's active treatment. Thus in this sense placebo may simply denote a procedure whose mode of action is not accounted for by the experimenter's theory. A placebo factor may also mean something that is "non-specific" or common to a number of treatments, such as the experience of confiding in a sympathetic person, compared with a "specific ingredient" that is unique to a single therapy. As Wilkins (1985) points out, the term "non-specific" is very vague. Does this mean a factor that is not unique to one treatment, or one that is common to all in differing amounts, or one that is common to all in equal amounts?

In drug studies placebo pills are used to control for expectancy effects that are independent of the mode of action of the drug. In psychotherapy research, by contrast, it is held by most cognitive theorists that therapies are effective at least in part by virtue of the expectations for improvement that they arouse. According to this view almost all therapies involve the manipulation of expectancies, whether directly or indirectly: the contribution of expectancies should therefore be investigated systematically and not "controlled for." It is not a question, they would argue, of devizing an "inert" placebo treatment but of comparing the results of a number of treatments differing among other things in the expectancies they arouse. Expectancies are also "non-specific" only in the sense that they are probably present in all therapies in differing amounts. But this is true of other factors, such as exposure to the phobic stimulus, which have been proposed as specific ingredients in successful fear reduction. On this criterion also the notion of a placebo appears to be problematic. Even supporters of the placebo concept, such as Critelli and Neumann (1984) concede that when evaluating treatments it is necessary to control for expectancy of improvement, credibility of rationale and procedures, demand for improvement, and therapist variables such as attention, enthusiasm, effort, belief in therapy, and commitment to client improvement!

In conclusion, there is considerable evidence that outcome expectations affect people's reactions to medical and psychological procedures both physiologically and in terms of their feelings and behaviour. These expectations are part of the fabric of psychological therapy and cannot readily be separated from other ingredients that might be contributing to their effectiveness. In this context, therefore, the concept of a placebo treatment may be misleading.

## Efficacy Expectations

From Tolman (1932) on, most expectancy theories have been concerned with the differing outcome expectancies associated with various actions and how these related to the decision to perform one action rather than another. In animal experiments rats selected which alley or which part of a maze to run down according, it was supposed, to their expectations of reward and punishment. The heavy emphasis on studies involving reinforcement was at the expense of studies involving skill acquisition, which involves expectancies about whether or not a behaviour can be performed at all. That this is not an exclusively human concern is evident from watching cats pausing before they opt whether or not to leap onto a high wall. Presumably memories of past jumps are being accessed and some assessment is being made of whether this wall is more like those that featured in successful or unsuccessful attempts. Note that this does not involve an outcome expectancy because the cat is not attempting to obtain a reward or escape a punishment that is distinct from the leap itself.

Bandura (1977b) has labelled these expectations about one's own performance "self-efficacy" beliefs. His "self-efficacy theory" is an attempt to provide a unifying mechanism to account for the changes brought about by psychological therapies. He does not claim that self-efficacy is the only variable necessary to explain behaviour (see Chapter 8 and Bandura, 1977a), but suggests that in the therapeutic situation it will be one of the most important. His thesis is that people vary greatly in the confidence that they feel when coping with difficult situations, particularly ones that produce unpleasant emotional arousal. The more confident they feel about responding skilfully to the varying demands of the situation or, in his terms, the greater their self-efficacy, the harder they will try to overcome the problem and the longer they will persist at it. From this Bandura deduces that successful psychological therapies are those that are most effective at increasing self-efficacy: it is a mechanism that accounts for why some therapies are generally better than others and why some people do better than others at the same therapy.

The contribution of self-efficacy theory is to specify more precisely than has been done before how expectations should be measured and also where they originate from. Bandura distinguishes between the magnitude of self-efficacy beliefs, i.e., how difficult a task can be performed; the strength of those beliefs, i.e., how confident people are about performing it; and the generality of the beliefs, i.e., whether or not they extend to other related situations. In most cases optimal prediction of behaviour will be obtained by considering the strength as well as the magnitude of expectations. He points out that most studies of therapy credibility simply measured faith in a procedure about which people had only heard or read, and failed to consider more specific beliefs about their personal capabilities. For this reason studies that only manipulate outcome expectations are insufficient to answer more general questions about the role of expectations in accounting for therapeutic change.

Bandura goes on to describe four main sources of beliefs about efficacy. The most important is information about how a person has actually performed in the past. This recognizes the fact that therapies such as participant modelling and *in vivo* desensitization, which emphasize actual performance accomplishments, are more effective than purely verbal or imaginal treatments. In his view their success is due to the fact that actual performance has a particularly strong influence on efficacy judgements. In other words, just because a therapy consists of altering behaviour does not mean that it has no effect on a person's cognitive processes, and it is the cognitive rather than the behavioural changes that are held to be therapeutic. Another source of information is vicarious learning. Self-efficacy may be altered by observing how others cope in similar situations, or through the medium of books or television. People are not dependent on their own experience but can profit from the successes and misfortunes of others. This principle forms the basis of modelling treatments aimed at fear reduction, in which the patient first observes the therapist interact with a feared object or cope with a feared situation.

Verbal persuasion is also widely used to influence the judgement of efficacy. Persuasion may be effective when people are uncertain about their capabilities and seeking further information, such as consensus data about the performance of the average person. Verbal persuasion frequently takes the form of an appeal to social norms or of a comparison with past performances or the performances of other patients. Finally, people derive information about efficacy from their experience of emotional arousal. Because high arousal often has a detrimental effect on performance, feeling upset or anxious is likely to undermine confidence in one's capability to perform effectively. In Chapter 6 there is a discussion of attempts to alter the way in which arousal is labelled, e.g., by attributing it to the effects of a pill. This procedure also assumes that it is the information provided by high arousal rather than the arousal itself that affects people's actions.

Information from these four sources (performance accomplishments, vicarious learning, verbal persuasion, and emotional arousal) is then appraised by the person. As we have noted, information from actual accomplishments will be given a lot of weight, but it may be modified by the circumstances in which they occurred. For instance, if a woman with an agoraphobic problem has only succeeded in travelling on a bus when accompanied by her husband, this information may have a positive or negative influence on efficacy estimates about travelling alone. Similarly, if she has travelled alone only when obliged to by compelling circumstances, this information is likely to have a different effect on efficacy estimates than if she has travelled exactly the same number of miles but entirely of her own accord. The amount of effort needed may be relevant to the appraisal. Information obtained from observing others will also be given different weight according to a number of factors such as the similarity and expertness of the model, and the degree to which the person feels able to emulate them. Persuasive communications will be heeded more if they come from authoritative and disinterested sources. In other words, self-efficacy judgements depend on an extremely complex integration of many sorts of information from both past and present, and the new information provided by the experience of therapy must be seen in this light. It is this distillation of experience that, according to Bandura, then determines how people respond to specific self-imposed or therapist-imposed tasks and ultimately determines the success or otherwise of therapy.

## Evidence for Self-efficacy Theory

Bandura and his colleagues have conducted a number of investigations into the relation between self-efficacy and avoidance behaviour that are described in Bandura (1977b; 1982). In these experiments phobic subjects are first given a behavioural avoidance test consisting of tasks organized in a hierarchy of difficulty. Snake phobics might perhaps be asked to stand progressively closer to a cage containing a snake, then to put their gloved hand on the cage, then to do the same with their bare hand, etc. Following this test subjects are given one of several treatments such as modelling alone, participant modelling, or desensitization in vivo. They then make efficacy judgements in which they state the tasks they believe they are now capable of and how certain they are that they can perform the tasks. Finally, they take another behavioural avoidance test to see which tasks they can actually perform. Bandura and his colleagues report that different treatments have widely varying effects on subjects' self-efficacy ratings. As one would expect, performance-based treatments increase efficacy more than imaginal treatments. Whatever the treatment, however, there is a close relation between the magnitude and strength of efficacy judgements and subsequent performance.

This relationship does not hold just for the correlation between the total number of tasks a person expects to perform and the total actually performed, but is also evident when, for each subject, the researcher considers individual tasks and whether there is agreement between expectation and performance on each one. Bandura argues that this "microanalytic" method examining each task individually permits much greater precision in measuring the relation between expectation and performance than does consideration of total scores alone. Typically the level of agreement is of the order of 80–90%. There is some dispute, however, about whether it is useful to examine performance on individual tasks. Kirsch and Wickless (1983) have argued that it is redundant because the behavioural test and the measure of expectations are both graded in order of difficulty. When measures are precisely ordered in this way they are known as Guttman scales, which have the property that if one knows the total number of items a person has passed one also knows their performance on each item (i.e., if they have passed 10 items out of 20 they have succeeded on items 1–10 and failed on items 11–20). Kirsch and Wickless present evidence that Bandura's measures do approximate to Guttman scales, in which case agreement on individual items should be no more informative than the correlation between total scores. They do not, however, dispute that expectancies and performance are related, only the manner in which this relation should be calculated.

In addition to demonstrating a relation between self-efficacy and performance, the onus is also on Bandura to show that his measures are better predictors than past performance. It has been argued that subjects' past performance on the behavioural tasks was the determinant both of their performance in the final behaviour test and of their reported expectations, thus denying any causal role for the cognitions. Bandura has used several strategies to counter this line of attack. First, he has shown that efficacy judgements are frequently better predictors of future performance than is past performance. Second, he has shown that when phobics are given imaginal desensitization until their emotional reactions to feared scenes are completely extinguished (or when they experience other psychological treatments), their efficacy judgements concerning actual encounters with snakes differ widely. Whereas they have all attained a similar level in treatment, it is their efficacy judgements that predict which tasks they will actually perform. Third, efficacy judgements are able to predict performance equally well on tasks that subjects have never done before, where there is no past performance to assist in making the judgement. In one study Bandura used only modelling treatments (in which subjects watched a therapist interacting with snakes) to manipulate efficacy and correspondingly reduce avoidance, thus proving his point that efficacy judgements are based on whatever information is available, not just on actual performance.

Self-efficacy has now been found to be related to a range of behaviours in several different situations. It predicts the performance of agoraphobics carrying out tasks they find difficult, such as walking alone, shopping, and dining in a restaurant. It predicts assertiveness, achievement behaviour, and the behaviour of socially anxious males. A series of interesting studies has linked self-efficacy to the self-control of addictive behaviours such as smoking. Interventions to reduce smoking enhance efficacy, which is also able to predict whether or not a person will relapse (Condiotte & Lichtenstein, 1981; DiClemente, 1981). From the results of a large population survey DiClemente, Prochaska, and Gibertini (1985) reported that current smokers have lower levels of efficacy than recent quitters (abstinent for less than six months), who in turn have lower levels of efficacy than long-term quitters (abstinent for longer than six months). When these smokers were followed up from three to five months later, initial efficacy scores were able to predict who of those contemplating giving up really did give up, and who of the recent quitters then relapsed. Self-efficacy therefore appears to be a construct that is not just relevant to the treatment of fear but that has a general motivational role. This is, of course, to be expected given its roots in expectancy–value theories of motivation.

## Critique of Self-Efficacy Theory

It is worth considering the status of the theory in some detail, not only because it is widely cited, but because the arguments used in its support are those used to justify many cognitive theories of behaviour. Many of the criticisms of self-efficacy theory have centred on alternative interpretations of Bandura's findings. It has been suggested that it is the amount of conditioned fear experienced by a person that determines both their avoidance of the phobic object and their report of efficacy. This explanation runs into difficulties because the relationship between fear and avoidance behaviour is known to be very variable (Bolles, 1972; Rachman & Hodgson, 1974). It is quite common for people to feel extremely anxious and yet not to avoid the feared situations: actors and musicians who experience stage fright provide a good example. Indeed, if fear was the sole determinant of behaviour it is hard to visualize how frightening situations would ever be mastered. Bandura has additionally cited evidence that self-efficacy is a better predictor of behaviour than anticipatory or performance anxiety. In his view conditioned anxiety is one source of information on which people base their efficacy judgements, and hence it would be expected to display a weak relationship to behaviour.

It has also been suggested that exposure to the unreinforced conditioned stimulus determines both avoidance and efficacy beliefs. This seems unlikely because people who have experienced the same treatment package emerge with widely differing efficacy beliefs. One would therefore have to argue that people were not equally exposed to the CS, perhaps because some of them were distracted or did not follow instructions. This argument is as hard to prove as it is to refute. Another suggestion is that the apparent influence of efficacy derives from self-generated or experimenter-generated demands for improvement. That is, the fact of being asked to make an efficacy judgement puts pressure on the person to live up to their own predictions. Bandura has shown, however, that it makes little difference whether efficacy judgements are made privately or publicly, which does not support the demand effect hypothesis.

Many of these criticisms seem to have missed the point that self-efficacy theory is about motivation in general and is not a theory of fear acquisition or reduction. Bandura is not really concerned with why a person originally became afraid of snakes nor with the ideal therapy for phobias. What he is concerned about is why people do not cope equally successfully with their fears, with their marital problems, with their careers, with their poor tennis service, or with anything else that constitutes a problem. It is therefore true, but irrelevant, to argue that Bandura places too little weight on the acquisition of conditioned emotional reactions or that exposure rather than self-efficacy is the mechanism of fear reduction. Therapy outcome depends not only on knowing the correct "treatment" but on persistently and determinedly performing it. Explanations of fear acquisition and reduction, such as conditioning theory, may be good at specifying what the correct action is (although in practice this has been a rather hit and miss process) but one also needs a motivational theory to explain why, when armed with the correct information, some people rapidly overcome their disability while others flounder and allow their lives to be ruled by unpleasant emotional states. It is to this problem, the maintenance rather than the origin of anxiety, that self-efficacy addresses itself.

The predictive power of self-efficacy is good in studies of snake phobics and smokers, but not all studies have got such good results. Lane and Borkovec (1984) asked speech anxious subjects to make efficacy judgements about aspects of performance such as voice quality, posture, degree of unnecessary hesitations or dysfluencies, and amount of eye contact. They found that these measures were related to self-report measures of outcome such as anxiety ratings, but not to measures of behaviour or physiological reactivity. Meier, McCarthy, and Schmeck (1984) obtained efficacy ratings from students commencing a writing course concerning their ability to avoid spelling errors and express themselves clearly. Although these ratings were predictive of their standard of writing at the beginning, at the end of the course the students overestimated their ability and there was no relationship between efficacy and performance. These findings suggest an important limitation to the theory. Predictive power is best when (a) the criteria of a successful performance are unambiguous; and (b) the behaviour necessary is under deliberate conscious control. The snake phobics in Bandura's studies were aware of precisely what each test consisted of, and could decide whether to do it or not. Similarly the smokers had a conscious decision whether or not to abstain. Controlling one's non-verbal behaviour or writing a good essay are, by contrast, tasks over which one has far less control. One may intend to perform well but by the nature of the task get little feedback about whether one is succeeding. Under these circumstances one may simply not realize if one's performance is failing to live up to one's expectations.

These limitations in their turn suggest two things. First, efficacy judgements may be no more than a statement of what a person intends to do and, second, people may only be able to make valid efficacy judgements under certain conditions. Obtaining self-efficacy judgements from smokers or phobics about to take a behavioural avoidance test appears very similar to measuring their intentions. Does the measurement of efficacy offer any advantage over simply asking people what they are going to do next? This is another way of expressing dissatisfaction that the theory appears to conform too closely to common sense, or indeed is completely tautological. Smedslund (1978) has raised a similar point in a thought-provoking article in which he proposes that Bandura's theory can be reduced to a set of common sense theorems. This accounts for its allegedly self-evident character. He argues that many if not all of the theoretical statements are not empirically testable but are logically necessary explications of conceptual relationships embedded in ordinary language. For instance, Smedslund considers the statement (Bandura, 1977b, p.194):

> People fear and tend to avoid threatening situations they believe exceed their coping skills, whereas they get involved in activities and behave assuredly when they judge themselves capable of handling situations that would otherwise be intimidating.

Smedslund argues that, as in all generally valid theoretical statements in psychology (such as the law of effect), the conclusions follow logically from the ordinary meaning of the terms involved, and therefore cannot be falsified. Failure to confirm the relationship empirically would be similar to a failure to confirm Pythagorus' Theorem in that it would simply mean that the appropriate conditions of measurement were not established.

Whereas it is indeed difficult to distinguish between efficacy judgements and statements of intention when the action is very shortly to follow, the distinction does become useful when people fail to do what they intend. We can then ask whether efficacy was higher in those who fulfilled their intentions than in those who did not fulfil them. The abovementioned study by DiClemente et al. (1985) indicates that people who fulfil their intention to give up smoking or to remain abstinent do have higher efficacy than those who fail to carry through their plans. This suggests that to know about a person's level of efficacy is more informative than simply to know about their intention (at least over longer periods). Smedslund (1978) accepts that the explication of ordinary language concepts may have considerable practical value. He cites the example of geometry which, although it consists of a formal system derived from deduction rather than empirical findings, is still of enormous use to mankind. One response to the "common sense" criticism would thus be to say that self-efficacy theory could be very useful in directing our attention to important cognitions and their relationship to behaviour, even though the theory may not actually be falsifiable.

Another response to this criticism would be to look more closely at what is meant by "common sense". This seems to contain the notion, at least according to Smedslund, that people have free will and can decide for themselves what they want to do. We may contrast this with the more deterministic thesis of behaviourism, which is that behaviour occurs in response to environmental rather than mental events, and that thoughts have no causal properties. Behaviourism therefore appears to be "anti-common sense", and cognitive theories of behaviour that have grown up in opposition to it appear only to be stating what ordinary people knew all along. However, one of the reasons that behaviourist explanations were popular in clinical psychology was precisely that the phenomena in question were "anti-common sense" and defied ordinary explanation. People have always found it difficult to explain why a person acts out a compulsion against their will or is frightened of something that they know is not intrinsically harmful. In the field of abnormal psychology we come face to face with the failure of "common sense" explanations, which all of a sudden become contingent (i.e., falsifiable) propositions rather than logically necessary truths.

The second point has to do with the criteria for accurate introspection (see Chapter 2). Bandura implies by his use of the term "self-referent thought" that self-efficacy is exclusively a conscious judgement that people introspect about when they are asked to make efficacy ratings. In any case, the ratings certainly reflect conscious thought processes. Presumably a person can much more easily make a judgement about whether they will perform a simple voluntary action, on its own and with no distractions, than they can predict the level of a complex performance, made up of some regulated and some unregulated constituent parts, which they are not in the habit of monitoring. This is similar to the argument, reviewed in Chapter 2, that accurate introspection or verbalization has to be based on information in short-term memory. In the same way, efficacy judgements will be inaccurate predictors of behaviour that cannot be fully attended to. As Bandura notes, they will also be inaccurate predictors of the performance of skills that have only partially been mastered.

Another way of looking at this is to consider the sorts of experiences that might influence dealing with a feared situation. The fact that people often do not know why they are frightened of something means that they may not be aware of many of these experiences, perhaps because they occurred in childhood. Self-efficacy as a conscious thought process must then be limited by people's access to those experiences that are indeed relevant. Psychological treatments provide them with new information of a more or less compelling kind, but the information still has to be appraised in the light of pre-existing information whose nature may be largely unknown and that may be in conflict with the evidence provided by the therapy. Bandura appears to assume that the products of this appraisal process will be available to consciousness, but this assumption is contentious. It is also possible that this pre-existing information, for instance in the form of learned associations between certain actions, rewards, and punishments, will exert its own influence on behaviour outside of conscious awareness.

## CONCLUSIONS

In considering how expectations of control are related to physical and mental health, it is worth recalling some of the ways in which situations differ from the typical laboratory investigation of control. Most experimental studies involve the manipulation of instrumental or behavioural control, or the perception of such control, over the occurrence of a threatening or painful external event. In these experiments the degree of control or perceived control is clear-cut. Real life health-related situations differ from this paradigm in 3 main ways: (1) the degree of control a person has is usually unclear and in the absence of specific information much will depend on self-generated feelings of control; (2) control may reside partly in the hands of others, e.g., medical staff; (3) there may be several different ways of exerting control and individuals may have preferences for one over another.

The lack of objective information, or the fact that what information there is comes from conflicting or less credible sources, means that people have to fall back on their own estimates of control. These are presumed to be derived from past experience, weighted according to its relevance to the current situation. Various methods exist to estimate beliefs about control, some of the most popular involving the construct of locus of control or, more specifically, health locus of control. Although these various measures have been criticized in many ways, locus of control is a consistent if weak predictor of many health behaviours including use of preventive services and information-gathering, and internals consistently report themselves as less anxious and depressed than do externals. When trying to predict behaviour in novel or unfamiliar settings these measures are probably as good as any, but they have serious limitations when it comes to situations in which people are informed or misinformed. In many chronic diseases, for instance, patients have extensive experience with the disease and with their own reactions to different kinds of intervention.

The sick role obviously involves a certain degree of transfer of control to medical staff. Going into hospital for an operation is a good illustration of a situation where a person may be personally helpless yet not hopeless. While helplessness may be near total in some situations, there are many others where there is scope for wide variation in the distribution of and preference for control between patient and medical staff. This is illustrated in a study of women in labour (Brewin & Bradley, 1982), who were divided into those who had and had not attended childbirth preparation classes. Class attenders were characterized by the belief that both they and the medical staff had greater control over the process of childbirth. Personal control over duration was significantly predictive of reported discomfort among attenders but not among non-attenders, whereas perceived staff control was significantly predictive of discomfort in non-attenders but not in attenders. These findings suggest that it is important not to assume that personal control is the only important kind of expectation.

The placebo effect in medicine also illustrates that being able to take effective action is not the only way of gaining control. Of the numerous ways in which a person may seek to gain control over a situation, Thompson (1981) has distinguished informational control (learning about an aversive experience), behavioural control (directly acting on the situation), cognitive control (thinking about the situation differently), and retrospective control (deciding after the fact that one could have controlled the aversive event and presumably can do so in the future). Whereas informational, cognitive, and behavioural control are particularly relevant to preparation for surgery, cognitive and retrospective control may be more important in dealing with accidents or disability. In a recent study of women with breast cancer Taylor et al. (1984) found that belief both in one's own and in others' control over one's cancer was associated with better adjustment. When specific strategies were investigated, informational and retrospective control proved to be unrelated to adjustment, whereas cognitive control and specific aspects of behavioural control (increasing the time devoted to exercise and leisure activities) were associated with adjustment.

It should therefore be borne in mind that there are many ways of trying to achieve control other than by direct action on the environment, and that the ability to exercise cognitive and retrospective control may be of great importance when faced with an apparently irremediable situation. In the context of psychological therapy or rehabilitation, however, where patients are given concrete tasks and objectives, beliefs in behavioural control (self-efficacy) appear to be strongly related to patients' achievements, and offer a unifying theoretical framework to explain variations in the efficacy of different types of therapy. I have suggested, though, that efficacy is not so likely to be a good long-term predictor of behaviour when there are strong contrary expectations outside of awareness or when the nature of the behaviour is such that it is difficult to achieve simply by regulating effort expenditure. Much of behaviour, particularly the complex, skilled variety, cannot be regulated by deliberately trying harder and should not reflect so readily the influence of self-generated motivation. In the following chapter I discuss in greater detail the value of having control over one's environment and people's reactions to being deprived of it.

# 8 Values and Goals

Important as expectancies are, they are far from being the only, or even the major, determinants of behaviour. According to social learning theories (e.g., Bandura, 1977a; Rotter, 1954), a person's values and goals also influence the direction, intensity, and persistence of behaviour. Goals are the ends for which behaviour is the means and, because people and animals will work harder for more attractive rewards, goals are often thought of as energizers of behaviour. Some goals can be objectively defined, such as being offered a place at university or getting to the church on time, whereas others, such as becoming rich and famous, are less specific. Values refer to preferences for certain modes of conduct or activity over others. For instance, a person may value being helpful to others over being successful in his or her career. (For a more detailed treatment of values and goals, see Feather, 1982, and Rokeach, 1973). Values and goals may be expressed either behaviourally in people's choice of activities or verbally in self-reports. They may derive from several sources, including innate approach–avoidance tendencies, but in this chapter we shall be mainly concerned with learned preferences that arise through cultural transmission and the individual's unique experience. In both cases it is assumed that values and goals are adopted because of their associations with rewarding and punishing experiences.

In practice, people have hierarchies of goals relating to different areas of their lives. On the most general level, people may wish to maximize pleasant experiences and minimize unpleasant experiences such as physical pain, fear, anxiety, guilt, and cognitive inconsistency or dissonance. In order to do this successfully they strive to gain accurate information about their own abilities and characteristics (Festinger, 1954), and to understand, predict, and control their environment (Heider, 1958; Kelley, 1967). More specifically, they may wish to have an interesting job, an involving family life, intelligent and well brought-up children, financial security, and a certain amount of excitement and unpredictability. These life goals must coexist with other objectives arising out of particular circumstances, such as the wish to uphold moral values and standards of conduct, fulfil social and family obligations, and pursue activities of personal interest such as sports or hobbies.

Before discussing the unique values and goals that characterize individuals, we will first consider two widely-held objectives likely to influence behaviour in clinical situations. These are the maintenance of control over one's environment and the maintenance of one's self-esteem.

## MAINTENANCE OF CONTROL

There are numerous lines of evidence that point to the desirability of having control over one's environment. Some studies show that enhancing control leads to improvements in people's health and well-being. Others report that people often over-estimate the degree of control they actually have (the "illusion of control"). There is also evidence that people respond to restrictions placed upon them by trying to reassert control, and that they prefer activities that they have freely chosen. Before discussing these studies in greater detail, it is worth making two general points. First, studies of perceived control can be divided into two main kinds. The first kind have already been discussed in the chapter on expectancies. These studies examine the relation between the expectation that a response will obtain the desired outcome (i.e., the perceived control associated with that response) and the likelihood of performing that response or the level of associated physiological arousal. The goal in these cases is to achieve some specific outcome such as passing an examination, overcoming symptoms of anxiety, or avoiding a painful shock. In this chapter we will be concerned with studies that show that the perception of having control may be a desirable goal *in its own right*. The second point is that, although there are obvious evolutionary advantages to exercizing control over potentially threatening situations, we should not jump to the conclusion that the perception of control is invariably desirable. There may be some situations where it will actually be aversive, and there may be some people who prefer not to feel constantly in control. We shall be returning to this point later.

Two very well-known studies with the institutionalized elderly are cited as evidence for the value of enhancing control over the environment. Schulz

(1976) arranged for elderly people to be visited by college students. The first group could determine the timing and duration of their visits, the second could predict the occurrence of the visits but not control them, the third received unpredictable vists, and the fourth group were not visited at all. Following this intervention the first two groups were significantly superior to the others on several measures of physical and psychological health as well as level of activity. What is particularly interesting is that the third group of elderly people, who were visited an equal amount and who reported enjoying their visits just as much as did the other two, were no better on the objective measures of health than the group who were not visited at all. In a separate study, Langer and Rodin (1976) investigated the effects of increasing choice and personal responsibility for some residents of a nursing home. Relative to a control group of residents who received an intervention stressing the staff's wish to make them happy, this procedure resulted in improved alertness, active participation, and well-being. Indeed, the results, in terms of health, activity levels, mood and mortality rates, were still evident eighteen months later (Rodin & Langer, 1977).

These studies suggest that enhancing control can have beneficial consequences that go far beyond the effects of improving a person's expectations of attaining or avoiding a specific aversive outcome. Krantz and Schulz (1980) have argued that perceptions of control are also important when the elderly are being relocated, and in other areas of health care such as rehabilitation from cardiac illness. It should be borne in mind, though, that these studies have not generally included before-and-after measures of perceived control. Thus it is not clear that an intervention that increases the amount of objective control a person has over their environment necessarily works by increasing the subjective experience of control.

Another reason to think that the perception of control may be desirable in its own right is that, as we have seen in Chapter 5, people often over-estimate the contingency between their actions and a particular outcome, believing that they can exercise control even when this is not the case. Abramson and Alloy (1980) have documented many studies in human learning and social psychology that investigated people's ability to judge the contingency between their responses and outcomes. A typical example is the experiment by Bruner and Revusky (1961), who seated their subjects in front of a keyboard with four telegraph keys and instructed them to press the keys in such a way as to maximize the delivery of rewards. The actual contingency in operation was that subjects were only rewarded when they responded with a specified inter-response time on the third key from the left, the other keys being unrelated to the rewards. No subject detected this contingency, and all developed complex ("superstitious") patterns of responding involving one or more of the non-functional keys that they were convinced were necessary to produce the rewards. Abramson and Alloy comment that the tendency to over-estimate control can be explained by recourse to motivational or cognitive theories. A motivational account would emphasize either the desire to avoid the negative consequences accompanying a belief in no control (see also Langer, 1975), or the desire to enhance or maintain self-esteem. A cognitive account would suggest that people are unclear about what would constitute evidence for control over an outcome, and that their errors arise from faulty reasoning. At present there are no good grounds for accepting either of these explanations to the exclusion of the other.

Another approach to control is to investigate people's reactions when they are deprived of it. Much of this research has been carried out using the framework of reactance theory (Brehm, 1966), which holds that a person will experience psychological reactance whenever any of his or her free behaviours is eliminated or threatened with elimination. Reactance is a motivational state that will be directed at restoring the threatened or eliminated freedom, and may result in aggression to any social agent who threatens those freedoms. In contrast to frustration, which is usually defined as not obtaining what one desires, reactance is assumed to occur whenever *any* behaviour, even a less desirable alternative, is threatened. The evidence for and clinical applications of reactance theory have been discussed in detail by Brehm (1976), who points out that there are many opportunities for clients to feel that their freedom is being restricted by their therapists. She argues that when the therapist attempts to persuade the client to give up certain symptoms and behaviours, or follow a certain course of action, the client may feel that their freedom not to do these things is threatened and hence may experience reactance. The associated feelings of dissatisfaction, whose cause the client may not be able to identify, could lead to lack of cooperation or failure to carry out therapeutic assignments.

It may appear counter-intuitive to suggest that clients are sometimes threatened by their therapists' advice. In fact there are a number of reasons why this might happen, even with a therapist perceived as able and with the client's best interests at heart. Accepting that someone else knows one better than one does oneself, even in a limited sphere, may induce feelings of incompetence and low self-esteem. Neither is self-esteem likely to be particularly enhanced by improvements in symptoms that are attributed to someone else's expertise rather than to one's own efforts. Reactance theory draws attention to the fact that praising or rewarding a person for a particular action may under some circumstances be experienced as a behavioural restriction. A similar point has emerged from Deci's research on intrinsic motivation. In Deci and Ryan's (1980) cognitive evaluation theory, a distinction is drawn between the informational and the controlling aspects of external events such as rewards and communications. These events may be experienced either as providing information about competence or as exerting pressure towards a specific outcome. Research shows that whereas informational rewards or communications tend to enhance intrinsic motivation, controlling rewards or communications tend to undermine it.

Not only does enhanced personal control have beneficial consequences but, it appears, reduced control may have adverse consequences. Brehm (1976) has suggested that therapists can minimize reactance by avoiding overly strong social pressure on clients to perform certain tasks or adopt a certain view of their problems, and by giving clients the opportunity to demonstrate freedom of choice. Therapists may also be able to capitalize on reactance effects by using paradoxical instructions, a technique described by Haley (1963), which has under some circumstances achieved symptomatic improvement by telling the client to deliberately *increase* the frequency or intensity of the unwanted behaviour.

## Individual Differences

People differ in the extent to which they report wanting to exercise control over their environment. This has been related to a personality construct termed "desire for control" (Burger & Cooper, 1979) and also to the Type A/Type B personality dimension, which distinguishes people according to how competitive, striving, and achievement-oriented they are. Relative to Type Bs, Type As work hard to succeed, suppress subjective states such as fatigue that might interfere with performance, conduct their activities at a rapid pace, and express hostility when frustrated. Glass and Carver (1980) have argued that these characteristics reflect the desire to assert and maintain control over environmental challenges and demands. While there is some empirical support for this suggestion, an alternative explanation of the findings is available in terms of self-esteem maintenance. Pittner and Houston (1980) exposed subjects to conditions of either low stress, self-esteem threat, or shock threat, and measured psychophysiological and cognitive differences between Type As and Type Bs. No physiological differences occurred in situations involving low stress or shock threat, but when self-esteem was threatened Type As showed significantly higher blood pressure than Type Bs.

## Is Control always Desirable?

A great deal has been written about the desirability of increasing perceptions of control. Whereas there is good evidence for the benefits of perceived control over specific pleasurable or aversive events, there is less to support the idea that the experience of control is intrinsically motivating, whatever the circumstances. The latter position has been examined by

Rodin, Rennert, and Solomon (1980), who report some experiments that show that people do not invariably wish to exercise choice and that having control may at times lead to reduced self-esteem. Having control is particularly likely to be aversive when people feel that they have insufficient information on which to base their decision and when they have to take responsibility for bad outcomes. Rodin et al. conclude that a great overlap probably exists between the factors involved in motivation for control and self-esteem enhancement, and those that mediate the relationship between stress and control. In other words, attempts to increase perceptions of control, for instance by providing more information to patients about their treatment, will not necessarily be desirable, particularly if they pose a potential threat to self-esteem.

Rotter (1975) has commented in similar vein on the widespread belief that it is better to be a person with an internal rather than an external locus of control. He writes (1975, p.61):

> It may be better for people who are in obvious difficulties, who are trying to cope with failing abilities, such as the aged and those who have become victims of addictions, to have a greater feeling that they can, in fact, control what happens to them. But there must also be a limit on personal control. Many people may already feel that they have more control than is warranted by reality, and they may be subject in the future (or may already have been subjected) to strong trauma when they discover that they cannot control such things as automobile accidents, corporate failure, diseases, etc.

## SELF-ESTEEM MAINTENANCE

In discussing perceived control, we encountered a number of times the suggestion that one of its benefits was to enhance a person's self-esteem. Many other writers have proposed that one of the most important ways in which people organize their priorities is in relation to the superordinate goal of self-esteem maintenance. According to this view, people are motivated to preserve a positive image of themselves, both in their own eyes and in those of other people. Knowledge of the processes involved in self-esteem maintenance is particularly important in clinical psychology because having to admit to unhappiness or to not being able to cope, or attending a psychiatric facility, are shaming to very many people. Even when patients have successfully entered the health care system, it is not uncommon for them to conceal major problems or worries for quite long periods of time until they are reassured that disclosure will not provoke criticisism or rejection. Shrauger and Turner (reported in Shrauger, 1982) found that, in their sample of 100 clients coming to an outpatient psychiatric setting, lack of self-confidence was the most commonly mentioned problem. Thirteen percent said that it was their most important problem, and a further thirty-one percent saw it as one of their three most important concerns. As we have seen in Chapter 5, low self-esteem is also a core symptom of depression.

The term "self-esteem" most commonly refers to the subjective evaluation that one is a person of worth or value as opposed to the evaluation that one is bad, incompetent, or worthless. Self-esteem is thus an evaluative component of the "self-concept", a broader term that embraces beliefs concerning relatively specific aspects of the self (such as musical ability, gender identity, etc.) as well as overall evaluations such as self-acceptance and self-esteem (Wylie, 1979). Self-esteem usually refers to a generalized feeling, which means that one can feel bad or incompetent in a specific area without necessarily feeling that one is bad overall. Self-esteem has additionally been thought of as a trait and as a state. In other words, people can be characterized according to their (relatively stable) level of self-esteem, but the self-esteem of any individual will also be expected to vary with their circumstances. In practice, therefore, it will generally be helpful to assess whether a person presenting themselves as low in self-esteem is reporting a chronic problem or a temporary response to circumstances. In this chapter we will not be concerned with all the implications of having chronically low self-esteem (it is likely, for instance, to be associated with low expectations of future success), but rather with the consequences for patients' behaviour of trying to maintain self-esteem in the clinical situation.

Self-esteem has been seen as deriving from three main sources, the discrepancy between actual self and ideal self, social comparison, and causal attribution. The self–ideal self discrepancy refers to the gap between what one would like to be (or feels one ought to be) and what one thinks one actually is. Large discrepancies may arise either because the standards one sets oneself are hopelessly "idealistic" and unattainable, or because one undervalues one's actual performance. The importance of this process can be illustrated by considering three case histories of managerial stress, in which adverse mood change was related to a breakdown in the normal system for evaluating actual performance against expected performance (Brewin, 1980). The managers studied had previously based their evaluations on familiarity with the job requirements or on positive feedback from a trusted superior. When they were promoted or changed jobs, they suddenly found themselves in a situation where the job requirements were ambiguous and where there was no longer any reassurance that they were succeeding. Under these circumstances they began to evaluate their performance as a failure, despite having no external evidence that this was the case. They progressively increased their workload to the point where tension, exhaustion, and ultimately breakdown were well-nigh inevitable.

The second major source of self-esteem is social comparison. Festinger (1954) proposed that people have an in-built drive to evaluate their opinions and abilities, and that to the extent that objective, non-social means are unavailable, they do so by comparing themselves with others. A person who has failed at something will experience greater negative self-evaluation when comparison others are perceived as successful than when they also are perceived as having failed. To the degree that psychiatric patients perceive themselves to be unique, and other people to have successfully avoided their unwanted feelings or symptoms, they should therefore experience lowered self-esteem. A recent experiment by Mac-Carthy and Furnham (1986) has shown that anxious patients (although not depressed patients) do tend to over-estimate extraversion and under-estimate neuroticism in the general population, thus apparently believing that the ordinary person is abnormally well adjusted. Other studies, however, have shown that the depressed also see themselves as dissimilar to others, even on attributes that are unrelated to depression, and that they think they are more likely to have negative experiences than the average person (e.g., Brewin & Furnham, 1986).

As we have seen in Chapter 6, patients are frequently in the position of having to explain why distressing events have occurred or why they are experiencing unwanted symptoms. This attributional process represents a third influence on self-esteem. One way in which people may attempt to preserve a positive image of themselves is through the use of "self-serving biases" (e.g., Bradley, 1978), the tendency to take personal credit for success and to attribute blame for failure externally. Typically, success is attributed to one's own ability and failure, to bad luck or the interference of other people, and in the laboratory this tendency is more prevalent, the more the outcome has implications for self-esteem. Particularly at the beginning of therapy, symptoms and problems are likely to be ascribed to external factors that function as excuses or justifications, and patients may be unwilling to consider actively factors within themselves that have contributed to their problem. Therapists should be aware of the implications their formulation may have for the patient's self-esteem, and be tentative in trying to reattribute problems to such factors, desirable though this reattribution might be on other grounds. It will usually be important to try and determine whether patients have genuinely not considered the relevant internal causes, or whether they are choosing not to consider them in the interests of protecting fragile feelings of self-worth.

At times, then, the goal of self-esteem maintenance may conflict with that of sharing problems with others, seeking professional help, and providing the clinician with a full account of the reasons for one's problems. There may also sometimes be conflict with the goal of symptom reduction, a possibility that has been explored in research on "self-handicapping strategies". Following Alfred Adler, Jones and Berglas (1978) suggested that symptoms might have value to a person faced with a threat to his or her self-esteem because they provide a potential alibi for failure, whereas any success would be enhanced by the knowledge that it was achieved despite a handicap. As Snyder and Smith put it (1982, p.106):

> By adopting a symptom, the person increases the ambiguity as to the 'real' underlying reason for a possible failure ... Behind the veil of ambiguity supposedly generated by the symptoms, the self-handicapper therefore is able to nurture a fantasy of self-esteem and competence.

Smith, Snyder, and Perkins (1983) argued that hypochondriacal individuals may use the symptoms of physical illness as a self-handicapping strategy. They selected female students who scored either high or low on the MMPI Hypochondriasis scale and told them that they would be taking a test of "social intelligence". Before completing the second part of this test, which they expected to be difficult, subjects were either instructed that symptoms of physical illness would not affect their performance, or were given no instructions about the relation between symptoms and performance. Subjects then completed a questionnaire about their health in the past year and over the previous twenty-four hours. Hypochondriacal subjects in the "illness has no effect" condition reported fewer health problems than those in the "no instructions" condition, whereas this manipulation had no effect on non-hypochondriacal subjects. These results are consistent with the use of symptom report as a self-handicapping strategy by hypochondriacal individuals.

Many symptoms and behaviours, such as shyness, depression, test anxiety, and drug and alcohol abuse, may be viewed in these functional terms. Of particular clinical importance is the possibility that effort withdrawal, or failure to cooperate fully with treatment, reflects a similar strategy. Although there are no studies investigating this possibility with clinical samples, a number of very suggestive findings have been reported. For instance, it has been found that students who expected to fail an achievement test reduced their intended effort, but only when the task was an ego-involving one (Pyszczynski & Greenberg, 1983). In another study, high and low self-handicapping members of a men's swimming team were found to practice a similar amount prior to an unimportant meet, but high self-handicappers practised much less than their low self-handicapping colleagues prior to an important meet (Rhodewalt, Saltzman, & Wittmer, 1984). An interesting corollary is that self-handicapping may be avoided, and performance enhanced, by providing people with a ready-made explanation for failure that does not cast doubt on their abilities. After failure on an insoluble task, Frankel and Snyder (1978) found that subjects worked harder and were more successful at solving anagrams described as extremely difficult than they were at anagrams described as moderately difficult. This effect is contrary to what one might intuitively expect and indicates effort is not only affected by expectancy of success but also by the anticipated consequences of failure.

So far it has appeared that trying to maintain self-esteem only interferes with clinical progress. It is important to redress the balance and emphasize its positive aspects, some of which are illustrated by the literature on transgression and compliance. Carlsmith and Gross (1969) induced subjects to believe that they had given painful electric shocks to a person in a learning experiment. Such subjects were subsequently more willing to comply with their victim's request for help in getting up a petition than were subjects who did not believe they had administered shocks. In a similar design, Freedman, Wallington, and Bless (1967) induced subjects to knock over a supposedly carefully arranged pile of cards. Later these subjects were more willing than non-guilty controls to help in a public opinion survey. These effects of transgression on compliance are quite robust, and it has been thought that generalized feelings of guilt are aroused that encourage individuals to engage in behaviours likely to restore or enhance their self-esteem. Patients may be similarly encouraged to make reparation for negligent behaviour, an effect noted in the study of industrial accident victims discussed in Chapter 6 (Brewin, 1984a). Feelings of obligation towards close family members and others may also be a significant incentive to seek or cooperate in therapy.

## INDIVIDUAL VALUES AND GOALS

So far we have examined the evidence that people's behaviour is directed towards two very general goals, the perception of control and the maintenance of self-esteem. What characterizes people, however, is their adherence to unique sets of values and goals that structure their activities and that help them to define what sort of a person they are by resolving conflict between alternative courses of action. For instance Beck (1983), Blatt et al. (1982), and other theorists have proposed that depressives can be classified according to whether their goals are primarily concerned with achievement ("self-critical" or "autonomous" type) or whether they concern relationships with other people ("dependent" or "sociotropic" type). Blatt et al. (1982, p.114) describe the self-critical type as "characterized by intense feelings of inferiority, guilt, worthlessness, and by a sense that one must struggle to compensate for having failed to live up to expectations and standards". The dependent type are "characterized by feelings of helplessness and weakness, by fears of being abandoned, and by wishes to be cared for, loved, and protected." In certain situations it may be useful to know what people's goal priorities are in order to predict their reactions. As noted in Chapter 5, there is some evidence that the "dependent" group are more likely to be depressed by a life event affecting their relationships than one affecting their work, whereas the "self-critical" group are more likely to show the opposite pattern of vulnerability (Hammen et al., 1985).

One way of investigating individual value systems is through the use of repertory grids, a technique associated with Personal Construct Theory (Bannister & Fransella, 1971; Kelly, 1955). According to PCT, each person organizes information by using a unique set of dichotomous personal constructs, bipolar categories such as good–bad, kind–cruel, and so on. These constructs are organized into a hierarchical structure in order that people may better anticipate and understand the events they experience. The repertory grid elicits the relations between constructs, indicating which are the most important dimensions used in categorization. Some idea of the person's values can be obtained from examination of individual constructs, and by rating liked and disliked "elements" (e.g., significant others) in terms of these constructs.

An example of this approach is given below. The patient was a 35-year-old self-employed man who complained of constant headaches, irritability, and sleep disturbance. Although his business appeared to be successful, he felt under continual pressure at work and even when at home worried about whether what he was doing was cost-effective. He typically felt inefficient and dissatisfied with himself, had a history of anxiety in childhood, and had never had many friends. In view of the obvious signs of tension the first step was to introduce relaxation training. This was effective in eliminating his headache during the consultation, but he did not persevere with the exercises over the following weeks and made little progress. A repertory grid was next completed to explore the pattern of constructs that he applied to himself, to the person he would like to be, and to other significant figures in his life. A simplified version of this grid (see Fig. 8.1) shows the two major dimensions used to characterize people. The first (vertical axis) has construct poles such as "complaining" and "unfriendly" at one end, with "uncomplaining" and "easy to live with" at the other. The second (horizontal axis) has construct poles such as "tense" and "perfectionist" at one end, with "slapdash", "easygoing", and "relaxed" at the other.

The organization of constructs along this second dimension immediately suggests a reason for the failure to carry out the relaxation exercises. In this patient's system of beliefs, relaxation is associated with a number of negative qualities such as being slapdash, unambitious, and self-satisfied. The construct "tense–relaxed" is most highly correlated with the construct "relies on self–exploits other people". Thus, for this patient, there is a danger that the desired goal of relaxation will be associated (consciously or unconsciously) with other, *undesired* goals. This analysis is supported by the position of the "ideal self" element, which lies towards the "tense" end

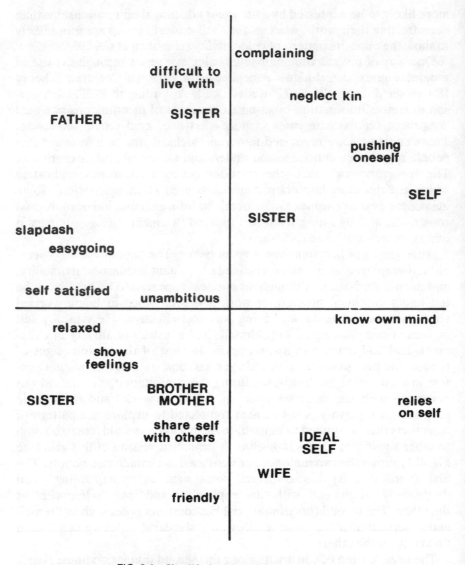

FIG. 8.1   Simplified version of the repertory grid.

of the dimension, and by the relative position of the "self" and "ideal self" elements, which indicates that whereas the patient does want to be somewhat less tense, his major goal is to be more friendly and easy to live with.

The grid also suggests some possible developmental reasons for this patient's pattern of behaviour. The element "father" is diametrically opposite to "ideal self" and close to "disliked person". "Father" is also rated towards the extreme end of the horizontal axis, and so may be seen to embody the construct cluster to do with being slapdash and unambitious. When questioned, the patient confirmed that he did see his father in this way, and that he regarded his father as having let down the family badly by not working and by providing inadequate financial support. This was something the patient was determined to avoid where his own family were concerned. It seems likely, therefore, that he was experiencing conflict between the goal of becoming more relaxed, which he consciously recognized as a desirable one, and the goal of not becoming more similar to his father on this important dimension. The conflict had remained unresolved because he was not aware of his negative associations to the idea of relaxation.

## GOALS AND SELF-REGULATION

So far we have considered some of the values and goals that may determine the direction of a person's behaviour, whether or not the person is consciously aware of them. In addition it is important to recognize people's capacity for deliberately regulating their own behaviour, a process that includes the setting of goals and the manipulation of values through self-reinforcement. As Bandura and Schunk note (1981, p. 586):

> Much human behaviour is directed and sustained over long periods, even though the external inducements for it may be few and far between. Under conditions in which external imperatives are minimal and discontinuous, people must partly serve as agents of their own motivation and action.

Kanfer (1970) has proposed that when people's behaviour is interrupted or fails to produce the intended effects, a process of self-regulation is initiated. This has three stages, of which the first is self-observation. People begin to attend to their behaviour and try to reconstruct or monitor their actions. The second stage is self-evaluation, in which they compare their actual performance with a subjective goal or level of aspiration, and try to correct any discrepancy. The final stage is self-reinforcement, when people either reward themselves for achieving their standards or punish themselves for failing to achieve them. This stage can be seen as one of investing certain outcomes with positive or negative value.

Rehm (1982) has developed a self-control model of depression based on Kanfer's ideas about self-regulation. He proposed that people who are depressed may show deficits in any or all of the three component processes. Their self-monitoring may, for example, be biased in that instances of negative outcomes are carefully attended to and logged, whereas positive outcomes are ignored. Their self-evaluation may be systematically affected by underestimating actual performance or by setting very high performance standards. Depressed people may also show low levels of self-reward and/or high levels of self-punishment that, Rehm suggests, could account in part for the typical behavioural features of less response initiation, longer latencies to respond, and reduced general activity. Some of the empirical support for this theory is presented below.

A similar view of self-regulation, but one not restricted to depression or interrupted behaviour sequences, is put forward in Bandura's (1977a) social learning theory. Bandura proposes that there are two major cognitive sources of motivation that influence intentional behaviour. The first is people's ability to keep in their minds an image of the desired goals towards which they are directing their efforts. The second derives from people's self-evaluative reactions to their performances. To quote Bandura and Schunk once more (1981, p. 586):

> This form of self-motivation, which operates largely through internal comparison processes, requires personal standards against which to evaluate ongoing performance. By making self-satisfaction conditional on a certain level of performance, individuals create self-inducements to persist in their efforts until their performances match internal standards. Both the anticipated satisfactions for matching attainments and the dissatisfactions with insufficient ones provide incentives for self-directed actions.

Like Kanfer, Bandura emphasizes the importance of accurate self-observation or self-monitoring. People cannot influence their actions so readily if they are not attending to the relevant dimensions of their behaviour. There is evidence, for instance, that intermittent self-monitoring produces less effective behaviour change than does more sustained attention to one's performance (Mahoney, Moore, Wade, & Moura, 1973). Self-monitoring provides the feedback about performance that is necessary for the next stage of evaluation. Setting goals in the absence of this feedback is unlikely to result in any improvements to performance (Bandura & Cervone, 1983). Bandura also notes that the judgmental process involved in evaluation includes a number of components, such as the comparison of one's performance with personal and social standards, and the attribution of the cause of one's performance to personal and external factors. Faced with the same objective outcome, there is thus scope for enormous differences in evaluations, which will depend *inter alia* on past experience in similar situations, the choice of others with whom to compare oneself, and predispositions to make certain kinds of attribution or set particular standards. The more performance falls short of what is expected, and the more this is attributed to internal factors, the more people will experience dissatisfaction and strive to make up the deficit.

## Goal-setting

In this section we will be mainly concerned with the way in which people set themselves standards and goals. This subject has been investigated by psychologists researching into such topics as level of aspiration, achievement motivation, and work performance. One question they have asked is whether people, when faced with a choice of tasks, tend to select easy ones, hard ones, or ones of intermediate difficulty. There are a number of interesting parallels between the achievement situation, in which people are required to discover their level of skill or ability, and the clinical situation, in which patients have to discover whether they are able to overcome their symptoms or minimize their handicaps. In both contexts a choice has to be made about how easy or difficult a target to aim at, and how to modify this target in the light of success and failure.

In Atkinson's (1966) theory of achievement motivation, for instance, behaviour is a joint function of motive, expectancy, and incentive. The theory predicts that, for people who in general have a stronger motive to achieve than to avoid failure, the most attractive tasks should be those of intermediate difficulty. These tasks (i.e., where the probability of success is close to .5) are the ones where the anxiety or uncertainty regarding the outcome are greatest. For people who in general are more concerned to avoid failure, however, the most attractive tasks should be *either* very easy *or* very difficult ones, because in both cases there is little uncertainty about the outcome. The assumption here is that the person is trying to avoid the anxiety associated with possible failure even more than actual failure. Atkinson's model also makes predictions about individual differences in reactions to success and failure. For instance, people who have a stronger motive to achieve should set their standards higher following success and should reduce them following failure. People who are anxious to avoid failure, however, should be less likely to lower their standards when they fail at a difficult task, and should be more likely to persist at an easy task they find themselves able to do.

It is quite well established that, whereas achievement-oriented people do prefer goals of moderate difficulty, the tendency to set oneself very high or very low standards of performance is typical of people who are anxious (Lewin, Dembo, Festinger, & Sears, 1944), or high in neuroticism (Eysenck & Himmelweit, 1946; Himmelweit, 1947). More recent research has documented the tendency to set oneself high performance standards among the depressed (Beck et al., 1979; Kanfer & Zeiss, 1983; Rehm, 1982), and among those with the Type A personality (Grimm & Yarnold,

1984; Snow, 1978). Grimm and Yarnold also noted that whereas Type Bs tended to alter their standards in accordance with prior performance, Type As exhibited a trait-like style of establishing high standards independent of prior outcomes. There are, of course, other theories that can provide a convincing account of these results. For example, Trope (1983) has argued that tasks are selected according to their potential for informing people about their abilities. Patients who are anxious about getting yet more information about their lack of ability (e.g., to perform well in social situations) should therefore select tasks so easy or so difficult that everybody would be expected to succeed or fail (i.e., tasks that were not diagnostic of ability). This is of course similar to an explanation in terms of self-handicapping, in which the tendency to set oneself unrealistically high standards of success would be seen as an attempt to preempt damaging internal attributions for failure.

What are the effects of setting people goals? A review of laboratory and field studies (Locke, Shaw, Saari, & Latham, 1981) found that in 90% of the studies, specific and challenging goals led to better performance than easy goals or no goals. Goal-setting was more effective when people were provided with feedback to show their performance in relation to the goal (see also Bandura & Cervone, 1983). Provided activities can be voluntarily controlled, therefore, higher standards will generally lead to greater effort expenditure. But in the majority of clinical situations, voluntary control is not so certain. Bandura and Simon (1977) investigated the effect of providing patients trying to lose weight with proximal goals (specifying maximum calorie intake at four points during each day), distal goals (specifying maximum intake for each week), or no goals. They found that setting goals resulted in much greater weight loss, and that this effect was only present for patients who had had set, or who had set themselves, proximal goals. They concluded that setting sub-goals that are relatively easily attainable is likely to sustain self-motivation. Bandura and Schunk (1981) examined the effects of goal-setting on children pursuing a programme of self-directed learning to overcome severe deficits in mathematical skills. Once again proximal goals proved superior to distal goals in improving the children's performance on mathematical problems, their feelings of efficacy, and their intrinsic interest in the tasks.

## Self-reinforcement

According to the theories of self-regulation discussed above, there should be a close relationship between actual–intended performance discrepancies and people's reactions of self-satisfaction and dissatisfaction. Grimm (1983) has confirmed that satisfaction is indeed related to the discrepancy between the standard and the actual performance rather than to either factor alone. It is important to note, however, that these affective reactions do not follow invariably from the perception of a discrepancy, but can to some extent be selectively engaged or disengaged. For instance, Simon (1979) has demonstrated that reactions to task performance vary according to whether the person believes that their performance reflects innate ability or the results of "automatic" conditioning processes. Awarding oneself praise or blame depends on the value or significance one attaches to the activity.

Bandura (1977a) argues that, as well as merely experiencing self-satisfaction and dissatisfaction, there is some scope for people to try to influence their own behaviour by creating self-incentives and rewarding or punishing themselves contingent on their performance. The conscious anticipation of feelings of pride or blame, he suggests, represents a deliberate strategy used by many people to assist greater effort at a chosen task or to inhibit unwanted behaviours. Just imagining how one is likely to feel later can act either as a spur or as a rein on one's activities. In addition, a number of studies have demonstrated the beneficial effects of making more tangible rewards, such as free time, food, or some leisure activity, contingent on one's performance. These can be as effective or more effective than incentives arranged by external agents such as one's therapist (Bandura, 1982).

There have been several studies examining levels of self-reinforcement in depressed patients. Rozensky et al. (1977) gave a word recognition task to depressed and non-depressed medical patients and found that the depressed group were less likely to reward themselves and more likely to punish themselves for their performance, despite the fact that there were no objective differences in the scores of the two groups. Similar findings were obtained by Nelson and Craighead (1977) with a sample of mildly depressed students. Lobitz and Post (1979) noted that neither of these studies were able to distinguish differences in self-evaluation from differences in patterns of self-reward: in neither was it clear whether depressed and non-depressed assessed their performances as similar but rewarded themselves differently, or whether the depressed also assessed their performances negatively relative to the non-depressed. In their own study they therefore collected self-report measures concerning expectations of success, assessment of performance, and level of deserved reward. Perhaps not surprisingly, in view of the close similarity in the type of measure and in the time at which they were collected, Lobitz and Post found very high correlations between all three. Their depressed patients had lower expectations, lower self-assessments, and lower levels of self-reward than non-depressed patients, but none of the measures were uniquely able to discriminate between the groups.

Finally, Gotlib (1981) reported that depressed psychiatric inpatients administered more self-punishment and less self-reward than a control group of hospital employees, but did not differ in either respect from a second control group of other psychiatric patients (mainly diagnosed as having anxiety neurosis or personality disorder). Psychiatric patients do, therefore, appear to be characterized by low rates of positive self-reinforcement, but there is little evidence that this is particular to any one diagnostic group, or that it can be usefully distinguished from other, related differences in self-perception. Studies that have attempted to isolate the self-reinforcement component in self-control therapy for depression have not found it to make a distinct contribution to clinical outcome (Kornblith et al., 1983).

The studies reviewed above emphasize that self-reinforcement is not an automatic consequence of self-evaluation, but rather a class of possible responses that can be learnt in various ways and that can be selectively engaged or disengaged. In particular, a number of mechanisms exist for dissociating negative self-reactions from the perception that one's performance has not lived up to one's internal standards. Bandura (1977a; 1982) has provided a useful review of these (see Fig. 8.2). To begin with, people may attempt to justify their behaviour, to make advantageous comparisons with behaviour that is far more reprehensible, or to relabel their behaviour in a way that makes it sound more acceptable. They may attempt to displace responsibility for their actions onto other people, or to diffuse it by appealing to collective responsibility. Finally, they may attempt to minimize the consequences of their actions, and to blame or dehumanize any victim of their actions. Whether or not these strategies are employed will depend on many factors, such as the ambiguity of the causal link between their actions and the consequences, the need to provide a public

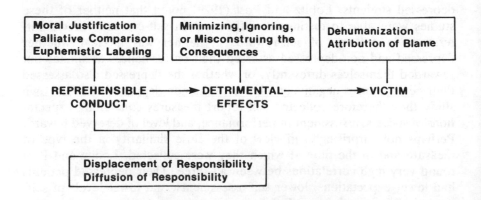
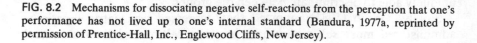

FIG. 8.2 Mechanisms for dissociating negative self-reactions from the perception that one's performance has not lived up to one's internal standard (Bandura, 1977a, reprinted by permission of Prentice-Hall, Inc., Englewood Cliffs, New Jersey).

account of their actions, and the degree of social consensus present for a particular account.

It would be helpful to know whether patients who show an excess of self-blame and register strong feelings of self-dissatisfaction have these techniques of dissociation in their repertoire of cognitive responses. Although self-blame may arise from the setting of excessively high performance standards, and from the discrepancy between these standards and actual performance, it is apparent that negative self-reactions need not necessarily follow. Knowledge of these mechanisms is also useful when trying to understand discrepancies between people's known standards and their actual behaviour. Schwartz and Howard (1980) have shown that the relation of internalized values concerning altruism to actual altruistic behaviour is moderated by responsibility denial. Personal norms correlate with behaviour for those who tend to accept responsibility, but not for those who deny responsibility. These findings are most readily interpretable in terms of a defensive strategy for minimizing the anticipated costs of violating internalized values.

## CONCLUSIONS

Values and goals are traditionally regarded as the energizers of behaviour, helping to provide direction, intensity, and persistence to people's actions. Goals are also central to theories of psychopathology, loss of an important goal having been linked by many writers to the experience of depression, and conflict between incompatible goals to the experience of anxiety. In this chapter we have described two kinds of generally desired goal, involving the maintenance of control and of self-esteem. Entering hospital or psychotherapy may involve threats to both, and for this reason we would expect some patients to behave in ways likely to restore both to acceptable levels. These may include selective non-cooperation with or forgetting of therapeutic suggestions, denial of the ability of the therapist to be helpful, denial of failure and of responsibility for failure, and the presentation of information about the self in the most favourable light. At times the therapist may suspect that the symptoms themselves serve the function of maintaining control over a particular situation or of protecting self-esteem. In the latter case they would be classed as a self-handicapping strategy.

Goal-setting and self-reinforcement are important components in the self-regulation of behaviour, and there is evidence that, particularly in depression, patients set themselves goals that are too easy, too difficult, or too distant. A useful therapeutic function may be simply to advise on more appropriate goals. Inappropriate goal-setting and lack of self-reinforcement may be an indication that there is a conflict between two or more goals, for example between having a medical condition treated and avoiding a worrying diagnosis, between being successful as a parent and in one's career, or between pleasing one's parents and following one's own inclinations. One important suggestion, given the most weight by psycho-analysts, is that this conflict may sometimes involve a conscious goal and a nonconscious goal, so that the patient does not know why he or she is having so much difficulty in achieving some objective.

The notion of a nonconscious goal, by which I mean one that the person is unaware of rather than one that is necessarily repressed, is quite com-patible with the cognitive theories and experiments described earlier in this book. In this chapter the example was given of the businessman who consciously wanted to relax but whose associations to the idea of relaxation suggested that he might, for reasons that were not immediately available to consciousness, find relaxation an unattractive goal. Other examples of occupational stress arising from the attempt to fulfil nonconscious goals are given by Firth (1985), who suggests that overwork and inability to delegate may sometimes stem from the hidden desire to please a demanding parent. Similarly, poor working relations and lack of cooperation with colleagues may stem from a wish to avoid close relationships in which the person runs the risk of being tricked or humiliated. In many instances these non-conscious goals seem to have been acquired in childhood and to represent aspects of the relationship between the child and one or both parents. The issue of how early relationships may come to be internalized and to affect behaviour later in life will be addressed in the next chapter.

# 9 Cognition and Interpersonal Relationships

Although cognitive theories of psychopathology are often formulated solely from the point of view of the individual, it is important not to lose sight of the fact that the individual exists in a social environment and that relationships with others are often critical for well-being. It is known that loss, separation, and other disruptions to close relationships, whether these occur early or late in life, are associated with many kinds of psychopathology. Equally, the existence of social support appears to reduce the impact of stressful experiences as diverse as rape and open heart surgery, and good support is associated with a better outcome in patients suffering from disorders such as cancer, multiple sclerosis, and chronic kidney disease. It is common for patients who consult psychologists to have low levels of support, whether because of poor social skills, isolation from others (self-imposed or situationally determined), or because of current difficulties in their intimate relationships or in relationships with people in authority. Many kinds of psychotherapy, whatever the theoretical model underlying them, share a common concern with improving patients' relationships with others, and take particular note of any difficulties that feature in their responses to the therapist's suggestions and interpretations. For these reasons some knowledge of the dynamics of interpersonal relationships is essential for any practising psychologist.

Since this is such a broad topic, we will focus in this chapter on just three aspects of the relation between cognition and social interaction. First, we will discuss the development of the self-concept from the perspective of attachment theory, which is concerned with how early social relationships influence people's perceptions of themselves and others. Then will follow an account of how two kinds of adult cognitive appraisal, explanation and social comparison, affect emotions such as anger and pity, helping behaviour, and the seeking-out or avoiding of social support. But no discussion of these processes can fail to acknowledge, unfortunately only briefly in this case, the substantial contribution of psychobiology and psychoanalysis. Situations involving loss or separation from the primary care-giver, and defeat by another animal in a social hierarchy, are associated with well-recognized neurochemical and behavioural responses in many different species (e.g., Gilbert, 1984; in press). For example, separation from the primary care-giver generally gives rise to a biphasic reaction involving agitated behaviour and distress vocalizations ("protest") followed by quiescence, retardation and vegetative activity ("despair"). The similarity of these states to the clinical disorders of anxiety and depression has been pointed out many times. Separation has also been found under certain circumstances to lead to later abnormalities in parenting.

A great deal has also been written about the human response to separation and loss from a psychoanalytic perspective, paying particular attention to the relation between early loss and psychopathology in children and adults. There is agreement on broad principles such as the importance of the child's stage of cognitive development in making sense of adverse experiences such as loss, the existence of defence mechanisms such as denial and repression to protect the individual against grief and threatening interpersonal emotions, and the influence of internalized models of close relationships on the patient's behaviour towards the therapist ("transference"). As yet there is little consensus on the exact mechanisms involved, although a number of important hypotheses have been put forward. The approach of attachment theory, reviewed below, is to assume that in many cases the behaviour observed by psychoanalysts can best be understood in terms of the functioning of an innate motivational system that has evolved to attach infants to care-givers. A review of psychoanalytic theories about interpersonal relationships is beyond the scope of this chapter, but in the first section we shall consider one of their central tenets, that the information extracted from early interpersonal disturbances influences subsequent relationships.

## MODELS OF SELF AND MODELS OF OTHERS

In our discussion of the self-concept in Chapter 5 it was stated that, developmentally, models of the self depend on actual experiences at the hands of other people. No mention was made at that point of the kind of experiences that are likely to be significant, or of the age at which they begin to be incorporated into the self-concept. The helplessness of the human infant means that it starts life totally dependent on the protection and nurturance provided by other people, and there appear to be a number of innate mechanisms that are designed to strengthen such relationships and to ensure their continuity. There is now a great deal of evidence that the success or failure of these early relationships has significant implications for later personality development and for the risk of psychopathology. The person most associated with this view is Bowlby (1973, 1980, 1982), who in his theory of attachment has synthesized the clinical observations of psychoanalysts and the experimental and naturalistic observations of ethologists and evolutionary biologists. In brief, Bowlby believes that infants possess a motivational system programmed to establish stable attachments with a small number of other individuals, and that the creation of secure affectional bonds promotes self-confidence and healthy psychological development. The breaking of these bonds by death or abandonment, or their disruption through temporary separations, produces well-recognized emotional patterns involving anxiety, anger, and despair, and behavioural patterns involving clinging and withdrawal. These feelings and behaviours, he believes, form the basis for many later psychiatric disorders, particularly depression and anxiety disorders such as agoraphobia.

Because of their biological significance and profound emotional consequences, experiences of attachment, separation, and loss are regarded as central to a child's development. From early infancy (particularly during the period from six months to five years) the presence of a primary attachment figure, and her (less often his) responsiveness to the child's needs, is a major factor in determining how much fear is created by a potentially alarming situation. Bowlby proposes that, largely on the basis of the responses of others in these kinds of situations, children gradually build up internal representations or working models of themselves and of their main attachment figures, which are used to appraise and guide behaviour in new situations. Crucial elements of the adult personality, including vulnerable cognitive styles and self-esteem, depend on the quality of early social interaction, and particularly on the inferences children draw about their acceptability or loveableness. Thus, the working model of the self is intimately connected to models of others, and confidence in the availability of attachment figures is gradually internalized as an important aspect of self-esteem. Working models continue to develop through infancy, childhood, and adolescence, and the expectations formed about self and others are thought to persist thereafter relatively unchanged, exerting an influence on the course of subsequent adult relationships. Theoretically, one of the functions of working models is to account for the intergenerational transmission of patterns of attachment behaviour. There are now a number of studies indicating that anxious attachment between a child and his or her mother is associated with the mother's reports of disruption or abandonment by her own early attachment figures (see Ricks, 1985, for a review).

Bowlby, in common with many psychoanalysts from Freud onwards, also suggests that individuals may sometimes have multiple models of themselves and of their attachment figures, and that these are not equally accessible to consciousness. Indeed, he argues that (1973, p.238):

> In a person suffering from emotional disturbance it is common to find that the model that has the greatest influence on his perceptions and forecasts, and therefore on his feeling and behaviour, is one that developed during his early years and is constructed on fairly primitive lines, but that the person himself may be relatively, or completely, unaware of; while, simultaneously, there may be operating within him a second, and perhaps radically incompatible, model, that developed later, that is much more sophisticated, that the person is more nearly aware of and that he may mistakenly suppose to be dominant.

It is thought that multiple models develop because the information from which they are constructed is not all consistent. Bowlby gives the example of a child who experiences his mother as unresponsive and unloving but who is told by her that she does love him and that any problems between them are due to his own contrary temperament. Under these circumstances, he argues, the child is faced with a grave dilemma. If the mother uses or implies threats of abandonment or withdrawal of love whenever her version is questioned, the child may adopt the solution of suppressing his own perceptions and accepting hers. In later life the two sets of perceptions are likely to be differentially accessible to consciousness.

The idea of constructing internal representations of one's experiences, whose effects can operate outside of awareness, is compatible with much of the experimental work reviewed earlier in this book. The existence of multiple representations of the self and of other people, differentially accessible to consciousness, is more speculative. From a clinical point of view, some explanation is needed for the fact that the emotions certain people feel towards their loved ones and their therapists alternate between the intensely positive and the intensely negative with no apparent justification. Studies of multiple personality (see Chapter 2) also suggest that it is possible to operate with a number of different selves who may be aware or unaware of each other. Multiple representations of self and others would certainly be feasible within a theory of cognitive organization such as Johnson-Laird's (1983) mental models approach. Applying this approach to depression, Power and Champion suggest that (1986, p.209):

A depressive could have a self-model that under certain conditions was positive and contained embedded negative aspects, but under other conditions the negative aspects could become superordinate and dominate any of the positive aspects. Furthermore, the depressive need not always be aware of the negative side, but only under these critical conditions (e.g., the loss of a significant relationship or important ambition) need they enter awareness.

To summarize, Bowlby's ideas about internal representations of the self and others anticipated recent developments in social cognition. This research is already providing an experimental basis for demonstrating nonconscious influences on behaviour, thereby buttressing his suggestion that individuals may sometimes operate with both conscious and unconscious models of themselves and others. Why some models remain unconscious, if they do, remains an open question. Although defensive processes may be involved, there are other explanations to do with the stage of cognitive development at which the critical events occurred. It is likely to be difficult or impossible to recall events before a differentiated consciousness of self and others has been present for some time, before linguistic categories are available to describe the experience, and before mechanisms are available for integrating different experiences. Whereas the building of a conscious model of self must wait upon this cognitive maturation, which may not be sufficiently developed until the fourth year of life or even later, simple conditioning can be demonstrated in utero. These kinds of simple contingency learning, that can occur in the absence of conscious awareness, may well form the basis of unconscious models of the self.

Bowlby's work, and that of other attachment theorists, is important in emphasizing that the roots of beliefs about the self lie in social relationships. Surprisingly, researchers investigating the cognitive changes that accompany depressed mood have tended to ignore this perspective, even though attachment theory makes it easier to understand why in later life loss events should be associated with major changes in levels of self-esteem.

## EXPLANATION AND ATTRIBUTION IN CLOSE RELATIONSHIPS

We turn now from social influences on cognitive development to consider some cognitive influences on adult social exchanges. Attribution theory suggests several ways in which cognitive appraisal might affect marital, family, and other close relationships. Jones and Nisbett (1972) proposed that the divergent perspective of actors and observers would lead a person explaining their own behaviour to place relatively greater weight on situational causes, whereas a person observing it would emphasize internal, dispositional causes. This is known as the "actor–observer bias." In a marital context, it would mean that a couple might differ in their explanation of negative behaviour such as arriving home later than promised: the one arriving late might see the cause as primarily related to the situation ("I had too much work to do"), whereas the partner might locate the cause in that person's negative personality characteristics ("You're selfish and unreliable"). The actor–observer bias is an example of the pervasive "fundamental attribution error" (Ross, 1977), the tendency to underrate situational influences on behaviour. They both indicate cognitive mechanisms that may underlie divergent beliefs and attributional conflict between family members.

The work of Weiner (1985a) has identified several specific emotional consequences of attributional judgements of internality–externality and controllability–uncontrollability. Weiner's theory proposes that when a person experiences a positive outcome, an attribution to the controllable (intentional) actions of another person elicits the emotion of gratitude. A negative outcome attributed to the controllable actions of another produces anger. When the negative outcome has been experienced by another person, on the other hand, attributions to causes external to and uncontrollable by that person elicit the emotion of pity. Interpersonal emotions such as gratitude, anger, and pity are important in understanding the tension and distress that arises in families and the willingness of family members to tolerate difficult behaviour and support each other at stressful times. There is now a considerable amount of research that supports the view that positive and negative emotions are based, at least in part, on specific patterns of causal belief.

## Couples and Marital Partners

Actor–observer biases were investigated by Orvis, Kelley, and Butler (1976), who got each member of a couple to write down their own explanation of areas of conflict as well as what they thought would be their partner's explanation. They found that actors more often explained their behaviour in terms of such causes as environmental circumstances, temporary internal states, and judgements of what was preferable or necessary, whereas the partner's explanation was more likely to be in terms of the actor's characteristics (lazy, forgetful, irresponsible, violent), and the actor's negative attitude toward the partner. These findings are consistent with the idea of an actor–observer bias, although actors also appear to emphasize reasons and justifications for their actions as well as situational constraints. A subsequent study by Harvey, Wells, and Alvarez (1978) obtained independent explanations for the same events from each member of a couple, as well as predictions about the partner's explanations. They found that even highly satisfied couples with relatively long-term relationships had inaccurate perceptions of each other's understanding of areas of conflict. Each member of the couple tended to think that the other's causal analysis would agree with their own, and both tended to be unaware of the existence of divergent explanations.

Neither of these studies found any difficulty in eliciting attributions, which is consistent with the principle that unusual or unwanted events attract greater attributional processing (see Chapter 6). This was strongly confirmed in a second study by Harvey et al. who concluded, after interviewing ten people recently separated from their partners (1978, p. 253):

> The more lonely and depressed the individual, the greater the concern with rehashing the issues... Furthermore, the less involved the individual in new experiences, the greater the continued review of the separation and its bases. These "why" questions and answers occurred regularly in the participants' records throughout the 6-month period.

This explicit concern over causes, together with the evidence for the existence of biases leading to attributional divergence, suggests that attributions may both contribute to marital distress and be a useful focus for marital counselling and therapy. A greater tendency to blame one's partner is certainly related to lower expressed satisfaction with one's relationship (Fincham & Bradbury, 1988).

The clinical significance of actor–partner differences was further investigated in a comparison of non-distressed couples with distressed couples seeking counselling (Fincham, Beach, & Baucom, 1987). Distressed spouses saw their own actions as more positively motivated and more deserving of praise than positive partner behaviour, whereas the causes of their own negative actions were rated as being more external, less stable, and less global than the causes of partners' negative actions. In contrast, non-distressed spouses made more benign attributions for their partner's behaviour than for their own behaviour. As Fincham et al. comment (1987, p. 746):

> It is precisely this pattern of attributions that is likely to maximize the impact of negative partner behavior for distressed spouses and positive partner behavior for non-distressed spouses...distressed spouses may discredit positive spouse behavior, because they do not believe it matches the motivation that characterizes their own behavior, and instead focus on negative partner behavior...this may account in part for the long chains of negative interchanges that distinguish distressed from non-distressed spouses.

Researchers have been at pains to point out that the highly-charged, emotion-laden attributions obtained from partners in distress do not represent a dispassionate assessment of causal factors, but embrace other aspects of explanation (see Chapter 6). On the basis of their evidence from young couples, Orvis et al. commented (1976, p. 379):

> Attributions are an integral part of the interpersonal evaluative process. The *reasons* for behavior are learned as part and parcel of the *evaluation* of behavior. Attributions are not simply handy auxiliary interpretive tags that permit the person to make adjustments in his evaluation of behavior, for example, shifting the judgement of theft towards the positive side if it occurred out of dire need. Rather, they enter into the very description of the behavior itself.

Similarly, Fincham, Beach, and Nelson (1987) found that distressed and non-distressed spouses were more clearly differentiated by responsibility judgements for partners' behaviour that focussed on negative intention, selfish motivation, and blameworthiness, than by judgements that were simply concerned with causes of that behaviour. Furthermore, only responsibility judgements predicted the affective impact and intended response to the behaviour.

The general conclusion from a large number of studies is that distressed spouses are more likely to see their partner and their relationship as the source of their difficulties. They also tend to see these causes as more global, i.e., affecting many areas of the marriage, as more blameworthy, and as more reflective of their spouse's negative attitude toward them. Recent evidence (Fincham & Bradbury, 1988) builds on these correlational findings and suggests that causal and responsibility attributions are predictive of future marital satisfaction (at least for wives). There are also promising indications that the experimental manipulation of attributions for one's partner's behaviour can lead to changes in behaviour, suggesting that this line of research is highly relevant to the practice of marital and family therapy.

## Parents and Children

An investigation of maternal attributions for a son or daughter's nocturnal enuresis (Butler, Brewin, & Forsythe, 1986) found that mothers endorsed a wide variety of causes for this upsetting and annoying condition. Interestingly, the most common attribution, to the child being a heavy sleeper, has received no support from empirical comparisons of the sleep patterns of enuretic and control children. Other common attributions, for example to a positive family history or to the child being a worrier, have been supported by research, however. Factor analysis indicated that the causes fell into three groups, one to do with anxiety and lack of confidence, one to do with lack of motivation and developmental constraints, and one to do with negative behaviour or negative characteristics on the part of the child. On average mothers rated the causes of the enuresis as internal to the child but as uncontrollable by him or her. A small minority perceived the behaviour as stemming from the child's laziness or disobedience, or as being a way of getting back at her. Consistent with Weiner's (1985a) analysis, mothers who perceived the cause as being more controllable by the child showed less tolerance for the enuresis. Mothers were also less tolerant of older children, who were expected to have more control over the problem.

Another study took parents who had demonstrated negative feelings towards their children and investigated whether their attributions differed from those of control families. Larrance and Twentyman (1983) presented mothers who had a prior history of child abuse, child neglect, or who had no known previous history of child maltreatment with a standardized sequence of photographic stimuli of their own child and another child. These photographs depicted children in situations where they either transgressed or were transgressed upon, toys were broken, walls were crayoned, and skill and chance games were performed. Mothers then had to evaluate and account for their child's behaviour. The comparison mothers attributed their child's positive behaviours to internal and stable causes such as enduring traits, whereas negative behaviours were attributed to external and unstable factors such as circumstances beyond their child's control. The abusing mothers demonstrated the opposite pattern of attributions, seeing their child's negative behaviours as due to internal and stable factors but their positive behaviours as unstable and externally caused. The scores of neglectful mothers fell in between these two groups. Larrance and Twentyman's results are consistent with the predictions of attribution theory, but it should be noted that they did not measure perceived controllability. Theoretically, internal and stable attributions for a child's misbehaviour should lead to hopelessness and lack of trying to effect change. They should not lead to anger, however, unless also associated with a cause that is in some way controllable by the child.

## Consequences of Interpersonal Attributions

The antecedents of positive emotions such as pity and pride, and negative emotions such as anger and guilt, are extremely relevant to understanding the tension and distress that sometimes arise between husbands and wives, doctors and patients, and so on. In addition they may have other quite specific consequences. Although what follows is of necessity speculative, there are at least two well-established findings that indicate how attributions and the emotions they engender might be related to clinically significant outcomes. The first concerns the antecedents of helping behaviour. Weiner (1985a) summarizes evidence that the decision whether or not to help another is largely the result of feelings of anger and pity towards that person, feelings that are based on perceptions of whether their predicament is, or was, under their own control. Thus maternal anger and intolerance over enuresis, shown above to be related to perceptions of the child's control over the causes, is also related to whether the parents withdraw their child prematurely from treatment (e.g., Butler, Brewin, & Forsythe, in press; Morgan & Young, 1975). Because the treatment of nocturnal enuresis demands a lot of effort on the part of the parents, premature drop-out can plausibly be seen as unwillingness to help the child.

Hospital staff may also be more or less willing to help (provide treatment for) different categories of patient. In a well-known study Sudnow (1967) described the differing attempts made to resuscitate patients brought in dead or on the point of death. Suicide victims, dope addicts, and prostitutes were likely to be pronounced dead more quickly than citizens regarded as more respectable by staff. In many other situations staff do have to allocate scarce resources between patients, and this will probably be done on the basis of notions of "deservingness". The patient's perceived responsibility for the cause of their admission is therefore likely to be a significant factor, and it would be expected that certain patients such as suicide attempters would attract staff hostility and correspondingly low levels of care and attention. The prescription of anti-anxiety and anti-depressive drugs by doctors may also be regarded as a form of helping behaviour. One study has found that medical students are more willing to prescribe such drugs to patients who have experienced uncontrollable life stress than to patients whose troubles are seen as being more of their own making (Brewin, 1984b).

The second set of findings that may be illuminated by an attributional approach concerns the effect of relatives' levels of expressed emotion (EE) on patients' probability of relapse. Two major components of high EE are hostility and criticism, and it is now well-established that depressed and schizophrenic patients are more likely to relapse when living with a high EE relative (Vaughn & Leff, 1976; Vaughn et al., 1984). It seems likely that the adverse effects of high EE are not confined to psychiatric patients, however, and may include patients who are simply trying to lose weight (Fischmann-Havstad & Marston, 1984). These findings suggest that relapse rates may be improved by intervening with relatives, and an initial study with the families of schizophrenic patients has shown that it is possible to lower relatives' levels of EE with beneficial effects (Leff et al., 1982). The processes affecting the development and modification of EE are as yet, however, poorly understood.

From an attributional perspective, hostility and criticism on the part of a relative stem from causal beliefs emphasizing the patient's control over and responsibility for their negative behaviours. Although this has yet to be demonstrated empirically, my colleague Brigid MacCarthy describes a natural experiment that illustrates this relationship. The father of a patient who was particularly severely handicapped by chronic schizophrenia had, on initial investigation, low levels of expressed emotion and believed that his son's problems were caused by an accident that had left him mentally impaired. Shortly afterwards a brain scan was carried out and the father was informed by medical staff that they had been unable to find any evidence of cerebral damage or abnormality. On re-assessment the father was found to express much higher levels of hostility and criticism. It is tempting to put this down to the effects of the test feedback, which may have undermined his belief in an important cause for which his son could not be held responsible and over which he had no control.

## COGNITION, SOCIAL INTERACTION, AND SOCIAL SUPPORT

The ability to interact with others in an appropriate and confident manner is extremely valuable if one is to have a satisfactory personal and professional life. To give only one example of the benefit of good personal relationships, social support from other people appears to be very important in protecting physical and mental health during stressful periods of one's life (e.g., Berkman & Syme, 1979; Cobb, 1976; Cohen & Wills, 1985). Yet many psychiatric patients, who would appear to be much in need of such support, have smaller social networks and interact less with others than do non-psychiatric controls. Even in the general population shyness, loneliness, and anxiety in social situations is very common, and in some cases social anxiety is so intense that the mere presence of other people becomes highly aversive and leads to social withdrawal.

Various explanations for social anxiety and social withdrawal have been put forward. These include a conditioning account that emphasizes the role of aversive past experiences in creating anxiety to social stimuli. There is also a social skills account based on the observation that anxious, isolated, or withdrawn individuals often display inappropriate non-verbal behaviour, initiate fewer conversations, fail to obey social rules about turn-taking, terminating conversations, etc. According to this view, their social difficulties arise from the discomfort produced in others by their inappropriate behaviour. Two main types of cognitive explanation have also been offered, one to do with beliefs about social competence, and one that emphasizes the role of social comparison processes. The various theories of social anxiety and withdrawal are not mutually exclusive, and all may be helpful in analyzing the problems of a particular individual. Their different causal focus does, however, point to different kinds of intervention strategy for improving social performance.

## Social Competence

Shy and lonely people tend to attribute interpersonal failures (but not necessarily other kinds of failure) to internal, stable, and uncontrollable factors such as lack of social ability (Anderson, Horowitz, & French, 1983; Teglasi & Hoffman, 1982). As we have seen earlier in this book, these kinds of attribution lead to low self-esteem and to low expectations of success or, in Bandura's (1977b) terms, to low self-efficacy. This in turn would be expected to reduce the amount of effort expended to initiate and persist at social encounters. Leary et al. (1986) have also investigated attributions for subjective feelings of nervousness, one of the factors claimed by Bandura to contribute to estimates of self-efficacy. In support of this model, Leary et al. showed that people who attribute their feelings of social anxiety to stable characteristics of themselves are more likely to avoid social encounters than people who attribute them to unstable characteristics of themselves or to situational factors.

The relevance of these cognitions to social behaviour has been further investigated in an elegant experiment by Anderson (1983). College students were first selected according to their tendency to make either uncontrollable, characterological attributions (character style) or controllable, behavioural attributions (behaviour style) for interpersonal failures. These two groups of subjects then took part in an interpersonal persuasion task (getting people to donate blood to a local blood bank) under one of three conditions. In one condition it was suggested that success at the task was due to abilities and personality traits, in another condition that success was due to using the right strategies and to effort; whereas in the third condition subjects received no prior attributional information. Anderson found that when attributions were not manipulated, behaviour style subjects had higher success expectancies, demonstrated greater motivation, and were more successful at the task than character style subjects. When attributions were manipulated, these group differences were abolished. Prior ascription of success to ability factors did not affect the character style group, but it reduced the performance of the behaviour style subjects to a level equal to that of the other group. Conversely, when the experimenter suggested in advance the importance of effort and choosing the correct strategies, there was no effect on the behaviour style subjects, but the performance of the character style group improved to a level equal to that of the behaviour style subjects. This experiment provides a convincing demonstration of the association between generalized causal beliefs and success in a novel interpersonal situation, and illustrates the potential impact on people's behaviour of changing their beliefs about the importance of various causal factors.

## Social Comparison, Affiliation, and Self-isolation

Theories based on beliefs about social competence are particularly relevant to those individuals who desire social interaction but have low expectations of being able to perform adequately. Other individuals may be socially competent, and know it, but actively avoid interaction because they have other attributes or experiences that they consider to be abnormal and of which they are embarrassed or ashamed. Goffman (1968) has described the many social difficulties experienced by stigmatized individuals who belong to a despised race or religion, or who have physical deformities or character blemishes. The adverse reactions of others may lead to a self-imposed isolation from society, as he illustrates in the following quotation from a 43-year-old unemployed mason: "How hard and humiliating it is to bear the name of an unemployed man. When I go out, I cast down my eyes because I feel myself wholly inferior. When I go along the street, it seems to me that I can't be compared with an average citizen, that everybody is pointing at me with his finger. I instinctively avoid meeting anyone" (p. 28).

Goffman's analysis is largely concerned with the social rejection experienced by stigmatized people and with the strategies they employ to avoid this. He distinguishes between "discredited" people such as paraplegic individuals, whose stigma is evident on the most casual acquaintance, and "discreditable" people who have a secret they are trying to conceal, such as their illiteracy. In many cases, however, a process of self-stigmatization may produce similar effects in a person who does not fall into one of Goffman's socially despised categories, and who has not experienced actual societal rejection. Ørner (1987) described these reactions in a group of British servicemen who had fought in the Falklands war five years previously and continued to experience the after-effects in the form of vivid memories or nightmares (post-traumatic stress disorder). According to Ørner, they felt marked out by their experiences and different from other people in an important way. In the absence of other servicemen with similar experiences, they felt unable to talk to others and chose rather to isolate themselves from society.

In a similar way, the teenager who has had an abortion, the woman who sometimes feels violent towards her child, and the man who feels self-conscious about his physique are all likely to experience some anxiety about a public revelation. Prompted by feelings of shame over some action or attribute, they must still estimate society's reaction if the secret is revealed. Expectations of censure and scorn, whether veridical or mistaken, may lead them to withdraw from social encounters. Even individuals who are obviously "discredited" must make similar estimates. If they are to avoid social isolation they may choose to focus on some feature of which they can feel proud and which emphasizes their comparability with others, as in the case of the physically handicapped who take part in sporting contests. Experimentally inducing feelings of shame and embarrassment in ordinary college students can also lead to a decreased desire for social interaction with peers (Sarnoff & Zimbardo, 1961). The fact that similar effects can be demonstrated in the laboratory with non-discredited subjects emphasizes that we are dealing with an intrapersonal process as well as a societal one.

The notion of stigma involves being classified as different from and inferior to one's peers. But, in the absence of continued rejection, how does a person arrive at the conclusion that their attributes or experiences make them different and inferior? The attitudes, values, and behaviour of those closest to them will obviously be important, but not necessarily crucial. As we have seen in Chapter 8, social comparison theory (Festinger, 1954) was originally developed to explain how people evaluate their opinions and abilities, but it can also be applied to the evaluation of actions, feelings, and experiences such as that of illness. According to Festinger, people who want to evaluate themselves first seek objective information and then turn to social comparison, preferring to compare themselves to similar others when doing so. This is because it is usually more informative to compare oneself with others who are similar on the relevant attributes than with others who are very dissimilar. The work of Schachter (1959) indicates that these affiliative tendencies increase when people are uncertain or fearful. Interestingly, animals low in a status hierarchy, which may be seen as an analogue of a social comparison situation, are characterized by increases in gaze aversion, in social avoidance, and in appeasement behaviour (Gilbert, in press).

Social comparison theory therefore suggests that people with a "problem" they are uncertain or fearful about should avoid "normal" (i.e., dissimilar) people and seek out similar others, sharing their problem with selected friends or perhaps joining self-help groups composed of people in related situations. Receiving information that others share their problems should increase their self-esteem and reduce self-stigmatization. Consistent with this view, Yalom (1975) has identified "universality," or the sharing of one's experiences with similar others, as one of the most potent factors for change in therapeutic groups. For people with a problem, information that it is a relatively common one also increases the probability of help-seeking (Snyder & Ingram, 1983). But many factors may interfere with this process of gaining consensus information via direct social comparison. The "discreditable" person may be unable to identify a group of similar others, and both "discreditable" and "discredited" may be prevented from mixing with their peers because of excessive shame and embarrassment, lack of social skills, etc.

A great deal will depend on the person's initial estimate of the frequency of their "problem". The more unusual the "discreditable" think themselves, the more likely they are to doubt the availability of similar others, and on this basis fear social interactions in which their "secret" might be unmasked. This process may account for the fact that depressed patients have smaller social networks than the non-depressed. The depressed believe that they are dissimilar to others and that negative experiences are more likely to happen to them than to other people (e.g., Brewin & Furnham, 1986; MacCarthy & Furnham, 1986). Brewin and Furnham suggested that these beliefs should lead the depressed to avoid others, thus restricting their access to normative or consensus information. In this way inaccurate consensus judgements would tend to persist through lack of disconfirmatory evidence, and social interaction would continue to be aversive. According to this approach, the reduced network size and relative lack of intimacy enjoyed by those prone to depression is explained by specific consensus beliefs that influence the attractiveness, and hence the probability, of social interaction. Consistent with this model, Brewin, MacCarthy, and Furnham (1987) found that the seeking of support following a stressful experience was associated with consensus beliefs independently of level of depression.

There is a strong case to be made that the frequency of different kinds of social interaction, including the seeking and utilization of social support, is linked to social comparison processes. But the relation between social comparison, social interaction, and negative emotions such as anxiety, depression, or embarrassment is a complex one. It does seem likely that inaccurate consensus beliefs are related to negative emotions and that these in turn are related to social withdrawal. For some patients the opportunity to gain consensus information, either in written form or by actually mixing with similar others, may therefore be extremely valuable. But mixing with similar others is less likely to appeal to those who do not wish to evaluate their feelings and experiences, either because they have access to adequate expert advice or because their coping strategies depend on attending to certain kinds of information and not others. For example, patients who use the "downward comparison" strategy to maintain their self-esteem (see Chapter 8) may find it upsetting to meet others who are managing better than they are and who make them feel like a failure. Patients who use the "upward comparison" strategy, on the other hand, may be uncomfortable mixing with others they perceive as worse off than themselves, since this may bring home the reality of their problem or disability.

This point is illustrated by studies of patients with chronic physical impairments such as multiple sclerosis (MS). Miles (1979) has identified two alternative coping strategies used by married couples with one partner suffering from MS. The "normalization" strategy involves continuing social relationships according to the pre-illness pattern and avoiding other sufferers. The "disassociation" strategy involves withdrawing from relationships with non-sufferers, sometimes by moving house. In an investigation of the association between social contact and well-being in MS sufferers, Maybury and Brewin (1984) reported that greater self-esteem and reduced psychological distress were related to greater contact with the able-bodied. Well-being was unrelated to the amount of contact with other MS sufferers, however, suggesting that the opportunity to obtain regular consensus information was not of great value to this group. It would be interesting to know whether there are certain times, for example immediately after the diagnosis is made, when consensus information would be useful for MS sufferers.

## CONCLUSIONS

In this chapter I have given some examples to illustrate the importance of a relatively neglected topic, the interrelation of cognition and social environment. This is very much a two-way traffic. Disruptions to early social relationships have been empirically shown to affect the later behaviour of humans and animals, and attachment theory suggests that this is mediated by internal working models of self and others. The relation of early experience to unconscious knowledge and to conscious beliefs remains an exciting topic for future research. If the psycho-analysts are correct, experimental studies of defence mechanisms (see Chapter 2) will once again assume a great deal of importance. In any event, the subject matter of a number of different disciplines such as evolutionary biology, experimental cognitive psychology, and psychoanalysis appears to be converging. In brain state theory (Gilbert, 1984; in press) certain kinds of stressful situation are viewed as precipitating a largely pre-programmed sequence of physiological and neurochemical reactions. Then, it is assumed, memories of previous experiences of this state become more accessible (state-dependent recall), amplifying these reactions or damping them down.

There is also increasing evidence from studies of adult beliefs and attitudes that cognitive appraisals, particularly explanations and social comparison estimates, are related to many dimensions of social functioning, including interpersonal emotions, helping behaviour, affiliation, and social withdrawal. The clinical evidence is largely correlational at present, but if the causal influence of cognitions can be established there will be important implications for counselling, psychotherapy, and medical practice more generally. First, research is needed into the effects of providing social comparison information to different clinical populations, whether in written form or through the medium of self-help groups. Studies with university students indicate that giving information that one's performance is normative (high consensus) can be effective in improving academic performance and self-esteem, and in reducing self-reported stress (Brewin & Furnham, 1986; Wilson & Linville, 1982). In one of the very few studies to have looked at the effects on social behaviour, Snyder and Ingram (1983) found that high consensus information facilitated help-seeking for a problem.

The presence of attributional discrepancies, such as arise from actor–observer biases, makes it likely that many types of interaction, whether between couples, parents and children, or patients and doctors, may be improved by paying explicit attention to the two partners' explanations for critical events. To give only two examples, research into attributional discrepancies in couples (Fincham, Beach, & Baucom, 1987) indicates that happy couples appear to view each other's behaviour through rose-coloured glasses. They suggest that distressed couples could be helped initially by encouraging them to make at least equally benign attributions for their own and their partner's behaviour. Similarly, a study comparing the causal beliefs held by patients with diabetes and clinical staff working in diabetes clinics (Gamsu & Bradley, 1987) indicates that these two groups differ markedly in their view of who should take the credit for therapeutic success and the blame for therapeutic failure. Follow-up research (Gillespie & Bradley, 1988) has shown that it is possible to overcome these discrepancies by encouraging the doctors to attend to the patients' beliefs and vice versa.

# 10 Therapy

In this final chapter I will review briefly earlier discussions of the major cognitive mechanisms believed to underlie anxiety, depression, low self-esteem, and abnormal behaviour. Then I will address the question of how unwanted feelings and behaviours can be prevented or modified by providing the person with certain kinds of information. One way to do this would be to describe, using their own terminology, the many kinds of therapy that are available. But it has been pointed out (e.g., Goldfried, 1980) that some clinical strategies are common to most therapeutic approaches. For example, most forms of therapy provide patients with new, corrective experiences, offer patients direct feedback, induce in patients the expectation that therapy can be helpful, create a therapeutic relationship in which therapist and patient participate, and provide patients with repeated opportunities to test reality. The ubiquity of these strategies suggests that many of the techniques employed by behaviour therapists, cognitive therapists, and humanistic and psychoanalytic psychotherapists, can be understood in terms of their effects on common mechanisms of information-processing, motivation, and emotion.

The framework I shall use rests on two fundamental contrasts that have already been much discussed. The first is the contrast between situational information and previously acquired knowledge. Many human judgements, including explanations, expectations, and contingency estimates, depend on the integration of these two types of information. It is therefore important to distinguish between novel situations, in which little previously acquired knowledge is applicable and situational information is given the greatest weight, and familiar situations, in which the influence of previous knowledge is much greater. Novelty or familiarity does not here refer to a person's subjective impression, but to the existence of related material in memory, of which the person may or may not be aware. The second contrast is between automatic cognitive processes operating out of awareness and conscious cognitive appraisal. Automatic processes are only likely to exert a systematic influence on behaviour in familiar situations, whereas conscious processes will be important in appraising and responding to situations that are both familiar and novel. It will therefore be convenient to group the theories, empirical findings, and potential therapeutic interventions under three headings: (a) the conscious appraisal of novel situations; (b) the automatic processing of familiar stimuli or situations; (c) the conscious appraisal of familiar situations.

The first group concerns the conscious appraisal of novel, or relatively novel, situations that are potentially threatening in some way. Good examples are the experience of going into hospital for the first time, or the recognition of unusual symptoms, both of which are likely to generate active attempts to understand the present and predict the future. An anxious or depressive reaction to such situations, or a reduction in self-esteem, will depend on the outcome of labelling and causal attribution ("What is the problem and why has it happened?"), and on perceptions of environmental resources and personal coping skills ("How controllable is this problem by medical staff and by myself?"). These aspects of appraisal, along with co-existing goals ("I must get better in order to play in the match on Saturday", or "If I have cancer, I really don't want to know about it"), also determine the decision to take various kinds of action. In the second example, the actions might be visiting a doctor, or learning about preventive care.

An account of the automatic processing of familiar situations would include theoretical structures, such as associative networks, schemata, and internal models, that contain summaries of prior learning. The structures most discussed are those containing fear memories and information about one's treatment at the hands of significant others. In some cases, for example after accidents or natural disasters experienced as an adult, individuals may be able to recall the significant event or events. In other cases individuals behave as though they are afraid of certain types of person or situation even though they have no memory of why this should be so. For many years an explanation of this kind of learning was provided by a fairly simple version of conditioning theory, but more recently interest has been focussed on the way in which events, together with their surrounding circumstances, are represented internally. These internal representations may be limited to fairly specific experiences (particularly traumatic ones) or, in the case of higher-order models of the self and significant others, may summarize experiences extending over a number of years. Through the medium of these representations, events involving fear, pain, loss, rejection, conflict, etc., may come to influence subsequent emotional reactions, behaviour, and conscious appraisals in various maladaptive ways.

The third general heading concerns the conscious appraisal and self-regulation of familiar feelings and behaviour. The effort and persistence with which people deal with recurrent or long-standing relationship problems, unwanted emotional reactions, physical disabilities, low self-esteem, and so on, depend on their causal analysis of the problem, the range of strategies and skills they have available, and on the expectations they hold about the effectiveness of these strategies and about their own ability to carry them out. They also depend on the importance of overcoming the problem, the existence of competing goals, and on the person's ability to motivate themselves by setting appropriate goals and reinforcing themselves for their achievements. Most forms of psychotherapy include procedures for raising patients' expectations and selectively reinforcing certain behaviours or ways of thinking. Although these procedures are not necessarily a central part of the therapeutic rationale, the frequency with which problems of resistance or "lack of motivation" are encountered suggests that they deserve more formal consideration.

## MODIFYING APPRAISAL IN NEW SITUATIONS

The scope for modifying emotional reactions to stressful situations not encountered before is virtually limitless, and in recent years counselling programmes have been set up for rape victims, for the victims of violent crime, for the bereaved, for the unemployed, and for women with an unwanted pregnancy, to name but a few. Underlying these various programmes are a small number of basic principles and procedures. These will be illustrated by considering the techniques employed in a situation that is potentially very threatening: psychological preparation for surgery.

Hospitalization for surgery is associated with increased levels of anxiety, and the greater the degree of pre-operative anxiety, the more likely the patient is to be distressed and in pain post-operatively. Much of this anxiety stems from common worries about pain and losing consciousness, but high levels of anxiety are associated with idiosyncratic worries that nurses are unlikely to identify accurately (Johnston, 1986). Interventions have therefore been designed to provide patients with reassurance, information, and advice about coping, through the medium of booklets, personal counselling, or films. Information about medical and surgical procedures is thought to be beneficial so that patients do not fear the worst when they wake up to find an intravenous drip in their arm. Alternatively, patients may be informed about the sensations they are likely to experience, such as a dry mouth or a burning pain along the incision. The latter type of information has generally been found to be more effective in reducing post-operative distress and enhancing recovery (e.g., Johnson et al., 1978).

Reassurance and information presumably act by providing consensus data about what should be considered normal, and by labelling procedures and experiences in a relatively non-threatening way. It should also be possible to increase patients' expectancies about coping with pain and distress by teaching them specific behavioural or cognitive strategies. Langer, Janis, and Wolfer (1975) asked a heterogeneous group of patients admitted for major and minor surgery to identify specific worries, and then encouraged them to counter these worries by questioning their factual basis and selectively attending to the positive aspects of going into hospital. These instructions were significantly more effective than information alone in reducing both distress and the use of pain-relieving and sedative drugs. More recently Ridgeway and Mathews (1982) randomly assigned women due for hysterectomy to one of three types of preparation: information about the surgery and its effects; training in the use of a cognitive coping method (involving increased emphasis on the positive and the minimization of anxiety); and general information about the ward. Patients receiving information about the surgery did end up knowing significantly more than the other groups but, as was found by Langer et al., the cognitive coping procedure was followed by the fewest days of pain and the least use of pain-relieving drugs.

This evidence suggests that modifying the cognitive appraisal of medical and surgical procedures can be of substantial benefit. The specific mechanisms responsible for the improved outcomes have not yet been established, however, and it would probably be unwise to make too many generalizations about such a heterogeneous set of situations. Hospitalizations vary considerably in the painfulness and the embarrassment of the procedures to be employed, in the likelihood that the patient will have been able to compare notes with other sufferers, in the ease with which the patient's sensations can be predicted, and in the scope for the patient to influence the amount of discomfort and the speed of recovery. The particular conditions would have to be very carefully analyzed before convincing tests could be made of the relative importance of consensus information, relabelling, reattribution, increasing expectancies, and other specific cognitive changes.

# MODIFYING SCHEMATIC KNOWLEDGE

## Uncovering Schemas and Rules

Several ways of inferring the content of nonconscious schemas and rules have already been mentioned. In very obvious cases, as we saw with the Manchester Airport disaster victims and with soldiers fresh off the battlefield, there are repeated thoughts and images that intrude into waking life and sometimes into dreams. The acutely depressed person often has repeated thoughts about their own worthlessness and about the hopelessness of their situation. Cognitive distortions may be evident, in which the person blames themselves for something that is not their fault, magnifies small setbacks into major disasters, and selectively focuses on what has gone wrong during the previous week or on the negative aspects of every situation. Schematic knowledge may also be inferred from the behaviour patterns of the phobic or obsessional patient. In these examples, the hypothesized schemas influence behaviour or the contents of consciousness in ways that are usually fairly evident to an outsider. They may, however, contain important additional information that is not currently available to conscious introspection.

In their work on depression, Beck et al. (1979) describe such schematic knowledge in the form of "depressogenic assumptions". As examples they give: "In order to be happy I have to be successful in whatever I undertake"; "To be happy, I must be accepted by all people at all times"; and "My value as a person depends on what others think of me". These are of course convenient verbal labels for knowledge that is in reality abstract and impalpable. Hypotheses about these assumptions are derived from general themes in the patient's automatic thoughts and in their other statements. For example, the patient may comment that a friend is unhappy because she has become too attached to her boyfriend. If this theme of attachment being linked to unhappiness appears in several different contexts, the therapist may draw the inference that it corresponds to schematic knowledge, whether or not the patient consciously holds to this belief. Similarly, a sequence of upsetting thoughts such as "My work is of poor quality", "I can't fix the bicycle", "I can't cut the grass", "I can't make a sale", and "The wallpaper wasn't lined up well enough" imply, Beck et al. suggest, underlying assumptions of the form "If I am not accomplishing anything, I am a loser" and "If I make a mistake, I am inept".

Schematic knowledge can also be inferred from observation of the conditions in which inappropriate feelings or behaviour occur. In psychoanalytic psychotherapy a major diagnostic tool is the transference, or reactions that the patient displays towards the therapist. Classically therapists are supposed to function as a "blank screen", giving away as little as possible about their own attitudes and personal characteristics in order that the patient's reactions be easier to interpret. Feelings such as anger, dependency, and rejection, provoked for example by the therapist going on holiday or having to cancel a session, provide clues about the patient's past experiences and current expectations. Evidence for similar reactions can be sought in the patient's other relationships in order to confirm or deny the hypothesis of a particular underlying belief or emotion. Other techniques include the use of projective tests such as the Rorschach or Thematic Apperception Test (TAT), and the analysis of resistance. The observation that a thought or suggestion is angrily rejected, or is followed by a disengagement from therapy, may signal that it plays an important part in underlying knowledge structures.

Another constant theme has been that in psychopathology cognition and affect are closely interlinked. Schematic knowledge includes a record of the specific emotional response—or the expressive-motor mechanism, to use Leventhal's (1984) terms—as well as a record of the environmental conditions associated with the occurrence of that response. Although it might be thought that people would know consciously when they were experiencing an emotion, and what emotion it was, this appears to be by no means always the case. One reason that has already been mentioned is that people acquire "feeling rules" that indicate when certain emotions are appropriate, and what emotions are acceptable. These feeling rules are sometimes at variance with their actual emotional responses. In some cases emotions the patient cannot consciously report may "leak" through non-verbal cues such as posture, gestures, and "micro-expressions", or through paralinguistic cues such as tone of voice. A short involuntary laugh accompanying a statement may indicate the presence of a concealed emotion such as anger (Greenberg & Safran, 1987).

One implication of the mood and memory experiments reviewed earlier is that, without the appropriate affect, the patient may find it hard to recall the thoughts and experiences that contributed to the development of important emotional schemata and that continue to reflect its contents. Although patients may spontaneously experience cathartic emotional releases in which related material is recalled, it may be necessary to help them access these emotions. A number of techniques may help, such as keeping patients focussed on their internal states, getting them to increase their respiration rate, having them shout or hit soft objects, role-playing feared situations, etc. The aim is not just to identify or express hidden feelings, although this may bring considerable relief in the short-term, but to reveal the content of emotional schemata so that these may be consciously appraised and modified.

Greenberg and Safran (1987) suggest that in addition it may be helpful to classify affective reactions into primary emotions, secondary reactive emotions, and instrumental emotions. Primary emotions such as anger, sadness, and fear are not long-lasting but are of adaptive significance, occurring in well-defined situations. Many humanistic and psychoanalytic psychotherapists believe that such emotions are typically unacknowledged or warded off by patients, and that one of the aims of therapy is to help them "get in touch" with these emotions. In contrast, secondary emotions such as despair, hopelessness, and anxiety are the product of learning experiences. They are frequently long-lasting, fully available to consciousness, and may be reactions to primary emotions. Aggression, for example, may be a way of warding off a primary experience of sadness. Behavioural and cognitive–behavioural therapies often attempt to reduce or eliminate secondary emotions by demonstrating that they are inappropriate, whereas humanistic and psychoanalytic approaches might attempt to locate an underlying primary emotion. Finally, instrumental emotions are responses that have been learned as ways of manipulating the environment. The "payoff" may be getting attention or sympathy, influencing others in desired ways, or avoiding responsibility. Clinical improvement may follow from making patients aware of the function of these emotions, and by encouraging them to explore different ways of attaining their goals.

In summary it must be said that uncovering the nature of patients' schemas and rules is often an extremely difficult process that requires great caution and tentativeness. Limitations on self-reports mean that attention must be paid to regularities in behaviour and speech, contexts in which inappropriate feelings and behaviour occur, and indirect cues to underlying emotional states. Guidano and Liotti (1983) suggest that clues to patients' tacit self-identity are usually to be found in sentences containing the five verbs to be, to have to, to be able to, to need, and to be worth. Single observations of this kind, like particular transference interpretations, emotional "leakage", and the results of projective tests, must be regarded as of dubious reliability, and judgement suspended until a consistent pattern begins to emerge that enables predictions about future behaviour to be made. A final caveat concerns the necessity for therapists to represent schematic knowledge to themselves in the form of verbal propositions. Therapists should not lose sight of the fact that these propositions are convenient simplifications that are unlikely to correspond to the way in which knowledge is actually represented internally, and that may themselves be a source of distortion.

## Exposure Treatments for Anxiety

Many therapeutic approaches contain the idea that psychopathology results from avoidance, whether of distressing thoughts, unacceptable feelings, or fear-eliciting situations, and they have developed procedures for exposing patients to the very things they are attempting to avoid.

Exposure is particularly associated with the modification of anxiety by behaviour therapists, who have devized techniques such as desensitization and flooding to ensure that patients expose themselves to their feared situation for sufficient periods of time. Whereas early behaviour therapists exposed patients to feared stimuli in their imagination only, it is now accepted that real-life or *in vivo* exposure is generally more effective (Marks, 1987). As discussed in Chapters 3 and 4, explanations for therapeutic improvement were originally couched in terms of a counter-conditioning process, but more recently favoured are explanations that talk about the modification of memory structures (Lang, 1977, 1979).

Foa and Kozak (1986) proposed that in therapy fear is reduced by the activation of the relevant memory structure and by the incorporation into it of incompatible information (see Chapter 4). Activation is inferred from physiological reactions (such as increased heart rate or electrodermal responsivity) to initial presentation of the feared stimulus. In their view the major type of incompatible information that is incorporated into the existing memory structure is provided by the habituation that takes place to the feared object within an exposure session. In addition to weakening the links between stimulus and response elements, so that presentation of the stimulus no longer produces such a marked physiological response, Foa and Kozak see exposure as altering representations of the severity and probability of harm associated with the stimulus. This is brought about by the experience of longer-term habituation over several exposure sessions as well as by short-term, within-session habituation.

It is important to note that exposure is not simply a matter of being in the presence of the feared object. Activation of the memory structure may not occur if the stimulus presented is too dissimilar to the memorial representation, or if the patient is not attending to the stimulus. Some patients may attempt to distract themselves by concentrating on non-feared aspects of the stimulus, or by imagining that they are really somewhere else. Experimental manipulations employing other methods of cognitive avoidance have shown that exposure to a feared object is less effective when patients are distracted by playing a video game or reading magazines than when they are encouraged to think actively about their experience (Grayson, Foa, & Steketee, 1982; Sartory, Rachman, & Grey 1982). Similarly, exposure will be ineffective when incompatible information is not generated, for example when no within-session habituation takes place because the period of exposure is too short. In this particular case the information would be compatible with that in memory and the fear structure would be expected to be strengthened.

Foa and Kozak's model places heavy emphasis on the information obtained from people's observation of their own behaviour and physiological reactions. Mineka's experiments on the social transmission of fear (described in Chapter 3) indicate that fear structures can in certain circumstances be altered by information derived from observing others in fear-eliciting situations. Also in Chapter 3 are reports of verbal instructions altering people's conditioned responses to mild aversive stimuli in the laboratory. However, clinical experience indicates that simple verbal instructions are not very effective at modifying well-established fears. One reason is that they may be contradicted by interoceptive information indicating enhanced physiological responding. Techniques such as hypnosis that dampen physiological responding are sometimes employed to enhance the impact of verbal messages, so that the patient can actively imagine being in the feared situation without a corresponding increase in arousal.

## Modifying the Self-schema

In depression, a more generalized mood disturbance, there is rarely such a simple one-to-one correspondence between a behaviour (avoidance) and an underlying situation-specific memory. Instead, the content of patients' maladaptive schemata is more complex and typically involves knowledge or beliefs about the relation between self and others. This knowledge can be brought to bear on the interpretation of many apparently quite different situations, although there are likely to be identifiable themes that link them together. As indicated above, a great deal of questioning and observation may be necessary to reveal the specific cognitions that are responsible. Once negative automatic thoughts and some initial depressogenic assumptions have been identified, cognitive therapy proceeds by distancing patients from their cognitions and getting them to test the reality of each one. This can be done within the therapy session by querying the evidence on which each thought is based, by generating alternative possibilities, and by rating the likelihood of each one.

For example, I questioned a depressed patient, who was convinced that she was unattractive and that none of her colleagues liked her, on why she held this belief. Her evidence was that they rarely spoke to her or smiled at her. However, she also admitted that she was extremely shy and reclusive, and would never take the initiative in making social advances, preferring to stay alone in her room. We explored the alternative explanation that her colleagues' lack of interest was related to her failure to emit the appropriate signals, and she agreed to test this hypothesis by smiling at certain people when she arrived at work in the morning. Rather to her surprise, her colleagues responded by smiling back, forcing some revision of her views. One event that produced negative automatic thoughts was when she knocked on a colleague's door but received no answer, even though she knew her colleague was in the room. The immediate explanation that came to mind was that this person did not like her and was trying to avoid her. This thought was so compelling that only in the therapy session did alternative explanations occur to her, for example that her colleague might have been on the telephone and had not heard her knock. In this example, it is reasonable to speculate that past experience had led to the development of a self-schema in which she was unattractive or unlovable. This schematic knowledge influenced her interpretation of other people's current behaviour, with the result that alternative, less damaging explanations did not come spontaneously to mind. Rather, her experience appeared to confirm her worst fears.

This example illustrates also how the self-evident quality of depressive thoughts can make it difficult for the patient to question them. Beck et al. (1979, p.255) cite the case of a man who was depressed, anxious, chronically irritable, and had difficulty asserting himself with his wife:

> He was asked what would happen if he told his wife about his unhappiness with the way she treated him. He said his wife would become angry and would threaten to leave him. He believed, 'If you want people to like you, you should always be nice to them'. 'If you find fault, they will punish you'. And further, he believed this rule applied at all times and in all situations.

This patient was given a series of graded task assignments that ran counter to these beliefs, learning how to confront his wife on first minor and then more major issues. By this reality testing he was able to prove that his fear of being left by his wife was unfounded, and that it was possible to express his own wishes without jeopardizing their relationship.

There have also been attempts to modify the self-schema by changing consistent patterns of causal beliefs about the self. Layden (1982) obtained information about the habitual attributional styles of low self-esteem and depressed college students from questionnaires and from programmed successes and failures on a number of tests of intellectual and social skills. She then discussed with each individual their tendency to internalize failure or externalize success, and the importance of accurate attribution. The therapy task was to keep a daily diary of successes and failures, examining each event thoroughly to see if there were internal causes for the successes and external causes for the failures. Subjects were not to make up causes, but to look for real, possible causes they normally missed. In other words, they were to try to acquire a healthier attributional style, by learning to analyze and re-evaluate everyday situations. Layden noted several reactions in her subjects that are consistent with the theoretical link between the self-schema, attributions, and self-esteem (1982, p.76):

> The responses individuals had to information about their attributional style and to the task they were to do were often dramatic. Some persons cried with

relief. One said to me that she had never been told that it was acceptable to like herself, to think she brought about successes. Some quoted parents or other authority sources to the effect that one should always feel responsible for all failures encountered to gain humility. Others were glad to be 'ordered' to do the task that they would have liked to do but felt uncomfortable giving themselves permission to do.

Layden's results indicated that, relative to a control group, subjects receiving attribution retraining over a four to five week period changed their attributions in the predicted directions and showed an increase in self-esteem. To the extent that attributional style changed, levels of self-reported depression also improved. Other investigators have subsequently confirmed that this method of supplying causes for everyday events can lead to changes in attributional style (Sober-Ain & Kidd, 1984).

One frequently mentioned rationale for cognitive therapy is that it deals explicitly with any tendency patients may have to discount or overlook successful experiences. As was noted in Chapters 4 and 5, the depressed are just as likely, if not more likely, to show biased processing of positive events and outcomes as they are to to show biased processing of negative outcomes. This may make it more difficult for them to incorporate the positive information provided by therapeutic assignments into their self-schemas. In addition to attributional style training, other techniques have been proposed to facilitate the processing of success experiences. Gold-fried and Robins (1982) suggest that patients should be constantly encouraged to compare present achievements with past performance, to weigh up their achievements in a deliberate fashion rather than make snap judgements about them, and to retrieve instances of past success. All these techniques are reminiscent of the need to avoid patients distracting themselves while being exposed to their feared situation. In both cases there is the suggestion that if incompatible information is to be incorporated into the relevant memory structure it must be held for a considerable time in focal attention.

Cognitive therapy for depression (Beck et al., 1979; Williams, 1984) includes many more specific behavioural and cognitive techniques that are targeted at specific symptoms in a highly structured way, but its essence lies in the uncovering and challenging of depressogenic thoughts and assumptions. Rather than being an exercise in simple verbal persuasion, it is a sophisticated and flexible procedure that does try and present the patient with new and incompatible information. This is achieved by a novel formulation of the problem ("Specific negative thoughts are making you feel worse"), by identifying cognitive patterns that summarize patients' experiences in ways they had not previously considered, and by presenting patients with hitherto unconsidered alternative strategies. To this extent the information is presented in verbal form. But by disrupting habitual patterns of automatic information processing it is hoped that the patient will be more able to incorporate incompatible information from everyday experiences. In addition there is the benefit to be gained from actively testing out assumptions. As Beck et al. (1979, p.644) state, "Acting against an assumption is the most powerful way to change it". The modification of the self-schema, like the modification of a fear memory, is probably best achieved by observations of one's own actions and of their consequences.

Many psychoanalytic writers have come to a similar conclusion, particularly with respect to the patient's difficulties in human relationships. The therapeutic relationship is often considered to provide the patient with a "corrective emotional experience", which is described by Alexander and French (1946, p.338) in the following terms:

> ... reexperiencing the old, unsettled conflict *but with a new ending* is the secret of every penetrating therapeutic result. Only the actual experience of a new solution in the transference situation or in his everyday life gives the patient the conviction that a new solution is *possible* and induces him to give up the old neurotic patterns.

This description clearly contains a reference to accessing disturbing memories, providing incompatible information, and raising expectations. Patients who come to therapy expecting to be dictated to or browbeaten, to be criticized for thoughts and feelings of which they are ashamed, or to be rejected unless they are "good", discover that their fears are not realized.

The essence of psychoanalytic psychotherapy has been summarized by Malan (1979). Symptoms are considered to represent a defence against mental pain or unacceptable hidden feelings such as anger towards a loved parent. The defence is necessary because of anxiety about the consequences of expressing these hidden feelings. The aim is to bring patients back in touch with these feelings by interpreting the links between their past experiences with parents, their current experiences with other people, and their behaviour towards the therapist. It is certainly possible to see this process in terms of accessing and altering emotional memories of which the patient is not aware but which are influencing their day-to-day behaviour. Where psychoanalytic theory chiefly differs from contemporary cognitive models is in its emphasis on defensive processes that keep certain material out of consciousness, and in its theories about the nature of that material. As stated earlier, there would appear to be other explanations that could account for many of the instances of emotional material being inaccessible. But this is not an issue to which cognitive therapists have properly addressed themselves.

## ENHANCING SELF-REGULATION

Even though the therapist may be clear about the kind of experiences that would be of benefit to the patient, it may be difficult to persuade the patient to undergo them initially and subsequently to continue behaving in the appropriate way. All depends on patients' willingness to disclose embarrassing or shameful facts to a stranger, to expose themselves to demanding situations or to upsetting thoughts, and to experiment with new coping strategies. They may well prefer to resist the therapist's suggestions or to drop out of therapy altogether rather than admit they find their therapeutic assignment has become too difficult or too onerous. This is not only true of anxiety and depression, but occurs in the treatment (or self-treatment) of addictions. Initial progress at losing weight or cutting down on cigarettes is frequently followed by a relapse. It is therefore of great importance to have a model of therapy with a motivational component.

The expectancy/value model of motivation put forward in this book is helpful in understanding the processes that make up many quite different types of psychological treatment. Chapter 8 described some approaches that have been used to increase the value of therapeutic targets by means of self-reinforcement, and to identify goals that might be in conflict with the aim of eliminating symptoms and unwanted behaviours. In addition, psychoanalytic approaches have been very concerned with the existence of competing or conflicting goals. Their assumptions have been nicely summed up by Wachtel (1982, p. xix):

> It is in the very nature of most psychological problems that the patient is hampered from doing what must be done to make things better. The very problems the patient comes to therapy to try to solve make it difficult for him to cooperate in their solution. This dilemma is the heart of the concept of resistance. The concept refers not to any willful malevolence or opposition on the patient's part but instead to the difficulties inherent in attempting to encounter and master feelings and experiences that have previously seemed so overwhelming they must be avoided and denied at all costs.

Whereas psychoanalytic psychotherapy is particularly concerned with the bringing of conflicting goals into conscious awareness, and makes little direct attempt to alter expectations, most behavioural and cognitive-behavioural therapies go to considerable lengths to increase expectations of improvement. When behaviour therapies were first being developed, this was not part of their theoretical rationale. Nevertheless, the procedures used seem certain to have had this effect. For example, a *functional analysis* of a patient's symptoms attempts to identify their consequences and the antecedent conditions, typically showing that the symptoms fluctuate in intensity over time and occur in some situations but not in others. In attribution theory terms, this is drawing patients' attention to low consistency and high distinctiveness information of which they may not previously have been fully aware. This pattern, particularly if combined with a reference to the frequency of the problem (high consensus information), would tend to encourage attributions to more external, unstable and specific factors, thereby increasing expectations of improvement. Expectations of being able to carry out the therapeutic task are addressed even more directly by the use of *graded hierarchies*, the technique of breaking down a task into small, manageable steps. In addition there is an explicit emphasis on encouragement and support from the therapist, who will often express confidence in the technique or in the patient's capacity to perform well.

Several cognitive therapy procedures have been developed to enhance self-regulation, including self-instructional training, stress-inoculation training, problem-solving training, and attribution training. Meichenbaum (1977) has drawn attention to the way in which behaviour is controlled at least partially by conscious thought, which he termed internal dialogue or inner speech. In his view one of the main aims of therapy is to alter what patients say to themselves when they experience obstacles or behave in undesired ways. Negative or task-irrelevant appraisals must be replaced by more adaptive self-talk specifying what the person's immediate goals are, what difficulties are likely to be encountered, and what action should be taken. These self-instructions help both to direct the patient's coping responses and, by challenging habitual ways of perceiving the world, to alter underlying cognitive structures in memory.

Self-instructions, based on such constructs as appraisal, expectancy, attribution, and self-perception, were explicitly incorporated by Meichenbaum into a procedure he called stress-inoculation training. Changing inner speech was accomplished by first making patients aware of anxiety-provoking or defeatist self-statements and then training them to counter these with adaptive self-statements. For example, in preparing for a stressor the patient might be told to say the following to themselves "Just think what you can do about it. That's better than getting anxious" or "Don't worry: worry won't help anything". Later, in actually confronting the stressor, the patient might be taught to say "One step at a time: you can handle the situation" or "Relax; you're in control. Take a slow deep breath." A patient concerned with being overwhelmed by fear might instruct themselves to "Label your fear from 0 to 10 and watch it change" or "Don't try to eliminate fear totally; just keep it manageable." And following the encounter the patient might say "It's getting better each time you use the procedures." The patient would be encouraged to practise using these self-instructions in a variety of different stressful situations, in the hope that they would then generalize.

Stress-inoculation training has been applied to a variety of conditions including anger and pain control. It is viewed as a way of acquiring a coping skill that can then be deliberately applied, as well as an experience that can alter learned associations or emotional memories. This emphasis on teaching self-regulatory skills is also part of problem-solving training (D'Zurilla & Goldfried, 1971; Goldfried & Goldfried, 1980). Problem-solving training involves at least five steps, the first of which is to orient people appropriately to their problem. They must recognize that a problem exists, assume that a solution is possible, and inhibit the temptation to act impulsively. The problem must then be formulated in a useful way, which often means making it more concrete. For example, rather than defining the problem as having a disobedient child it might be more helpful to define it as having a child who left his room untidy and was late for meals. The next step is to defer judgement about the right solution, and instead to generate as many alternative solutions as possible. The advantages and disadvantages of these alternatives are then weighed up and the most promising solution adopted. Finally, the correctness of the solution is verified in the light of results, with a repetition of the whole process if the outcome has not been satisfactory. Problem-solving approaches have proved to be useful in dealing with such diverse issues as marital and family conflict, with preventing relapse among heroin addicts, and with preparing long-stay psychiatric patients about to be discharged from hospital into the community.

Most behavioural and cognitive-behavioural interventions consist of a complex set of procedures, so that it is difficult to know which element is responsible for their success or failure. In contrast, attribution training approaches have focussed specifically on the effects of modifying causal beliefs in one single direction. Perhaps for this reason, with the exception of the few studies aimed at modifying the self-schema, they have mainly confined themselves to improving various aspects of academic and intellectual achievement. In a pioneering study, Dweck (1975) undertook the retraining of children who had extreme reactions to failure and easily became helpless in the classroom. These children took less personal responsibility for the outcomes of their behaviour and tended to place relatively little emphasis on the role of effort in determining success and failure. Dweck provided them with a series of problems into which she had pre-programmed a number of failures. Whenever a child failed, he or she was explicitly told that this was because they should have tried harder. As predicted, this reattribution of failure to an unstable and controllable cause led to increased persistence and enhanced performance. Theoretically, this effect should have been mediated by an increase in expectations of a successful outcome.

Försterling (1985) has reviewed fifteen subsequent studies that aimed to improve reading, arithmetic, general academic performance, and performance on a variety of more specific tasks, mainly by getting subjects to reattribute failure to lack of effort. A variety of techniques have been used, including an operant approach with positive reinforcement of effort attributions, explicit mention or modelling by an experimenter of effort attributions, and the provision of antecedent or "pre-attributional" information. In spite of the fact that the subjects were mainly selected for their poor levels of performance or low levels of achievement motivation, all bar one of the fifteen studies reviewed by Försterling reported very promising results, producing changes in self-report measures and in measures of persistence and performance. In one of the studies to encourage unstable (but not effort) attributions for failure, Wilson and Linville (1982) were able to improve long-term academic performance and improve drop-out rates by simply giving freshman college students two types of information. First, they were told that grades tended to be low at first but improved in later years (information about low consistency); and secondly they were shown videotaped interviews with older students reporting improvement in their grades (information about high consensus). Most studies, however, relied on a number of structured sessions in which subjects worked on a task and were instructed how to explain the occurrence of success and failure.

The processes involved in self-regulation may become clearer if we examine the conditions under which people fail to carry out their plans. A recent review (Kirschenbaum, 1987) of relapse and self-regulatory failure indicates that this often occurs in the context of social stress, social pressures (e.g., to join in the consumption of alcohol or drugs), physiological pressures such as cravings, and the first failure to meet therapeutic targets. Whatever the trigger, a subsequent relapse is associated with depressogenic cognitions, negative emotions such as guilt and hopelessness, and the discontinuation of self-monitoring. Kirschenbaum argues that some form of systematic attention to the self-regulated target behaviour must be sustained to avoid self-regulatory failure. This will not be possible when individuals are actively brooding on their mistakes and deficiencies, a process also implicated in the maintenance of depression by Lewinsohn et al. (1985). Cognitive–behavioural interventions may help to cut down the risk of relapse by providing explicit attributions or other self-statements to counter the depressogenic cognitions, and by specifying a series of simple steps or procedures to which people can switch their attention in case of failure.

## EFFICACY OF COGNITIVE THERAPY

A number of controlled studies of "cognitive" therapies have now been carried out. As will be clear from reading this chapter, however, to call a therapy "cognitive" may be misleading unless the specific mechanism of change targeted by the therapy is identified. Most so-called "cognitive therapies" employ a mixture of verbal persuasion and encouragement, behavioural task assignments, and attempts to identify and change habitual thinking patterns. Some of these components may be aimed at altering conscious appraisals and others at altering underlying schematic knowledge. So-called behavioural treatments, on the other hand, typically involve giving patients an explicit rationale and a certain amount of encouragement, before embarking on task assignments such as graded exposure. From a cognitive point of view, these components would also be expected to alter cognitive appraisal and underlying schematic knowledge. In other words, there is invariably a high degree of overlap between the two approaches. The main difference is that so-called cognitive therapies typically spend longer eliciting patients' beliefs, challenging them, and providing an alternative explanatory framework before embarking on behavioural assignments.

Marks (1987) examined thirty-three studies that compared "behavioural" and "cognitive" treatments for phobias and obsessional–compulsive disorders. The behavioural treatments relied mainly on therapist-aided exposure or self-exposure, whereas the cognitive treatments explicitly challenged patients' beliefs and assumptions or encouraged them to use self-instructions, with or without the addition of an exposure component. On the whole, with the possible exception of social anxiety treatments, the extra "cognitive" procedures added little to the effectiveness of exposure alone. What can we conclude from this review? First, the results do not tell us whether exposure works by modifying schematic knowledge or by some other mechanism. They do tell us that the cognitive procedures were largely redundant, but we still do not know whether this means that altering conscious appraisals is an unnecessary part of therapy. One reason is that the behavioural treatments may have contained a convincing rationale that altered these appraisals as effectively as the more formal cognitive procedures. The second is that patients who agree to take part in and successfully complete therapy trials may be those who find the therapeutic rationale convincing in the first place. It is conceivable that the cognitive procedures would be of particular use with a reluctant or sceptical patient who would not normally volunteer for such a trial or who would only participate in a half-hearted manner.

The efficacy of Beck's cognitive treatment for depression, compared with existing treatments such as tricyclic anti-depressant medication, has been reviewed by Teasdale (1986). In the five outcome studies carried out cognitive therapy was as effective or more effective than pharmacotherapy in all cases. There was also some evidence that cognitive therapy had a prophylactic effect, reducing the likelihood of relapse. These outcome studies did not include an attention placebo condition to control for the greater amount of professional contact received by the cognitive therapy groups. Nevertheless, independent evidence indicates that highly structured interventions such as cognitive therapy are more effective in the treatment of depression than relaxation or less focussed psychological treatment. These findings offer encouraging evidence for the value of cognitive therapy, but as yet little is known about which components of this complex package are the effective ones, and which cognitive mechanisms are mediating change.

## CONCLUSIONS

In this chapter I have summarized a wide variety of therapeutic procedures in terms of their effects on a small number of cognitive mechanisms. It is important to remember that these mechanisms are hypothetical ones, and stand or fall on their ability to account for clinical and laboratory findings in an economical and internally consistent way. I do not wish to claim that these are the only mechanisms that mediate clinical change, but I do suggest that they are important ones and worthy of further study. The concept of an emotional memory that is partly or completely inaccessible to consciousness, whether in the form of an association, a schema, or a mental model, appears essential to understand the intense emotional reactions, and the concurrent avoidance behaviour, that occur in a small number of well-defined situations. Good progress has been made in identifying the characteristics of the emotional memories and self-schemas associated with depression, and similar attempts are now being made to characterize the schematic knowledge of people with agoraphobia, obsessional–compulsive disorder, and anorexia (Guidano & Liotti, 1983). Different therapeutic approaches are broadly in agreement in emphasizing the importance of activating the emotional memories, bringing their contents fully into consciousness, and getting the patient to attend fully to information or to an experience that is incompatible with the memory.

Similarly, many forms of therapy rely on modifying the patient's conscious appraisal of threatening situations. This is used to reduce the intensity of emotional reactions to life crises of all kinds, although the specific cognitive mechanisms are likely to vary quite widely. For example, surgical patients may benefit most from information that enhances predictability and control, whereas the victims of disasters or personal assaults may need information about the experiences and reactions of others in a similar situation. Modifying conscious appraisal is also important for therapies that depend on the patient's preparedness to experiment actively with new coping strategies rather than simply providing incompatible information within a therapeutic session. Because this approach depends on the patient's capacity for deliberate self-regulation, they often include procedures for enhancing motivation. These procedures typically involve the use of reinforcement, the elimination of competing goals, the raising of the expectancy of success, and the mental rehearsal of adaptive thoughts and coping strategies. Particular attention is being increasingly paid to strategies for dealing with the emotional and attentional consequences of setbacks and disappointments.

Most forms of behavioural and cognitive–behavioural therapy attempt to influence both conscious and nonconscious cognitive systems. For example, Beck's cognitive therapy of depression has the initial aim, providing the depression is not too severe, of getting the patient to identify, evaluate, and consciously argue against negative automatic thoughts. At a later stage a combination of behavioural assignments and rational argument is used to modify underlying depressogenic assumptions. Other therapies, such as stress inoculation training (Meichenbaum, 1977), systematic rational restructuring (Goldfried et al., 1974), and anxiety management (Suinn & Richardson, 1971), contain a self-talk component in which patients deliberately try to counter anxiety-provoking cognitions and rehearse their coping strategies, as well as a behavioural component in which feedback from their own performance provides information incompatible with that in memory. A better theoretical understanding of these two elements of therapy, and of their interaction, would lead to an enormous advance in the effectiveness of psychological treatments.

# References

Abramson, L.Y. & Alloy, L.B. (1980). Judgment of contingency: Errors and their implications. In A.Baum & J.E.Singer (Eds.), *Advances in environmental psychology. Vol. 2. Applications of personal control*. Hillsdale, N.J.: Lawrence Erlbaum Associates Inc.

Abramson, L.Y., Seligman, M.E.P., & Teasdale, J.D. (1978). Learned helplessness in humans: Critique and reformulation. *Journal of Abnormal Psychology, 87*, 49–74.

Alexander, F. & French, T.M. (1946). *Psychoanalytic therapy*. New York: Ronald Press.

Alloy, L.B. & Abramson, L.Y. (1979). Judgments of contingency in depressed and nondepressed students: Sadder but wiser? *Journal of Experimental Psychology: General, 108*, 441–485.

Alloy, L.B. & Abramson, L.Y. (1982). Learned helplessness, depression, and the illusion of control. *Journal of Personality and Social Psychology, 42*, 1114–1126.

Alloy, L.B. Abramson, L.Y., Metalsky, G.I., & Hartlage, S. (1988). The hopelessness theory of depression: Attributional aspects. *British Journal of Clinical Psychology, 27*, 3–18.

Alloy, L.B. & Ahrens, A.H. (1987). Depression and pessimism for the future: Biased use of statistically relevant information in predictions for self versus others. *Journal of Personality and Social Psychology, 52*, 366–378.

Alloy, L.B. & Tabachnik, N. (1984). Assessment of covariation by humans and animals: The joint influence of prior expectations and current situational information. *Psychological Review, 91*, 112–149.

American Psychiatric Association (1980). *Diagnostic and statistical manual of mental disorders* (3rd Edition), Washington, D.C.: APA.

Anderson, C.A. (1983). Motivational and performance deficits in interpersonal settings: The effect of attributional style. *Journal of Personality and Social Psychology, 45*, 1136–1147.

Anderson, C.A., Horowitz, L.M., & French, R. (1983). Attributional style of lonely and depressed people. *Journal of Personality and Social Psychology, 45*, 127–136.

Anderson, J.R. & Bower, G.H. (1974). A propositional theory of recognition memory. *Memory and Cognition, 2*, 406–412.

Antaki, C. (1985). Ordinary explanation in conversation: Causal structures and their defence. *European Journal of Social Psychology, 15,* 213–230.

Antaki, C. & Brewin, C.R. (Eds.) (1982). *Attributions and psychological change: Applications of attributional theories to clinical and educational practice.* London: Academic Press.

Archibald, W.P. (1974). Alternative explanations for self-fulfilling prophecy. *Psychological Bulletin, 81,* 74–84.

Atkinson, J.W. (1966). Motivational determinants of risk-taking behavior. In J.W.Atkinson & N.T.Feather (Eds.), *A theory of achievement motivation.* New York: Wiley.

Bandura, A. (Ed.) (1971). *Psychological modeling: Conflicting theories.* Chicago: Aldine-Atherton.

Bandura, A. (1977a). *Social learning theory.* Englewood Cliffs, N.J.: Prentice-Hall.

Bandura, A. (1977b). Self-efficacy: Toward a unifying theory of behavioral change. *Psychological Review, 84,* 191–215.

Bandura, A. (1982). The self and mechanisms of agency. In J.Suls (Ed.), *Psychological perspectives on the self. Vol. 1.* Hillsdale, N.J.: Lawrence Erlbaum Associates Inc.

Bandura, A. & Cervone, D. (1983). Self-evaluative and self-efficacy mechanisms governing the motivational effects of goal systems. *Journal of Personality and Social Psychology, 45,* 1017–1028.

Bandura, A. & Schunk, D.H. (1981). Cultivating competence, self-efficacy, and intrinsic interest through proximal self-motivation. *Journal of Personality and Social Psychology, 41,* 586–598.

Bandura, A. & Simon, K.M. (1977). The role of proximal intentions in self-regulation of refractory behaviour. *Cognitive Therapy and Research, 1,* 177–193.

Bannister, D. & Fransella, F. (1971). *Inquiring man: The theory of personal constructs.* Harmondsworth: Penguin.

Bargh, J.A. (1982). Attention and automaticity in the processing of self-relevant information. *Journal of Personality and Social Psychology, 43,* 425–436.

Beck, A.T. (1967). *Depression: Clinical, experimental, and theoretical aspects.* New York: Hoeber.

Beck, A.T. (1983). Cognitive therapy of depression: New perspectives. In P.J. Clayton & J.E. Barrett (Eds.), *Treatment of depression: Old controversies and new approaches.* New York: Raven Press.

Beck, A.T. & Emery, G. (1985). *Anxiety disorders and phobias: A cognitive perspective.* New York: Basic Books.

Beck, A.T., Rush, A.J., Shaw, B.F., & Emery, G. (1979). *Cognitive therapy of depression.* New York: Wiley.

Becker, M.H. & Maiman, L.A. (1975). Sociobehavioral determinants of compliance with health and medical care recommendations. *Medical Care, 13,* 10–24.

Berkman, L.F. & Syme, S.L. (1979). Social networks, host resistance, and mortality: A nine-year follow-up study of Alameda County residents. *American Journal of Epidemiology, 109,* 186–204.

Berry, D.C. & Broadbent, D.E. (1984). On the relationship between task performance and associated verbalizable knowledge. *Quarterly Journal of Experimental Psychology, 36A,* 209–231.

Blaney, P.H. (1986). Affect and memory: A review. *Psychological Bulletin, 99,* 229–246.

Blatt, S.J., Quinlan, D.M., Chevron, E.S., McDonald, C., & Zuroff, D. (1982). Dependency and self-criticism: Psychological dimensions of depression. *Journal of Consulting and Clinical Psychology, 50,* 113–124.

Bolles, R.C. (1972). The avoidance learning problem. In G.Bower (Ed.), *The psychology of learning and motivation. Vol. 6.* New York: Academic Press.

Bower, G.H. (1981). Mood and memory. *American Psychologist, 36,* 129–148.

Bower, G.H. & Mayer, J.D. (1985). Failure to replicate mood-dependent retrieval. *Bulletin of the Psychonomic Society, 23*, 39–42.

Bower, G.H., Monteiro, K.P., & Gilligan, S.G. (1978). Emotional mood as a context for learning and recall. *Journal of Verbal Learning and Verbal Behavior, 17*, 573–585.

Bowlby, J. (1973). *Attachment and loss: Vol. 2. Separation*. London: Hogarth Press.

Bowlby, J. (1980). *Attachment and loss: Vol. 3. Loss, sadness and depression*. London: Hogarth Press.

Bowlby, J. (1982). *Attachment and loss: Vol. 1. Attachment*. (2nd Edition). London: Hogarth Press.

Bradley, B. & Mathews, A. (1983). Negative self-schemata in clinical depression. *British Journal of Clinical Psychology, 22*, 173–181.

Bradley, B. & Mathews, A. (1987). *Memory bias in recovered clinical depressives*. Unpublished manuscript. London: Institute of Psychiatry.

Bradley, C., Brewin, C.R., Gamsu, D.S., & Moses, J.L. (1984). Development of scales to measure perceived control of diabetes mellitus and diabetes-related health beliefs. *Diabetic Medicine, 1*, 213–218.

Bradley, C., Gamsu, D., Moses, J.L., Knight, G., Boulton, A.J.M., Drury, J., & Ward, J.D. (1987). The use of diabetes-specific perceived control and health belief measures to predict treatment choice and efficacy in a feasibility study of continuous sub-cutaneous insulin infusion pumps. *Psychology and Health, 1*, 133–146.

Bradley, G.W. (1978). Self-serving biases in the attribution process: A re-examination of the fact or fiction question. *Journal of Personality and Social Psychology, 36*, 56–71.

Brehm, J.W. (1966). *A theory of psychological reactance*. New York: Academic Press.

Brehm, S.S. (1976). *The application of social psychology to clinical practice*. Washington, D.C.: Hemisphere.

Breuer, J. & Freud, S. (1895/1955). *Studies on hysteria*. London: Hogarth Press.

Brewin, C.R. (1980). Work role transitions and stress in managers: Illustrations from the clinic. *Personnel Review, 9*, 27–30.

Brewin, C.R. (1984a). Attributions for industrial accidents: Their relationship to rehabilitation outcome. *Journal of Social and Clinical Psychology, 2*, 156–164.

Brewin, C.R. (1984b). Perceived controllability of life events and willingness to prescribe psychotropic drugs. *British Journal of Social Psychology, 23*, 285–287.

Brewin, C.R. (1985). Depression and causal attributions: What is their relation? *Psychological Bulletin, 98*, 297–309.

Brewin, C.R. (1986). Internal attribution and self-esteem in depression: A theoretical note. *Cognitive Therapy and Research, 10*, 469–475.

Brewin, C.R. & Antaki, C. (1982). The role of attributions in psychological treatment. In C.Antaki & C.R.Brewin (Eds.), *Attributions and psychological change*. London: Academic Press.

Brewin, C.R. & Antaki, C. (1987). An analysis of ordinary explanations in clinical attribution research. *Journal of Social and Clinical Psychology, 5*, 79–98.

Brewin, C.R. & Bradley, C. (1982). Perceived control and the experience of childbirth. *British Journal of Clinical Psychology, 21*, 263–270.

Brewin, C.R. & Furnham, A. (1986). Attributional versus pre-attributional variables in self-esteem and depression: A comparison and test of learned helplessness theory. *Journal of Personality and Social Psychology, 50*, 1013–1020.

Brewin, C.R., MacCarthy, B., & Furnham, A. (1987). *Social support in the face of adversity: The role of cognitive appraisal*. Unpublished manuscript. London: Institute of Psychiatry.

Brewin, C.R. & Shapiro, D.A. (1984). Beyond locus of control: Attributions of responsibility for positive and negative outcomes. *British Journal of Psychology, 75*, 43–49.

Broadbent, D.E., Fitzgerald, P., & Broadbent, M.H.P. (1986). Implicit and explicit knowledge in the control of complex systems. *British Journal of Psychology, 77*, 33–50.

Brown, G.W., Adler, Z., & Bifulco, A. (In press). Life events, difficulties, and recovery from chronic depression. *British Journal of Psychiatry*.

Brown, G.W., Andrews, B., Harris, T.O., Adler, Z., & Bridge, L. (1986). Social support, self-esteem and depression. *Psychological Medicine, 16*, 813–831.

Brown, G.W., Bifulco, A., & Harris, T.O. (1987). Life events, vulnerability and onset of depression: Some refinements. *British Journal of Psychiatry, 150*, 30–42.

Brown, G.W. & Harris, T.O. (1978). *The social origins of depression*. London: Tavistock.

Bruner, A. & Revusky, S.H. (1961). Collateral behavior in humans. *Journal of the Experimental Analysis of Behavior, 4*, 349–350.

Bruner, J.S. & Postman, L. (1947). Emotional selectivity in perception and reaction. *Journal of Personality, 16*, 69–77.

Bulman, R.J. & Wortman, C.B. (1977). Attributions of blame and coping in the 'real world': Severe accident victims react to their lot. *Journal of Personality and Social Psychology, 35*, 351–365.

Burger, J.M. & Cooper, H.M. (1979). The desirability of control. *Motivation and Emotion, 3*, 381–393.

Butler, R.J., Brewin, C.R., & Forsythe, W.I. (1986). Maternal attributions and tolerance for nocturnal enuresis. *Behaviour Research and Therapy, 24*, 307–312.

Butler, R.J., Brewin, C.R., & Forsythe, W.I. (In press). A comparison of two approaches to the treatment of nocturnal enuresis and the prediction of effectiveness using pre-treatment variables. *Journal of Child Psychology and Psychiatry*.

Carlsmith, J.M. & Gross, A.E. (1969). Some effects of guilt on compliance. *Journal of Personality and Social Psychology, 11*, 232–239.

Carver, C.S., Ganellen, R.J., & Bihar-Mitrani, V. (1985). Depression and cognitive style: Comparisons between measures. *Journal of Personality and Social Psychology, 49*, 722–728.

Clark, D.M., Salkovskis, P.M., & Chalkley, A.J. (1985). Respiratory control as a treatment for panic attacks. *Journal of Behavior Therapy and Experimental Psychiatry, 16*, 23–30.

Clark, D.M. & Teasdale, J.D. (1982). Diurnal variation in clinical depression and accessibility of memories of positive and negative experiences. *Journal of Abnormal Psychology, 91*, 87–95.

Clark, D.M. & Teasdale, J.D. (1985). Constraints on the effects of mood on memory. *Journal of Personality and Social Psychology, 48*, 1595–1608.

Cobb, S. (1976). Social support as a moderator of life stress. *Psychosomatic Medicine, 38*, 300–314.

Cobb, L.A., Thomas, G.I., Dillard, D.H., Merendino, K.A., & Bruce, E.A. (1959). An evaluation of internal–mammary–artery ligation by a double-blind technic. *New England Journal of Medicine, 260*, 1115–1118.

Cohen, S. & Wills, T.A. (1985). Stress, social support, and the buffering hypothesis. *Psychological Bulletin, 98*, 310–357.

Collins, A.M. & Loftus, E.F. (1975). A spreading-activation theory of semantic processing. *Psychological Review, 82*, 407–428.

Collins, B.E. (1974). Four components of the Rotter internal–external scale: Belief in a difficult world, a just world, a predictable world, and a politically responsive world. *Journal of Personality and Social Psychology, 29*, 381–391.

Condiotte, M.M. & Lichtenstein, E. (1981). Self-efficacy and relapse in smoking cessation programs. *Journal of Consulting and Clinical Psychology, 49*, 648–658.

Cook, E.W. III, Hodes, R.L., & Lang, P.J. (1986). Preparedness and phobia: Effects of stimulus content on human visceral conditioning. *Journal of Abnormal Psychology, 95*, 195–207.

Critelli, J.W. & Neumann, K.F. (1984). The placebo: Conceptual analysis of a construct in transition. *American Psychologist, 39*, 32–39.

Davey, G.C.L. (1983). An associative view of human classical conditioning. In G.C.L. Davey (Ed.), *Animal models of human behavior*. Chichester: Wiley.

Davey, G.C.L. (1987). An integration of human and animal models of Pavlovian conditioning: Associations, cognitions, and attributions. In G.C.L. Davey (Ed.), *Cognitive processes and Pavlovian conditioning in humans*. Chichester: Wiley.

Davey, G.C.L., Gordon, J., & Smith, H. (1986). Attributional effects in human autonomic conditioning. Unpublished paper. London: City University.

Dawson, M.E. & Schell, A.M. (1987). Human autonomic and skeletal classical conditioning: The role of conscious cognitive factors. In G.C.L.Davey (Ed.), *Cognitive processes and Pavlovian conditioning in humans*. Chichester: Wiley.

Deci, E.L. & Ryan, R.M. (1980). The empirical exploration of intrinsic motivational processes. In L.Berkowitz (Ed.), *Advances in experimental social psychology. Vol.13*. New York: Academic Press.

DeMonbreun, B.G. & Craighead, W.E. (1977). Distortion of perception and recall of positive and neutral feedback in depression. *Cognitive Therapy and Research, 1*, 311–329.

de Silva, P., Rachman, S., & Seligman, M.E.P. (1977). Prepared phobias and obsessions: Therapeutic outcome. *Behaviour Research and Therapy, 15*, 65–77.

Dickinson, A. (1980). *Contemporary animal learning theory*. Cambridge: Cambridge University Press.

Dickinson, A. (1985). Actions and habits: The development of behavioural autonomy. In L.Weiskrantz (Ed.), *Animal intelligence*. Oxford: Clarendon Press.

Dickinson, A. (1987). Animal conditioning and learning theory. In H.J.Eysenck & I.Martin (Eds.), *Theoretical foundations of behavior therapy*. New York: Plenum.

DiClemente, C.C. (1981). Self-efficacy and smoking cessation maintenance: A preliminary report. *Cognitive Therapy and Research, 5*, 175–187.

DiClemente, C.C., Prochaska, J.O., & Gibertini, M. (1985). Self-efficacy and the stages of self-change of smoking. *Cognitive Therapy and Research, 9*, 181–200.

Dixon, N.F. (1958). Apparent changes in the visual threshold as a function of subliminal stimulation. *Quarterly Journal of Experimental Psychology, 10*, 211–215.

Dixon, N.F. (1981). *Preconscious processes*. Chichester: Wiley.

Dixon, N.F. & Haider, M. (1961). Changes in the visual threshold as a function of subception. *Quarterly Journal of Experimental Psychology, 13*, 229–235.

Dohrenwend, B.S. & Dohrenwend, B.P. (Eds.) (1974). *Stressful life events: Their nature and effects*. New York: Wiley.

Dweck, C.S. (1975). The role of expectations and attributions in the alleviation of learned helplessness. *Journal of Personality and Social Psychology, 31*, 674–685.

Dweck, C.S. & Reppucci, N.D. (1973). Learned helplessness and reinforcement responsibility in children. *Journal of Personality and Social Psychology, 25*, 109–116.

D'Zurilla, T.J. & Goldfried, M.R. (1971). Problem solving and behavior modification. *Journal of Abnormal Psychology, 78*, 197–226.

Ekman, P. (1973). Cross-cultural studies of facial expression. In P.Ekman (Ed.), *Darwin and facial expression: A century of research in review*. New York: Academic Press.

Ekman, P. (1986). *Telling lies*. New York: Berkley Books.

Ekman, P. & Friesen, W.V. (1974). Detecting deception from the body or face. *Journal of Personality and Social Psychology, 29*, 288–298.

Ekman, P., Levenson, R.W., & Friesen, W.V. (1983). Autonomic nervous activity distinguishes among emotions. *Science, 221*, 1208–1210.

Ellis, A. (1962). *Reason and emotion in psychotherapy*. New York: Lyle Stuart.

Epstein, S. (1983). The unconscious, the preconscious, and the self-concept. In J.Suls & A.G.Greenwald (Eds.), *Psychological perspectives on the self (Vol. 2)*. Hillsdale, N.J.: Lawrence Erlbaum Associates Inc.

Ericsson, K.A. & Simon, H.A. (1980). Verbal reports as data. *Psychological Review, 87*, 215–251.

Eysenck, H.J. (1967). *The biological basis of personality.* Springfield, Illinois: C.C. Thomas.

Eysenck, H.J. (1979). The conditioning model of neurosis. *Behavioral and Brain Sciences, 2*, 155–199.

Eysenck, H.J. (1987). Behavior therapy and neurosis. In H.J. Eysenck & I.Martin (Eds.), *Theoretical foundations of behavior therapy.* New York: Plenum.

Eysenck, H.J. & Himmelweit, H.T. (1946). An experimental study of the reactions of neurotics to experiences of success and failure. *Journal of General Psychology, 35*, 59–75.

Eysenck, H.J. & Rachman, S. (1965). *Causes and cures of neurosis.* London: Routledge & Kegan Paul.

Eysenck, M.W. (1984). *A handbook of cognitive psychology.* London: Lawrence Erlbaum Associates Inc.

Fazio, R.H., Sanbonmatsu, D.M., Powell, M.C., & Kardes, F.R. (1986). On the automatic activation of attitudes. *Journal of Personality and Social Psychology, 50*, 229–238.

Feather, N.T. (Ed.) (1982). *Expectations and actions: Expectancy-value models in psychology.* Hillsdale, N.J.: Lawrence Erlbaum Associates Inc.

Festinger, L. (1954). A theory of social comparison processes. *Human Relations, 7*, 117–140.

Field, D. (1976). The social definition of illness. In D.Tuckett (Ed.), *An introduction to medical sociology.* London: Tavistock.

Fincham, F.D. Beach, S., & Baucom, D. (1987). Attribution processes in distressed and nondistressed couples: 4. Self–partner attribution differences. *Journal of Personality and Social Psychology, 52*, 739–748.

Fincham, F.D., Beach, S., & Nelson, G. (1987). Attribution processes in distressed and nondistressed couples: 3. Causal and responsibility attributions for spouse behavior. *Cognitive Therapy and Research, 11*, 71–86.

Fincham, F.D. & Bradbury, T.N. (1988). The impact of attributions in marriage: Empirical and conceptual foundations. *British Journal of Clinical Psychology, 27*, 77–90.

Firth, J. (1985). Personal meanings of occupational stress: Cases from the clinic. *Journal of Occupational Psychology, 58*, 139–148.

Firth-Cozens, J., & Brewin, C.R. (1988). Attributional change during psychotherapy. *British Journal of Clinical Psychology, 27*, 47–54.

Fischmann–Havstad, L. & Marston, A.R. (1984). Weight loss maintenance as an aspect of family emotion and process. *British Journal of Clinical Psychology, 23*, 265–272.

Fishbein, M. & Ajzen, I. (1975). *Belief, attitude, intention, and behavior: An introduction to theory and research.* Reading, Mass.: Addison–Wesley.

Fisher, C.B., Glenwick, D.S., & Blumenthal, R.S. (1986). Subliminal Oedipal stimuli and competitive performance: An investigation of between-groups effects and mediating subject variables. *Journal of Abnormal Psychology, 95*, 292–294.

Foa, E.B. & Kozak, M.J. (1986). Emotional processing of fear: Exposure to corrective information. *Psychological Bulletin, 99*, 20–35.

Foon, A.E. (1986). Locus of control and clients' expectations of psychotherapeutic outcome. *British Journal of Clinical Psychology, 25*, 161–172.

Försterling, F. (1985). Attributional retraining: A review. *Psychological Bulletin, 98*, 495–512.

Frankel, A. & Snyder, M.L. (1978). Poor performance following unsolvable problems: Learned helplessness or egotism? *Journal of Personality and Social Psychology, 36*, 1415–1423.

Freedman, J.L., Wallington, S.A., & Bless,E. (1967). Compliance without pressure: The effect of guilt. *Journal of Personality and Social Psychology, 7*, 117–124.

Frith, C.D. (1979). Consciousness, information processing and schizophrenia. *British Journal of Psychiatry, 134*, 225–235.

Furnham, A., Hillard, A., & Brewin, C.R. (1985). Type A behavior pattern and attributions of responsibility. *Motivation and Emotion, 9*, 39–51.

Gamsu, D.S. & Bradley, C. (1987). Clinical staff's attributions about diabetes: Scale-development and staff vs. patient comparisons. *Current Psychological Research and Reviews, 6*, 69–78.

Gatchel, R.J. (1980). Perceived control: A review and evaluation of therapeutic implications. In A.Baum & J.E.Singer (Eds.), *Advances in environmental psychology. Vol. 2. Applications of personal control.* Hillsdale, N.J.: Lawrence Erlbaum Associates Inc.

Geer, J.H., Davison, G.C., & Gatchel, R.J. (1970). Reduction of stress in humans through nonveridical perceived control of aversive stimulation. *Journal of Personality and Social Psychology, 16*, 731–738.

Gilbert, P. (1984). *Depression: From psychology to brain state.* London: Lawrence Erlbaum Associates Ltd.

Gilbert, P. (in press). Psychobiological interactions in depression. In S.Fisher & J.Reason (Eds.), *Handbook of life stress, cognition, and health.* Chichester: Wiley.

Gillespie, C. & Bradley, C. (1988). Causal attributions of physician and patients in a diabetes clinic. *British Journal of Clinical Psychology, 27*, 67–76.

Glass, D.C. & Carver, C.S. (1980). Environmental stress and the Type A response. In A.Baum & J.E.Singer (Eds.), *Advances in environmental psychology. Vol.2. Applications of personal control.* Hillsdale, N.J.: Lawrence Erlbaum Associates Ltd.

Goffman, E. (1968). *Stigma.* London: Penguin Books.

Goldfried, M.R. (1980). Toward a delineation of therapeutic change principles. *American Psychologist, 35*, 991–999.

Goldfried, M.R., Decenteceo, E., & Weinberg, L. (1974). Systematic rational restructuring as a self-control technique. *Behavior Therapy, 5*, 247–254.

Goldfried, M.R. & Goldfried, A.P. (1980). Cognitive change methods. In F.H.Kanfer & A.P.Goldstein (Eds.), *Helping people change* (2nd Edition). New York: Pergamon.

Goldfried, M.R. & Robins, C. (1982). On the facilitation of self- efficacy. *Cognitive Therapy and Research, 6*, 361–380.

Gotham, A-M., Brown, R.G., & Marsden, C.D. (1986). Depression in Parkinson's disease: A quantitative and qualitative analysis. *Journal of Neurology, Neurosurgery, and Psychiatry, 49*, 381–389.

Gotlib, I.H. (1981). Self-reinforcement and recall: Differential deficits in depressed and nondepressed psychiatric in-patients. *Journal of Abnormal Psychology, 90*, 521–530.

Gotlib, I.H. (1983). Perception and recall of interpersonal feedback: Negative bias in depression. *Cognitive Therapy and Research, 7*, 399–412.

Graham, S., Doubleday, C., & Guarino, P.A. (1984). The development of relations between perceived controllability and the emotions of pity, anger, and guilt. *Child Development, 55*, 561–565.

Gray, J.A. (1971). *The psychology of fear and stress.* London: World University Library.

Gray, J.A. (1979). Is there any need for conditioning in Eysenck's conditioning model of neurosis? *Behavioral and Brain Sciences, 2*, 169–171.

Gray, J.A. (1982). *The neuropsychology of anxiety.* Oxford: Clarendon Press.

Grayson, J.B., Foa, E.B., & Steketee, G. (1982). Habituation during exposure treatment: Distraction versus attention-focusing. *Behaviour Research and Therapy, 20*, 323–328.

Greenberg, L.S. & Safran, J.D. (1987). *Emotion in psychotherapy.* New York: Guilford.

Grimm, L.G. (1983). The relation between self-evaluation and self-reward: A test of Kanfer's self-regulation model. *Cognitive Therapy and Research, 7*, 245–250.

Grimm, L.G. & Yarnold, P.R. (1984). Performance standards and the Type A behavior pattern. *Cognitive Therapy and Research, 8*, 59–66.

Grings, W.W. & Dawson, M.E. (1973). Complex conditioning. In W.F. Prokasy & D.C.Raskin (Eds.), *Electrodermal activity in psychological research.* New York: Academic Press.

Groeger, J.A. (1986). Predominant and non-predominant analysis: Effects of level of presentation. *British Journal of Psychology, 77*, 109–116.

Guidano, V.F. & Liotti, G. (1983). *Cognitive processes and emotional disorders*. New York: Pergamon.

Gurin, P., Gurin, G., & Morrison, B.M. (1978). Personal and ideological aspects of internal and external control. *Social Psychology, 41*, 275–296.

Haley, J. (1963). *Strategies of psychotherapy*. New York: Grune and Stratton.

Hammen, C., Marks, T., deMayo, R., & Mayol, A. (1985). Self-schemas and risk for depression: A prospective study. *Journal of Personality and Social Psychology, 49*, 1147–1159.

Hammen, C., Marks, T., Mayol, A., & deMayo, R. (1985). Depressive self-schemas, life stress, and vulnerability to depression. *Journal of Abnormal Psychology, 94*, 308–319.

Hardy, G.R. & Legge, D. (1968). Cross-modal induction of changes in sensory thresholds. *Quarterly Journal of Experimental Psychology, 20*, 20–29.

Harvey, J.H. & Galvin, K.S. (1984). Clinical implications of attribution theory and research. *Clinical Psychology Review, 4*, 15–33.

Harvey, J.H., Wells, G.L., & Alvarez, M.D. (1978). Attribution in the context of conflict and separation in close relationships. In J.H.Harvey, W.J.Ickes, & R.F.Kidd (Eds.), *New directions in attribution research* (Vol. 2). Hillsdale, N.J.: Lawrence Erlbaum Associates Inc.

Heider, F. (1958). *The psychology of interpersonal relations*. New York: Wiley.

Hilgard, E.R. & Hilgard, J.R. (1975). *Hypnosis in the relief of pain*. Los Altos, Ca.: William Kaufman.

Hilton, D.J. & Slugoski, B.R. (1986). Knowledge-based causal attribution: The abnormal conditions focus model. *Psychological Review, 93*, 75–88.

Himmelweit, H.T. (1947). A comparative study of the level of aspiration of normal and neurotic persons. *British Journal of Psychology, 37*, 41–59.

Holender, D. (1986). Semantic activation without conscious identification in dichotic listening, parafoveal vision, and visual masking: A survey and appraisal. *Behavioral and Brain Sciences, 9*, 1–66.

Holland, P.C. & Rescorla, R.A. (1975). The effects of two ways of devaluing the unconditioned stimulus after first- and second-order appetitive conditioning. *Journal of Experimental Psychology: Animal Behavior Processes, 5*, 65–78.

House, W.C. (1983). Variables affecting the outcome between depression and attribution of outcomes. *Journal of Genetic Psychology, 142*, 293–300.

Ickes, W.J. & Layden, M.A. (1978). Attributional styles. In J.H. Harvey, W.J.Ickes, & R.F.Kidd (Eds.), *New directions in attribution research* (Vol. 2). Hillsdale, N.J.: Lawrence Erlbaum Associates Inc.

Ingram, R.E. (1984). Toward an information-processing analysis of depression. *Cognitive Therapy and Research, 8*, 443–478.

Isen, A.M. (1984). Toward understanding the role of affect in cognition. In R.S.Wyer & T.K.Srull (Eds.), *Handbook of social cognition* (Vol. 3). Hillsdale, N.J.: Lawrence Erlbaum Associates Inc.

Isen, A.M., Shalker, T.E., Clark, M., & Karp, L. (1978). Affect, accessibility of material in memory, and behavior: A cognitive loop? *Journal of Personality and Social Psychology, 36*, 1–12.

Jacobs, W.J. & Nadel, L. (1985). Stress-induced recovery of fears and phobias. *Psychological Review, 92*, 512–531.

Janoff-Bulman, R. (1979). Characterological versus behavioral self-blame: Inquiries into depression and rape. *Journal of Personality and Social Psychology, 37*, 1798–1809.

Jaspars, J., Hewstone, M., & Fincham, F.D. (1983). Attribution theory and research: The state of the art. In J.Jaspars, F.D.Fincham, & M.Hewstone (Eds.), *Attribution theory and research: conceptual, developmental, and social dimensions*. London: Academic Press.

Johnson, J.E., Rice, V.H., Fuller, S.S., & Endress, M.P. (1978). Sensory information, instruction in a coping strategy, and recovery from surgery. *Research on Nursing and Health, 1,* 4–17.

Johnson-Laird, P.N. (1983). *Mental models: Towards a cognitive science of language, inference, and consciousness.* Cambridge: Cambridge University Press.

Johnston, M. (1986). Pre-operative emotional states and post-operative recovery. *Advances in Psychosomatic Medicine, 15,* 1–22.

Jones, E.E. & Berglas, S. (1978). Control of attributions about the self through self-handicapping strategies: The appeal of alcohol and the role of underachievement. *Personality and Social Psychology Bulletin, 4,* 200–206.

Jones, E.E. & Nisbett, R.E. (1972). The actor and the observer. In E.E.Jones, D.E.Kanouse, H.H.Kelley, R.E.Nisbett, S.Valins, & B. Weiner (Eds.), *Attribution: Perceiving the causes of behavior.* New Jersey: General Learning Press.

Kamin, L.J. (1969). Predictability, surprise, attention, and conditioning. In B.M.Campbell & R.M.Church (Eds.), *Punishment and aversive behavior.* New York: Appleton-Century-Crofts.

Kammer, D. (1984). Attributional processing style differences in depressed and nondepressed individuals. *Motivation and Emotion, 8,* 211–220.

Kanfer, F.H. (1970). Self-regulation: Research, issues, and speculations. In C. Neuringer & J.L. Michael (Eds.), *Behavior Modification in Clinical Psychology.* New York: Appleton-Century-Crofts.

Kanfer, R. & Zeiss, A.M. (1983). Depression, interpersonal standard setting, and judgments of self-efficacy. *Journal of Abnormal Psychology, 92,* 319–329.

Kassin, S.M. & Baron, R.M. (1985). Basic determinants of attribution and social perception. In J.H.Harvey & G.Weary (Eds.), *Attribution: Basic issues and applications.* Orlando, Fl.: Academic Press.

Kelley, H.H. (1967). Attribution theory in social psychology. In D.Levine (Ed.), *Nebraska symposium on motivation. Vol.15.* Lincoln: University of Nebraska Press.

Kelley, H.H. & Michela, J.L. (1980). Attribution theory and research. *Annual Review of Psychology, 31,* 457–501.

Kelly, G.A. (1955). *The psychology of personal constructs. Vols. 1 & 2.* New York: W.W.Norton.

Kihlstrom, J.F. (1984). Conscious, subconscious, unconscious: A cognitive perspective. In K.S.Bowers & D. Meichenbaum (Eds.), *The unconscious reconsidered.* New York: Wiley.

Kihlstrom, J.F. & Cantor, N. (1984). Mental representations of the self. In L.Berkowitz (Ed.), *Advances in experimental social psychology* (Vol. 17). Orlando, Fl.: Academic Press.

Kimble, G. & Perlmuter, L.C. (1970). The problem of volition. *Psychological Review, 77,* 361–384.

King, J.B. (1982). The impact of patients' perceptions of high blood pressure on attendance at screening: An attributional extension of the Health Belief Model. *Social Science and Medicine, 16,* 1079–1092.

King, J.B. (1983). Attribution theory and the Health Belief Model. In M.Hewstone (Ed.), *Attribution theory: Social and functional extensions.* Oxford: Blackwell.

Kirsch, I. (1978). The placebo effect and the cognitive–behavioral revolution. *Cognitive Therapy and Research, 2,* 255–264.

Kirsch, I. & Wickless, C.V. (1983). Concordance rates between self-efficacy and approach behavior are redundant. *Cognitive Therapy and Research, 7,* 179–188.

Kirschenbaum, D.S. (1987). Self-regulatory failure: A review with clinical implications. *Clinical Psychology Review, 7,* 77–104.

Kline, P. (1981). *Fact and fantasy in Freudian theory*. 2nd Edition. London: Methuen.

Kornblith, S.J., Rehm, L.P., O'Hara, M.W., & Lamparski, D.M. (1983). The contribution of self-reinforcement training and behavioral assignments to the efficacy of self-control therapy for depression. *Cognitive Therapy and Research, 7*, 499–528.

Krantz, D.S. & Schulz, R. (1980). A model of life crisis, control, and health outcomes: Cardiac rehabilitation and relocation of the elderly. In A.Baum & J.E.Singer (Eds.), *Advances in environmental psychology. Vol.2. Applications of personal control*. Hillsdale, N.J.: Lawrence Erlbaum Associates Inc.

Kuiper, N.A., MacDonald, M.R., & Derry, P.A. (1983). Parameters of a depressive self-schema. In J.Suls & A.G.Greenwald (Eds.), *Psychological perspectives on the self* (Vol. 2). Hillsdale, N.J.: Lawrence Erlbaum Associates Inc.

Kuiper, N.A., Olinger, L.J., MacDonald, M.R., & Shaw, B.F. (1985). Self-schema processing of depressed and nondepressed content: The effects of vulnerability to depression. *Social Cognition, 3*, 77–93.

Lane, T.W. & Borkovec, T.D. (1984). The influence of therapeutic expectancy/demand on self-efficacy ratings. *Cognitive Therapy and Research, 8*, 95–106.

Lang, P.J. (1977). Imagery in therapy: An information processing analysis of fear. *Behavior Therapy, 8*, 862–886.

Lang, P.J. (1979). A bio-informational theory of emotional imagery. *Psychophysiology, 16*, 495–512.

Langer, E.J. (1975). The illusion of control. *Journal of Personality and Social Psychology, 32*, 311–328.

Langer, E.J., Janis, I.L., & Wolfer, J.A. (1975). Reduction of psychological stress in surgical patients. *Journal of Experimental Social Psychology, 11*, 155–165.

Langer, E.J. & Rodin, J. (1976). The effects of choice and enhanced personal responsibility for the aged: A field experiment in an institutional setting. *Journal of Personality and Social Psychology, 34*, 191–198.

Larrance, D.T. & Twentyman, C.T. (1983). Maternal attributions and child abuse. *Journal of Abnormal Psychology, 92*, 449–457.

Latané, B. & Darley, J.M. (1970). *The unresponsive bystander: Why doesn't he help?* New York: Appleton–Century–Crofts.

Layden, M.A. (1982). Attributional style therapy. In C.Antaki & C.R.Brewin (Eds.), *Attributions and psychological change*. London: Academic Press.

Lazarus, R.S. (1966). *Psychological stress and the coping process*. New York: McGraw-Hill.

Lazarus, R.S. (1982). Thoughts on the relations betweeen emotion and cognition. *American Psychologist, 37*, 1019–1024.

Lazarus, R.S., Averill, J.R., & Opton, E.M. (1970). Towards a cognitive theory of emotion. In M. Arnold (Ed.), *Feelings and emotions*. New York: Academic Press.

Lazarus, R.S., Kanner, A.D., & Folkman, S. (1980). Emotions: A cognitive-phenomenological analysis. In R.Plutchik & H.Kellerman (Eds.), *Emotion: Theory, research and experience*. (Vol. 1). New York: Academic Press.

Leary, M.R., Atherton, S.C., Hill, S., & Hur, C. (1986). Attributional mediators of social avoidance and inhibition. *Journal of Personality, 54*, 704–716.

Leff, J., Kuipers, L., Berkowitz, R., Eberlein-Vries, R., & Sturgeon, D. (1982). A controlled trial of social intervention in the families of schizophrenic patients. *British Journal of Psychiatry, 141*, 121–134.

Levenson, H. (1974). Activism and powerful others: Distinctions within the concept of internal–external control. *Journal of Personality Assessment, 38*, 377–383.

Leventhal, H. (1984). A perceptual-motor theory of emotion. In L.Berkowitz (Ed.), *Advances in experimental social psychology* (Vol. 17). Orlando, Fl.: Academic Press.

Lewin, K., Dembo, T., Festinger, L., & Sears, P.S. (1944). Level of aspiration. In J.McV.Hunt (Ed.), *Personality and the behavior disorders*. New York: Ronald Press.

Lewinsohn, P.M., Hoberman, H., Teri, L., & Hautzinger, M. (1985). An integrative theory of depression. In S.Reiss & R.R.Bootzin (Eds.), *Theoretical issues in behavior therapy.* New York: Academic Press.

Lewinsohn, P.M., Mischel, W., Chaplin, W., & Barton, R. (1980). Social competence and depression: The role of illusory self-perceptions. *Journal of Abnormal Psychology, 89,* 203–212.

Libet, B. (1973). Electrical stimulation of cortex in humans, and conscious sensory aspects. In A.Iggo (Ed.), *Handbook of sensory physiology.* (Vol. 2). New York: Springer.

Lick, J. & Bootzin, R. (1975). Expectancy factors in the treatment of fear: Methodological and theoretical issues. *Psychological Bulletin, 82,* 917–931.

Lobitz, G.K. & Johnson, S.M. (1975). Normal versus deviant children: A multimethod comparison. *Journal of Abnormal Child Psychology, 3,* 353–374.

Lobitz, W.C. & Post, R.D. (1979). Parameters of self-reinforcement and depression. *Journal of Abnormal Psychology, 88,* 33–41.

Locke, E.A., Shaw, K.N., Saari, L.M., & Latham, G.P. (1981). Goal setting and task performance: 1969–1980. *Psychological Bulletin, 90,* 125–152.

Lowe, C.F. (1983). Radical behaviorism and human psychology. In G.C.L.Davey (Ed.), *Animal models of human behavior.* Chichester: Wiley.

Lowery, C.R., Denney, D.R., & Storms, M.D. (1979). Insomnia: A comparison of the effects of pill attributions and nonpejorative self-attributions. *Cognitive Therapy and Research, 3,* 161–164.

MacCarthy, B. & Furnham, A. (1986). Patients' conceptions of psychological adjustment in the normal population. *British Journal of Clinical Psychology, 25,* 43–50.

Mackintosh, N.J. (1973). Stimulus selection: Learning to ignore stimuli that predict no change in reinforcement. In R.A.Hinde & J.Stevenson Hinde (Eds.), *Constraints on learning.* London: Academic Press.

Mackintosh, N.J. (1983). *Conditioning and associative learning.* New York: Oxford University Press.

MacLeod, C., Mathews, A., & Tata, P. (1986). Attentional bias in emotional disorders. *Journal of Abnormal Psychology, 95,* 15–20.

Mahoney, M.J., Moore, B.S., Wade, T.C., & Moura, N.G.M. (1973). The effects of continuous and intermittent self-monitoring on academic behavior. *Journal of Consulting and Clinical Psychology, 41,* 65–69.

Manstead, A.S.R. & Wagner, H.L. (1981). Arousal, cognition and emotion: An appraisal of two-factor theory. *Current Psychological Reviews, 1,* 35–54.

Marcel, A.J. (1983). Conscious and unconscious perception: Experiments on visual masking and word recognition. *Cognitive Psychology, 15,* 197–237.

Marks, I.M. (1977). Phobias and obsessions. In J.Maser & M.E.P. Seligman (Eds.), *Experimental psychopathology.* San Francisco: Wiley.

Marks, I.M. (1987). *Fears, phobias and rituals: Panic, anxiety, and their disorders.* New York: Oxford University Press.

Markus, H. (1977). Self-schemata and processing information about the self. *Journal of Personality and Social Psychology, 35,* 63–78.

Markus, H. & Sentis, K. (1982). The self in social information processing. In J.Suls (Ed.), *Psychological perspectives on the self* (Vol. 1). Hillsdale, N.J.: Lawrence Erlbaum Associates Inc.

Martin, I. & Levey, A. (1985). Conditioning, evaluations, and cognitions: An axis of integration. *Behaviour Research and Therapy, 23,* 167–175.

Martin, M., Ward, J.C., & Clark, D.M. (1983). Neuroticism and the recall of positive and negative personality information. *Behaviour Research and Therapy, 21,* 495–503.

Mathews, A. & Eysenck, M.W. (1987). Clinical anxiety and cognition. In H.J.Eysenck & I.Martin (Eds.), *Theoretical foundations of behavior therapy.* New York: Plenum.

Mathews, A. & MacLeod, C. (1985). Selective processing of threat cues in anxiety states. *Behaviour Research and Therapy, 23*, 563–569.

Mathews, A. & MacLeod, C. (1986). Discrimination of threat cues without awareness in anxiety states. *Journal of Abnormal Psychology, 95*, 131–138.

Maybury, C.P. & Brewin, C.R. (1984). Social relationships, knowledge, and adjustment to multiple sclerosis. *Journal of Neurology, Neurosurgery, and Psychiatry, 47*, 372–376.

Meichenbaum, D. (1977). *Cognitive-behavior modification.* New York: Plenum.

Meier, S., McCarthy, P.R., & Schmeck, R.R. (1984). Validity of self-efficacy as a predictor of writing performance. *Cognitive Therapy and Research, 8*, 107–120.

Melamed, B.G. & Siegel,L.J. (1975). Reduction of anxiety in children facing surgery by modeling. *Journal of Consulting and Clinical Psychology, 43*, 511–521.

Miles, A. (1979). Some psychosocial consequences of multiple sclerosis: Problems of social interaction and group identity. *British Journal of Medical Psychology, 52*, 321–331.

Miller, J.Z. & Rose, R.J. (1982). Familial resemblance in locus of control: A twin-family study of the internal-external scale. *Journal of Personality and Social Psychology, 42*, 535–540.

Miller, S.M. (1979). Controllability and human stress: Method, evidence and theory. *Behaviour Research and Therapy, 17*, 287–304.

Mineka, S. (1987). A primate model of phobic fears. In H.J. Eysenck & I.Martin (Eds.), *Theoretical foundations of behavior therapy.* New York: Plenum.

Mineka, S. & Kihlstrom, J.F. (1978). Unpredictable and uncontrollable events: A new perspective on experimental neurosis. *Journal of Abnormal Psychology, 87*, 256–271.

Minkoff, K., Bergman, E., Beck, A.T., & Beck, R. (1973). Hopelessness, depression, and attempted suicide. *American Journal of Psychiatry, 130*, 455–459.

Mischel, W. (1973). Toward a cognitive social learning reconceptualization of personality. *Psychological Review, 80*, 252–283.

Mogg, K., Mathews, A., & Weinman, J. (1987). Memory bias in clinical anxiety. *Journal of Abnormal Psychology, 96*, 94–98.

Morgan, R.T.T. & Young, G.C. (1975). Parental attitude and the conditioning treatment of childhood enuresis. *Behaviour Research and Therapy, 13*, 197–199.

Morris, P.E. (1981). The cognitive psychology of self-reports. In C. Antaki (Ed.), *The Psychology of Ordinary Explanations of Social Behaviour.* London: Academic Press.

Neisser, U. (1963). The multiplicity of thought. *British Journal of Psychology, 54*, 1–14.

Neisser, U. (1967). *Cognitive psychology.* New York: Appleton-Century-Crofts.

Nelson, R.E. & Craighead, W.E. (1977). Selective recall of positive and negative feedback, self-control behaviors, and depression. *Journal of Abnormal Psychology, 86*, 379–388.

Nisbett, R.E. & Ross, L. (1980). *Human inference: Strategies and shortcomings of social judgement.* Englewood Cliffs, N.J.: Prentice-Hall.

Nisbett, R.E. & Wilson, T.D. (1977). Telling more than we can know: Verbal reports on mental processes. *Psychological Review, 84*,231–259.

Nunn, J.D., Stevenson, R.J., & Whalan, G. (1984). Selective memory effects in agora-phobic patients. *British Journal of Clinical Psychology, 23*, 195–202.

Oatley, K. & Bolton, W. (1985). A social-cognitive theory of depression in reaction to life events. *Psychological Review, 92*, 372–388.

Öhman, A., Dimberg, U., & Öst, L.-G. (1985). Animal and social phobias: Biological constraints on learned fear responses. In S.Reiss & R.R.Bootzin (Eds.), *Theoretical issues in behavior therapy.* New York: Academic Press.

Öhman, A., Frederikson, M., & Hugdahl, K. (1978). Towards an experimental model of simple phobic reactions. *Behavioural Analysis and Modification, 2*, 97–114.

Ørner, R.J. (1987). Post-traumatic stress disorders in victims of the Falklands War: Syndrome and treatment. Paper delivered at the British Psychological Society Annual Conference, Brighton.

Orvis, B.R., Kelley, H.H., & Butler, D. (1976). Attributional conflict in young couples. In J.H.Harvey, W.J.Ickes, & R.F. Kidd (Eds.), *New directions in attribution research* (Vol. 1). Hillsdale, N.J.: Lawrence Erlbaum Associates Inc.

Parry, G. & Brewin, C.R. (1988). Cognitive style and depression: Symptom-related, event-related, or independent provoking factor? *British Journal of Clinical Psychology, 27,* 19–31.

Perry, C. & Laurence, J-R. (1984). Mental processing outside of awareness: The contributions of Freud and Janet. In K.S.Bowers & D.Meichenbaum (Eds.), *The unconscious reconsidered.* New York: Wiley.

Peterson, C. & Seligman, M.E.P. (1984). Causal explanations as a risk factor for depression: Theory and evidence. *Psychological Review, 91,* 347–374.

Pietromonaco, P.R. & Markus, H. (1985). The nature of negative thoughts in depression. *Journal of Personality and Social Psychology, 48,* 799–807.

Pittner, M. & Houston, B. (1980). Response to stress, cognitive coping strategies and the type A behavior pattern. *Journal of Personality and Social Psychology, 39,* 147–157.

Posner, M.I. & Snyder, C.R. (1975). Attention and cognitive control. In R.L.Solso (Ed.), *Information processing and cognition: The Loyola symposium.* Hillsdale, N.J.: Lawrence Erlbaum Associates Inc.

Power, M.J. (1986). *The unconscious: A brief history and a contemporary cognitive approach.* Unpublished manuscript. London: Institute of Psychiatry.

Power, M.J. & Champion, L.A. (1986). Cognitive approaches to depression: A theoretical critique. *British Journal of Clinical Psychology, 25,* 201–212.

Pylyshyn, Z.W. (1973). What the mind's eye tells the mind's brain: A critique of mental imagery. *Psychological Bulletin, 80,* 1–22.

Pyszczynski, T. & Greenberg, J. (1983). Determinants of reduction in intended effort as a strategy for coping with anticipated failure. *Journal of Research in Personality, 17,* 412–422.

Quattrone, G.A. (1985). On the congruity between internal states and action. *Psychological Bulletin, 98,* 3–40.

Rachman, S. (1977). The conditioning theory of fear acquisition: A critical examination. *Behaviour Research and Therapy, 15,* 375–387.

Rachman, S. (1980). Emotional processing. *Behaviour Research and Therapy, 18,* 51–60.

Rachman, S. (1981). The primacy of affect: Some theoretical implications. *Behaviour Research and Therapy, 19,* 279–290.

Rachman, S., & Hodgson, R. (1974). Synchrony and desynchrony in fear and avoidance. *Behaviour Research and Therapy, 12,* 311–318.

Rehm, L.P. (1982). Self-management in depression. In P.Karoly & F.H.Kanfer (Eds.), *Self-management and behavior change: From theory to practice.* New York: Pergamon.

Reisenzein, R. (1983). The Schachter theory of emotion: Two decades later. *Psychological Bulletin, 94,* 239–264.

Rescorla, R.A. (1968). Probability of shock in the presence and absence of the CS in fear conditioning. *Journal of Comparative and Physiological Psychology, 66,* 1–5.

Rescorla, R.A. (1980). *Pavlovian second-order conditioning: Studies in associative learning.* Hillsdale, N.J.: Lawrence Erlbaum Associates Inc.

Rescorla, R.A. & Heth, D.C. (1975). Reinstatement of fear to an extinguished conditioned stimulus. *Journal of Experimental Psychology: Animal Behavior Processes, 1,* 88–96.

Rhodewalt, F., Saltzman, A.T., & Wittmer, J. (1984). Self-handicapping among competitive athletes: The role of practice in self-esteem protection. *Basic and Applied Social Psychology, 5,* 197–209.

Rickard, K.M., Forehand, R., Wells, K.C., Griest, D.L., & McMahon, R.J. (1981). Factors in the referral of children for behavioral treatment: A comparison of mothers of clinic-referred deviant, clinic-referred non-deviant and non-clinic children. *Behaviour Research and Therapy, 19,* 201–205.

Ricks, M.H. (1985). The social transmission of parental behavior: Attachment across generations. In I.Bretherton & E.Waters (Eds.), *Growing points of attachment: Theory and research*. Monograph of Society of Child Development, Vol. 50. Chicago: University of Chicago Press.

Ridgeway, V. & Mathews, A. (1982). Psychological preparation for surgery: A comparison of methods. *British Journal of Clinical Psychology, 21*, 271–280.

Rodin, J. & Langer, E.J. (1977). Long-term effects of a control-relevant intervention with the institutionalized aged. *Journal of Personality and Social Psychology, 35*, 897–902.

Rodin, J., Rennert, K., & Solomon, S.K. (1980). Intrinsic motivation for control: fact or fiction. In A.Baum & J.E.Singer (Eds.), *Advances in environmental psychology. Vol.2. Applications of personal control*. Hillsdale, N.J.: Lawrence Erlbaum Associates Inc.

Rokeach, M. (1973). *The nature of human values*. New York: Free Press.

Rollman, G.B. & Nachmias, J. (1972). Simultaneous detection and recognition of chromatic flashes. *Perception and Psychophysics, 12*, 309–314.

Rosenstock, I.M. (1966). Why people use health services. *Milbank Memorial Fund Quarterly, 44*, 94–127.

Ross, L. (1977). The intuitive psychologist and his shortcomings. In L.Berkowitz (Ed.), *Advances in experimental social psychology* (Vol. 9). New York: Academic Press.

Ross, M. & Olson, J.M. (1982). Placebo effects in medical research and practice. In J.Eiser (Ed.), *Social psychology and behavioral medicine*. Chichester: Wiley.

Rotter, J.B. (1954). *Social learning and clinical psychology*. Englewood Cliffs, N.J.: Prentice-Hall.

Rotter, J.B. (1966). Generalised expectancies for internal versus external control of reinforcement. *Psychological Monographs, 80*(1), Whole no. 609, 1–28.

Rotter, J.B. (1975). Some problems and misconceptions related to the construct of internal versus external control of reinforcement. *Journal of Consulting and Clinical Psychology, 43*, 56–67.

Rozensky, R.H., Rehm, L.P., Pry, G., & Roth, D. (1977). Depression and self-reinforcement behavior in hospitalised patients. *Journal of Behavior Therapy and Experimental Psychiatry, 8*, 35–38.

Rushton, J.P., Fulker, D.W., Neale, M.C., Nias, D.K.B., & Eysenck, H.J. (1986). Altruism and aggression: The heritability of individual differences. *Journal of Personality and Social Psychology, 50*, 1192–1198.

Salkovskis, P.M. & Clark, D.M. (1986). Cognitive and physiological approaches in the maintenance and treatment of panic attacks. In I.Hand & H-U.Wittchen (Eds.), *Panic and Phobias*. Berlin: Springer-Verlag.

Sarnoff, I. & Zimbardo, P.G. (1961). Anxiety, fear, and social affiliation. *Journal of Abnormal and Social Psychology, 62*, 356–363.

Sartory, G., Rachman, S., & Grey, S.J. (1982). Return of fear: The role of rehearsal. *Behaviour Research and Therapy, 20*, 123–133.

Schachter, S. (1959). *The psychology of affiliation*. Stanford, Ca.: Stanford University Press.

Schachter, S. (1964). The interaction of cognitive and physiological determinants of emotional state. In L.Berkowitz (Ed.), *Advances in experimental social psychology* (Vol. 1). New York: Academic Press.

Schachter, S. & Singer, J.E. (1962). Cognitive, social, and physiological determinants of emotional state. *Psychological Review, 69*, 379–399.

Schare, M.L., Lisman, S.A., & Spear, N.E. (1984). The effects of mood variation on state-dependent retention. *Cognitive Therapy and Research, 8*, 387–408.

Schneider, W. & Shiffrin, R.M. (1977). Controlled and automatic human information processing: I. Detection, search, and attention. *Psychological Review, 84*, 1–66.

Schulz, R. (1976). Effects of control and predictability on the physical and psychological well-being of the institutionalized aged. *Journal of Personality and Social Psychology, 33*, 563–573.

Schwartz, S.H. & Howard, J.A. (1980). Explanations of the moderating effect of responsibility denial on the personal norm–behavior relationship. *Social Psychology Quarterly, 43*, 441–446.

Segal, Z.V. & Shaw, B.F. (1986). Cognition in depression: A reappraisal of Coyne & Gotlib's critique. *Cognitive Therapy and Research, 10*, 671–694.

Seligman, M.E.P. (1971). Phobias and preparedness. *Behavior Therapy, 2*, 307–320.

Seligman, M.E.P. (1975). *Helplessness: On depression, development, and death.* San Fransisco: Freeman.

Shapiro, A.K. (1971). Placebo effects in medicine, psychotherapy, and psychoanalysis. In A.E. Bergin & S.L.Garfield (Eds.), *Handbook of psychotherapy and behavior change: An empirical analysis.* New York: Wiley.

Shiffrin, R.M. & Schneider, W. (1977). Controlled and automatic human information processing: II. Perceptual learning, automatic attending, and a general theory. *Psychological Review, 84*, 127–190.

Shrauger, J.S. (1982). Selection and processing of self-evaluative information: Experimental evidence and clinical implications. In G.Weary & H.L.Mirels (Eds.), *Integrations of clinical and social psychology.* New York: Oxford University Press.

Silverman, L.H. (1983). The subliminal psychodynamic activation method: Overview and comprehensive listing of studies. In J.Masling (Ed.), *Empirical studies of psychoanalytic theories. Vol 1.* Hillsdale, N.J.: Analytic Press.

Simon, K.M. (1979). Self-evaluative reactions: The role of personal valuation of the activity. *Cognitive Therapy and Research, 3*, 111–116.

Smedslund, J. (1978). Bandura's theory of self-efficacy: A set of common-sense theorems. *Scandinavian Journal of Psychology, 19*, 1–14.

Smith, E.R. & Lerner, M. (1986). Development of automatism of social judgments. *Journal of Personality and Social Psychology, 50*, 246–259.

Smith, T.W., Snyder, C.R., & Perkins, S.C. (1983). The self-serving function of hypochondriacal complaints: Physical symptoms as self-handicapping strategies. *Journal of Personality and Social Psychology, 44*, 787–797.

Snow, B. (1978). Level of aspiration in coronary prone and noncoronary prone adults. *Personality and Social Psychology Bulletin, 4*, 416–419.

Snyder, C.R. & Ingram, R.E. (1983). "Company motivates the miserable": The impact of consensus information on help seeking for psychological problems. *Journal of Personality and Social Psychology, 45*, 1118–1126.

Snyder, C.R. & Smith, T.W. (1982). Symptoms as self-handicapping strategies: The virtues of old wine in a new bottle. In G. Weary & H. Mirels (Eds.), *Integrations of clinical and social psychology.* New York: Oxford University Press.

Sober-Ain, L. & Kidd, R.F. (1984). Fostering changes in self-blamers' beliefs about causality. *Cognitive Therapy and Research, 8*, 121–138.

Spence, K.W. (1966). Cognitive and drive factors in the extinction of the conditioned eyeblink in human subjects. *Psychological Review, 73*, 445–458.

Storms, M.D. & McCaul, K.D. (1976). Attribution processes and the emotional exacerbation of dysfunctional behavior. In J.H.Harvey, W.J.Ickes, & R.F.Kidd (Eds.), *New directions in attribution research.* (Vol. 1). Hillsdale, N.J.: Lawrence Erlbaum Associates Inc.

Storms, M.D. & Nisbett, R.E. (1970). Insomnia and the attribution process. *Journal of Personality and Social Psychology, 16*, 319–328.

Stratton, P., Heard, D., Hanks, H.G.I., Munton, A.G., Brewin, C.R., & Davidson, C. (1986). Coding causal beliefs in natural discourse. *British Journal of Social Psychology, 25*, 299–314.

Strickland, B.R. (1978). Internal–external expectancies and health-related behaviors. *Journal of Consulting and Clinical Psychology*, *46*, 1192–1211.

Sudnow, D. (1967). *Passing on: The social organisation of dying*. New York: Prentice Hall.

Suinn, R. & Richardson, F. (1971). Anxiety management training: A nonspecific behavior therapy program for anxiety control. *Behavior Therapy*, *2*, 498–510.

Sweeney, P., Anderson, K., & Bailey, S. (1986). Attributional style in depression: A meta-analytic review. *Journal of Personality and Social Psychology*, *50*, 774–791.

Taylor, S.E., Lichtman, R.R., & Wood, J.V. (1984). Attributions, beliefs about control, and adjustment to breast cancer. *Journal of Personality and Social Psychology*, *46*, 489–502.

Teasdale, J.D. (1983). Negative thinking in depression: Cause, effect, or reciprocal relationship? *Advances in Behaviour Research and Therapy*, *5*, 3–25.

Teasdale, J.D. (1986). Non-pharmacological treatments for depression. Unpublished manuscript. Cambridge: MRC Applied Psychology Unit.

Teasdale, J.D. & Dent, J. (1987). Cognitive vulnerability to depression: An investigation of two hypotheses. *British Journal of Clinical Psychology*, *26*, 113–126.

Teasdale, J.D. & Russell, M.L. (1983). Differential effects of induced mood on the recall of positive, negative and neutral words. *British Journal of Clinical Psychology*, *22*, 163–171.

Teasdale, J.D., Taylor, R., & Fogarty, S.J. (1980). Effects of induced elation-depression on the accessibility of memories of happy and unhappy experiences. *Behaviour Research and Therapy*, *18*, 339–346.

Teglasi, H. & Hoffman, M.A. (1982). Causal attributions of shy subjects. *Journal of Research in Personality*, *16*, 376–385.

Tetlock, P.E. (1980). Explaining teacher explanations of pupil performance: An examination of the self-presentation position. *Social Psychology Quarterly*, *43*, 283–290.

Thompson, S.C. (1981). Will it hurt less if I can control it? A complex answer to a simple question. *Psychological Bulletin*, *90*, 89–101.

Tolman, E.C. (1932). *Purposive behavior in animals and men*. New York: Century.

Totman, R.G. (1979). *Social causes of illness*. London: Souvenir Press.

Trope, Y. (1983). Self-assessment in achievement behavior. In J. Suls & A.G.Greenwald (Eds.), *Psychological perspectives on the self* (Vol. 2). Hillsdale, N.J.: Lawrence Erlbaum Associates Inc.

Turner, S.M., McCann, B.S., Beidel, D.C., & Mezzich, J.E. (1986). DSM-III classification of the anxiety disorders: A psychometric study. *Journal of Abnormal Psychology*, *95*, 168–172.

Tversky, A. & Kahneman, D. (1974). Judgement under uncertainty: Heuristics and biases. *Science*, *185*, 1124–1131.

Vaughn, C.E. & Leff, J.P. (1976). The influence of family and social factors on the course of psychiatric illness. *British Journal of Psychiatry*, *129*, 125–137.

Vaughn, C.E., Snyder, K.S., Jones, S., Freeman, W.B., & Falloon, I.R.H. (1984). Family factors in schizophrenic relapse: Replication in California of British research on expressed emotion. *Archives of General Psychiatry*, *41*, 1169–1177.

Vazquez, C. (1987). Judgment of contingency: Cognitive biases in depressed and nondepressed subjects. *Journal of Personality and Social Psychology*, *52*, 419–431.

Wachtel, P. (1977). *Psychoanalysis and behavior therapy: Toward an integration*. New York: Basic Books.

Wachtel, P. (Ed.) (1982). *Resistance: Psychodynamic and behavioral approaches*. New York: Plenum.

Wallston, K.A., Wallston, B.S., & DeVellis, R. (1978). Development of the multidimensional health locus of control (MHLC) scales. *Health Education Monographs*, *6*, 160–170.

Watts, F.N., McKenna, F.P., Sharrock, R., & Trezise, L. (1986). Colour naming of phobia-related words. *British Journal of Psychology*, *77*, 97–108.

Weiner, B. (1980). *Human motivation.* New York: Holt, Rinehart, & Winston.

Weiner, B. (1985a). An attributional theory of achievement motivation and emotion. *Psychological Review, 92,* 548–573.

Weiner, B. (1985b). "Spontaneous" causal thinking. *Psychological Bulletin, 97,* 74–84.

Weiner, B. (1986). *An attributional theory of motivation and emotion.* New York: Springer-Verlag.

Weiner, B., Amirkhan, J., Folkes, V.S., & Verette, J.A. (1987). An attributional analysis of excuse giving: Studies of a naive theory of emotion. *Journal of Personality and Social Psychology, 52,* 316–324.

Weiskrantz, L. (1977). Trying to bridge some neuropsychological gaps between monkey and man. *British Journal of Psychology, 68,* 431–435.

Wilkins, W. (1985). Therapy credibility is not a nonspecific event. *Cognitive Therapy and Research, 9,* 119–126.

Williams, J.M.G. (1984). *The psychological treatment of depression.* London: Croom Helm.

Williams, J.M.G. & Broadbent, K. (1986). Autobiographical memory in suicide attempters. *Journal of Abnormal Psychology, 95,* 144–149.

Wilson, T.D. (1985). Strangers to ourselves: The origins and accuracy of beliefs about one's own mental states. In J.H.Harvey & G.Weary (Eds.), *Attribution: Basic issues and applications.* Orlando, Fl.: Academic Press.

Wilson, T.D., Dunn, D.S., Bybee, J.A., Hyman, D.B., & Rotondo, J.A. (1984). Effects of analyzing reasons on attitude-behavior consistency. *Journal of Personality and Social Psychology, 47,* 5–16.

Wilson, T.D., Lassiter, G.D., & Stone, J.I. (1984). *Regulated versus unregulated nonverbal behaviour in social interaction: Evidence for limited access to mental states.* Unpublished manuscript, University of Virginia.

Wilson, T.D. & Linville, P.W. (1982). Improving the academic performance of college freshmen: Attribution therapy revisited. *Journal of Personality and Social Psychology, 42,* 367–376.

Wolpe, J. (1973). *The practice of behavior therapy.* (2nd Edition). New York: Pergamon.

Wylie, R.C. (1979). *The self-concept. Vols. 1 & 2.* (revised edition). Lincoln: University of Nebraska Press.

Yalom, I.D. (1975). *The theory and practice of group psychotherapy.* New York: Basic Books.

Yarrow, M.R., Schwartz, C.G., Murphy, H.S., & Deasy, L.C. (1956). The psychological meaning of mental illness in the family. *Journal of Social Issues, 11,* 12–24.

Zajonc, R.D. (1980). Feeling and thinking. Preferences need no inferences. *American Psychologist, 35,* 151–175.

Zuckerman, M., Larrance, D.T., Spiegel, N.H., & Klorman, R. (1981). Controlling nonverbal cues: Facial expressions and tone of voice. *Journal of Experimental Social Psychology, 17,* 506–524.

# Indices

## AUTHOR INDEX

# SUBJECT INDEX